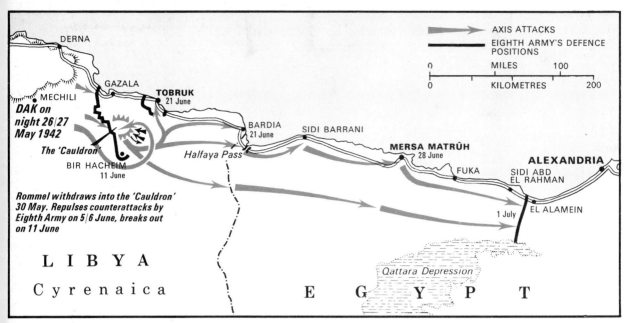

Rommel's drive to El Alamein

The Fall of Tobruk

Eighth Army's pursuit to Tunisia

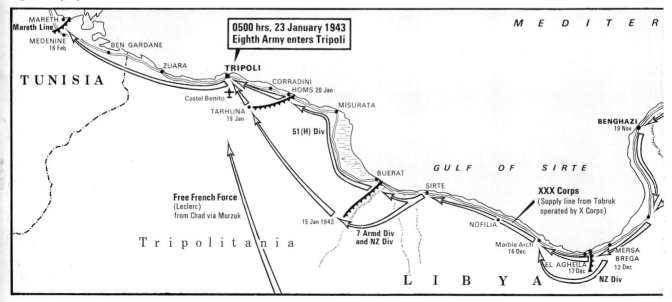

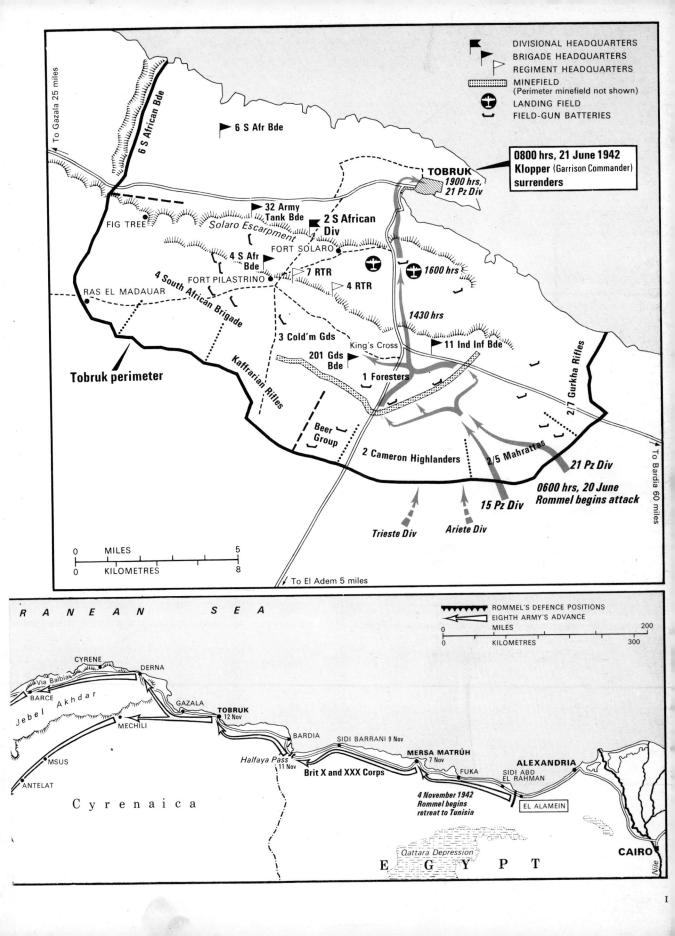

DIVISIONAL HEADQUARTERS
BRIGADE HEADQUARTERS
REGIMENT HEADQUARTERS
MINEFIELD (Perimeter minefield not shown)
LANDING FIELD
FIELD-GUN BATTERIES

To Gazala 25 miles

6 S African Bde

6 S Afr Bde

0800 hrs, 21 June 1942
Klopper (Garrison Commander)
surrenders

TOBRUK
1900 hrs,
21 Pz Div

32 Army Tank Bde

2 S African Div

FIG TREE

Solaro Escarpment

FORT SOLARO

4 S Afr Bde

7 RTR

1600 hrs

RAS EL MADAUAR

4 South African Brigade

FORT PILASTRINO

4 RTR

1430 hrs

Kaffrarian Rifles

3 Cold'm Gds

King's Cross

11 Ind Inf Bde

Tobruk perimeter

201 Gds Bde

1 Foresters

2/7 Gurkha Rifles

Beer Group

2 Cameron Highlanders

2/5 Mahrattas

21 Pz Div

15 Pz Div

0600 hrs, 20 June
Rommel begins attack

Trieste Div   *Ariete Div*

0   MILES   5
0   KILOMETRES   8

To El Adem 5 miles

To Bardia 60 miles

R A N E A N   S E A

ROMMEL'S DEFENCE POSITIONS
EIGHTH ARMY'S ADVANCE

0   MILES   200
0   KILOMETRES   300

CYRENE

DERNA

Via Balbia

BARCE

Jebel Akhdar

GAZALA

TOBRUK 12 Nov

BARDIA

SIDI BARRANI 9 Nov

MECHILI

Halfaya Pass 11 Nov

Brit X and XXX Corps

MERSA MATRÛH 7 Nov

ALEXANDRIA

MSUS

FUKA

SIDI ABD EL RAHMAN

ANTELAT

4 November 1942
Rommel begins
retreat to Tunisia

EL ALAMEIN

C y r e n a i c a

Qattara Depression

E G Y P T

CAIRO

Nile

I

SIDGWICK & JACKSON
LONDON

THE NORTH AFRICAN WAR

Warren Tute/Foreword by Manfred Rommel

CONTENTS

PHOTO CREDITS: United States National Archives 22–23; 68–69; 144–146; 152–153; 154–155; 172–173; 182; 186–189; 200–203; 206–207; 208–209. Paul Popper 16. Camera Press 14–15. Associated Press 51; 66; 88–89; 93 top; 148; 184–185. Ullstein 58–59; 70–71. Novosti 64. Keystone 86. Facetti 142. Bundersarchiv 22; 96; 190–195. Robert Hunt library 10–11; 18; 20–21; 24; 38–41; 44 bottom; 45 bottom; 46–47; 60–61; 65; 67; 72–73; 81 top; 82; 92 top right; 93 bottom; 139 bottom; 156–157; 166–167; 170–171; 196–197; 204–205. Imperial War Museum 17; 18–19; 26–37; 44 top; 45 top; 48–50; 52–57; 62–63; 68; 69; 74–80; 81 bottom; 84–85; 87; 92 top left; 92 bottom left and right; 94–95; 129–138; 139 top; 143; 149–151; 153; 160–165; 168; 174–181; 183; 196; 198–199; 208; 212–215.

© Warren Tute and Sidgwick and Jackson Limited 1976
Foreword © Manfred Rommel 1976

Designed by Anna Tryon and Sarah Kingham

ISBN 0.283.98240.3

Printed in Great Britain by
Jarrold & Sons Ltd., Whitefriars, Norwich NR3 1SH
for Sidgwick and Jackson Limited
1 Tavistock Chambers, Bloomsbury Way
London W.C.1A 2SG

FOREWORD

Every war is a tragedy for the victims and their relatives, and this is as true for the North African campaign as for any other. But it is in the nature of man to forget the miseries and recall only the pleasures, and it is no platitude to remind ourselves that in war there is not only chivalry but also viciousness, heroism as well as cowardice, brilliance as well as stupidity. One could wish that the self-sacrifice that war encourages was as common in the solving of peacetime problems.

It is generally agreed that the North African theatre was, by and large, characterized by a degree of mutual respect and probity which did not always apply on other fronts. This fairness must stand to the credit of all ranks, both German and British, and it was an attitude which was repeatedly evident in the speeches and writings of the British Prime Minister, Winston Churchill.

There are two temptations which I wish to resist: I do not want to summarize, for this book is itself a magnificent and lively account of very complicated events; nor can I make any value judgements of the campaign, for I only achieved the rank of Air Force Auxiliary N.C.O. (*Luft-waffenoberhelfer*), about equivalent to the rank of Corporal. I do, however, want to say a little about my father who, together with the British Field-Marshals Wavell, Auchinleck and Montgomery, and the German General von Arnim, was one of the military leaders in North Africa.

My father was born on 15 November 1891 in Heidenheim, a small Swabian town where my grandfather was employed as a grammar school teacher. He grew up with his sister and two brothers there until the family moved to Aalen, not very far away, when my grandfather was appointed headmaster of the grammar school.

Those who knew my father as a young man describe him as good-natured and gentle, with an exceptional aptitude for mathematics and science. I had much to suffer from this for he was unable to accept that others were not so gifted. He learnt to play the violin, and though he believed that this tuition was successful, this view was not shared by those who had to listen. His

interest in the arts generally was limited, though he was a natural draughtsman, a talent he used almost exclusively for the drawing of military sketches and maps.

My father originally wanted to become an engineer, but, as a result of pressure from my grandfather, he finally decided on a military career. He later described his training with a Swabian Infantry Regiment as extremely hard and unpleasant, but useful. He was good at sports, a fine horseman and one of the best bayonet fencers in the regiment.

The First World War, during which he served as Company Commander and Battalion Commander in France, Italy and Romania and earned the highest military medal the Kaiser could bestow, affected him greatly. Talking about his experiences, he remarked that he not only discovered that he appeared to lack the emotion fear, but that he had the knack of acquiring and keeping the trust and affection of his troops. It was then also that he discovered his flair for tactics. From that moment he became a difficult subordinate who treated orders from above with considerable mistrust.

He also learnt that for soldiers to withstand the dangers of bestialization which a long war can produce it was first necessary for their military superiors to strengthen by example their moral behaviour. This was a principle which guided him throughout his life – for him conscience was a reality. His ethics were simple and incorruptible; flexible as he was in matters of tactics and strategy, his principles of morality were unshakeable.

In the field of tactics he always defended his view that in a conflict between theory and prac-tice, the correct solution would almost always be in favour of practice. He realized that a principle can become detached from its basis of fact far too easily and can begin to lead a life of its own, removed from reality. This was a danger which had been repeatedly stressed by both the German military theoretician von Clausewitz and by Liddell Hart, but nonetheless it did not prevent military leaders from applying out-of-date principles which only led to the destruction of their troops. My father's approach to a better understanding of these dangers lay through meticulous self-criticism. To this end he wrote a book on infantry tactics based on his own experiences and adventures in the First World War. To write this book he used his own detailed notes and sketch maps and undertook detailed research by means of voluminous correspondence with his former colleagues. He made a similar study of his campaigns in North Africa, Normandy and Italy, hoping by this means to arrive at the practical principles of leadership.

My father was a planner because he knew the limits of planning. He once said that the best plan is the one made after a battle, for only the past is certain, while planning has to be carried out on the basis of the more-or-less probable. A plan must not, consequently, become gospel in the sense that it must be carried out no matter what events might dictate. Far too often this is what does happen, and, inevitably, it will be to the detriment of the soldiers who are unlucky enough to have to trace with their blood what is written on a piece of paper.

True to his principle, my father never hesitated to alter his plans when he thought they were no longer in tune with events, or if he should have meanwhile thought of a better plan. He continually encouraged his troops to accustom themselves to this kind of flexibility, even though his fluid planning often caused him to be accused of a lack of principle by other generals. My father maintained, however, that it was this fluidity which was the major cause of his successes, and he was disdainful towards those who thought that strategy and tactics are best created on the basis of an orthodox edifice of theory.

His constant presence on the front line, his contact with fighting troops, and his austere standards of living were not the result of any desire for mercenary rewards or a search after adventure. He had definite leanings towards an ascetic way of life, which, if my mother had not objected so strongly, he would have carried over into his home. My father's familiarity with the opinion of the front-line troops, who believed that the Staff thought themselves smarter the further they were from the fighting, led him to take great pains to demand of himself everything that he required of his troops and never more than what he himself could do. His preference was for the ordinary soldier and on innumerable occasions he supported a subordinate against a superior officer. They rewarded him, despite the German catastrophe, with affectionate memory for more than thirty years.

Until 1939 my father held the mistaken idea that another war was not possible as long as the generation that had fought in the First World War was still alive, but then my father understood little of politics because he did not wish to; he considered himself only a soldier whom politics did not concern. It was not until his return to the European theatre of war that he first became aware, day after day, of the true nature of National Socialist leadership. And as the information he received of the atrocities that had been committed in the name of National Socialism accumulated, so his decision hardened to take part in the planned rising against Hitler. It was a decision for which he would have to pay with his life. On 14 October 1944, while he was recovering from the wounds he had received in Normandy on 17 July of that year, Hitler had him killed.

My father's consolation was that the troops which he had sadly seen surrender at the capitulation of Tunis were spared – as prisoners of war – from being senselessly sacrificed in the final battles which Hitler had ordered.

The North African campaign has now been over for more than thirty years and its scars have long vanished. Since 1953 the face of Europe has changed more rapidly than ever before in history. In such a short time enemies have become friends and allies, and we have to thank the honourable attitude of the Western Allies towards a defeated Germany for making this possible; but it is also the determination of Germany never again to surrender her reclaimed democracy to a dictatorship. Despite all the changes that have taken place in the years since the ending of the North African War, the actors in the campaign deserve to be remembered. That is the purpose of this book.

August 1975   MANFRED ROMMEL

ACKNOWLEDGEMENTS

Acknowledgements are due to the following for granting permission to reproduce extracts from the books listed below: to Cassell & Co. Ltd for *The Second World War* by Winston S. Churchill and *Panzer Battles 1939* by F. W. von Mellenthin; to George Weidenfeld and Nicolson for *Patton* by Ladislas Farago; to William Collins Sons & Co. for *The Rommel Papers* by B. H. Liddell Hart, *The Memoirs of Field Marshal Montgomery* and *Diplomat Among Warriors* by Robert Murphy; to William Heinemann Ltd for *Crusade in Europe* by Dwight D. Eisenhower; to the Estate of Lord Cunningham for *A Sailor's Odyssey* by Lord Cunningham; to the Estate of Rear-Admiral W. H. Chalmers for *Full Cycle* by Chalmers; to the Controller of Her Majesty's Stationery Office for *The Eighth Army*; to George G. Harrap & Co. for *With Rommel in the Desert* by H. W. Schmidt and to A. M. Heath & Co. Ltd for *The War and Colonel Warden* by Gerald Pawle.

AUTHOR'S PREFACE

Any historian, however objective and impartial we all try to be, inevitably tends to exhibit a personal opinion in the matters he deals with especially if he has had some part in the events about which he is writing. I claim no exception to this. Naturally I take full responsibility for anything I have written and that, of course, includes any apparent bias, stress or, on the other hand, omission which there may be in this account of the vast panorama of the North African War.

Before publication I have tried to put right anything which might be thought to be unfair in comments, direct or implied, which appear in this book. But no writer can satisfy the particular prejudices of every reader – he can only hope that he has got his facts right, after meticulous checking, and where a judgement of those facts is inescapable that he has been as balanced as possible. In short I have no axe to grind.

Many, many books have been written about every aspect of the North African War and an attempt to compress a struggle stretching over three years and involving millions of men on both sides is fraught with danger, some of it obvious and some of it only visible when the story is considered as a whole.

Whatever conclusions a changing fashion in analysis may lead each generation of historians to take, all arguably valid, the basic material remains very much unaltered. In early accounts of the fighting written by generals, admirals, air marshals and politicians, there is inevitably a certain amount of special pleading which is usually refuted by subsequent writers. For instance there is a feeling today that the contribution of Wavell and Auchinleck, who bore the brunt of the most tricky part of the Desert War and who were then replaced, has not received adequate credit.

This may very well be true. The reader must make up his own mind. However, I have quoted extensively from Churchill, Eisenhower, Montgomery and Rommel because they made the running and because they saw the scene, albeit from their own points of view, with clarity and force. Moreover the giant, Churchill, whatever his defects, was consistently generous not only to his adversaries but also to those on his own side who disagreed with his point of view. And when all is said and done, Churchill and Roosevelt remain the summit personalities of the war.

As a further comment I would like to put in a word about the role which the United States played in the North African War. At first sight and because the United States only entered the war in December 1941, when the British and their allies had already been hard at it in the desert for eighteen months, American participation seems to be confined to the 'Torch' operation and what followed from that. So far as physical combat is concerned, this is true. But there is more to it than that.

On the longer haul, had it not been for the immense American potential, we might still have been fighting the war for another five years. Indeed it was as a result of General Eisenhower's success in North Africa that the United States subsequently became the senior partner on the Allied side. This fact and its deeper implications were fully appreciated by Rommel, a realist if ever there was one, and this change in the Allied relationship marks the point at which the Axis powers had, in essence, lost the war – though this was obviously not a politic opinion to bring out into the open in front of Hitler and the Oberkommando der Wehrmacht.

The vast shadow of the United States needs to be remembered through all the early chapters of this book. Until Pearl Harbor the Americans had supported the Allies almost surreptitiously and with a deference to protocol. Eleven months later the colossus came into sharp focus with the American landings in North Africa. The risks were shattering, the outcome by no means sure and the 'blooding process' costly and painful. But the torch had been well and truly lit, the drama was intense and the results proved to be decisive. It was in North Africa that those American generals who were to distinguish themselves so greatly later in the war – Eisenhower, Patton, Bradley and Mark Clark – first came into the limelight which was never to leave them till the war was over.

The Desert Fox. Rommel discusses movements with General von Bismarck

I
ROMMEL

To: All Commanders and Chiefs of Staff
From: Headquarters, B.T.E. and M.E.F.

There exists a danger that our friend Rommel is becoming a kind of magician or bogey-man to our troops, who are talking far too much about him. He is by no means a superman, although he is undoubtedly very energetic and able. Even if he were a superman, it would still be highly undesirable that our men should credit him with supernatural powers.

I wish you to dispel by all possible means the idea that Rommel represents something more than an ordinary German General. The important thing now is to see to it that we do not always talk of Rommel when we mean the enemy in Libya. We must refer to 'the Germans' or 'the Axis powers' or 'the enemy' and not always keep harping on Rommel.

Please ensure that this order is put into immediate effect, and impress upon all Commanders that, from a psychological point of view, it is a matter of the highest importance.

(*Signed*)
C. J. Auchinleck,
General,
Commander-in-Chief, M.E.F.

Erwin Rommel was the central character of the North African War. His personality induced an apprehensive fascination in his adversaries and an almost religious loyalty in his own men. He called for – and received – efforts and endurances which came near to being 'superhuman'. His final departure from the scene in the spring of 1943 signalled the fact that there could no longer be any hope for the Wehrmacht in North Africa. Long before that the Italians had wanted to pack it in. They would have done so had not the German presence stiffened them into continuing a reluctant resistance. The end of the Tunisian campaign saw the surrender of some 250,000 men.

Why was he called the Desert Fox? A fox to the hunting British, perhaps, but if a symbolic animal is required then Lion would have been a better choice. Rommel's own character was far from sly. Indeed his moral courage, his impetuous energy and his blunt outspokenness – attributes carrying a somewhat low profile in Nazi Germany – although they stood him in well with Hitler himself, caused him to be regarded with jealousy and dislike by the German General Staff. The toadies who surrounded the Fuehrer called him disdain-

fully a *Feldherr* – a Field Gentleman – as if practical soldiering in the appalling conditions of North Africa could scarcely be worth their attention. Yet this arrogance had a certain justification because of Rommel's predilection for committing himself to hazardous moves without fully considering their logistic implications. This brusque habit could scarcely be expected to endear him to the people who had to keep him supplied with rations, fuel and ammunition.

The arrival of Rommel brought a new dimension to the Desert War. The Italians had suffered a major defeat and the impact of a successful, aggressive German general on Axis morale was immediate, though not especially welcome to the Italian officers concerned. Once he had established himself, Rommel's presence near the front line came to be sensed instinctively by the British as the summer of 1941 wore on and, so far as fighting troops were concerned, the myth of Rommel began to take hold.

The North African War lasted from the summer of 1940 to the spring of 1943. Rommel and the German Panzers did not arrive in the theatre of operations till February 1941. How did they come to be sent there at all? Libya and Tripolitania were Italian colonies supposedly capable of defending themselves or even of becoming the springboard necessary for a lunge into Egypt where the main British forces in the Middle East were established. What had happened to Mussolini's 'eight million steel-hearted fighters'? The Duce was always boasting about them when Italy entered the war – late, as usual, and only just in time, as the rest of the world cynically observed, to qualify for a share of the pickings after the collapse of France in June 1940. The Mediterranean, according to Mussolini, was 'mare nostrum'. Theoretically the Italian forces in North Africa could be kept supplied – in spite of Royal Naval interference – via the short sea route from Sicily to Tripoli. Yet by February 1941 the British had advanced west over 1,000 miles from Egypt to within striking distance of Tripoli itself.

At this point the Germans stepped in. There was now a reasonable chance of the Italians being pushed out of North Africa altogether so that they had now to be shored up at all cost. How had this grave reflection on the fighting capabilities of the Italian armed forces come about?

The Second World War began in September 1939 and by June 1940 Germany alone had over-run the greater part of Western Europe, with the exception of the Iberian peninsula which remained neutral. When Mussolini declared war on the Allies a few days before France collapsed, the Rome–Berlin axis became a military as well as a political fact. But late though he was, the Duce remained sensitive about certain aspects of his relationship with Hitler. In particular the Duce had no intention of allowing his German friend to poach on Italian preserves.

Thus after July 1940 the only remaining Axis enemy in a condition to continue the fight was Great Britain. To deal with the British, Hitler had decreed that the Germans would make war north of the Alps, the south being taken care of by the Italians. This division of the world in the manner of a medieval Pope must have surprised the German General Staff and flattered the Italians, and would have delighted the British had they known about it since the British Mediterranean Fleet effectively guarded and kept open the short sea route to the Far East via Gibraltar and the Suez Canal, daring the Italian Navy to leave the

safety of its mainland ports – a gage picked up but rarely and with understandable reluctance.

By the autumn of 1940 the strategic map looked as follows. All Western Europe except for Spain, Portugal and Greece had become Axis controlled. The British possessed Egypt, the Near East, the island of Malta, which was the pivot of the Mediterranean, and Gibraltar, which dominated the western end. The 1940 armistice between Germany and France had sliced metropolitan France into two zones – one occupied by German troops and one technically unoccupied. French North Africa, comprising French Morocco, Algeria and Tunisia, remained nominally free and neutral.

The master key to control of the Mediterranean was the island of Malta. This lay ninety miles south of Sicily and plumb across supply routes to Italian possessions in Tripolitania and Cyrenaica. With Italian air power virtually supreme – at least locally – the British watched to see which way the Axis would move. Would they try and press on into Egypt? Or would an attempt to capture the island of Malta be made? Or both? Perhaps these moves might be timed to coincide with Hitler's projected invasion of England. Not only the British but Mussolini's German ally waited to see what practical aggressive measures the Duce would order. They had a long time to wait.

In September 1940, under strong pressure from Mussolini, Marshal Graziani decided to launch an attack on Egypt with the eight infantry divisions he commanded in Libya. Hitler sent General von Thoma to see Graziani and discuss the possible dispatch of German forces to the North African theatre. Von Thoma reported that not less than four armoured divisions would be needed and that supplying them would be difficult or even impossible in the face of British sea power. Nevertheless Hitler offered Mussolini anti-tank units, but these were brushed aside. Mussolini would manage alone. The Duce's innate arrogance was to colour German–Italian relations for the next three years, until, in fact, Italy collapsed. However, Mussolini was made aware of the possibility that German troops might be sent to Africa whether the Duce wanted them or not. Collaterally, so to speak, German aircraft were sent to Sicily to help the Italians dispute control of the adjacent waters with the British. At a summit conference in January 1941, the Italians accepted Hitler's offer of the 5th Light Division. On the first day of the Italian débâcle at Beda Fomm, Hitler decided to send an armoured division as well. However, long before the end of 1940, there came an early warning of the dangers facing the Axis powers.

On his autumn advance towards Egypt, Graziani encountered – somewhat to his surprise – only weak British outposts on the frontier. The Italians penetrated as far east as Sidi Barrani. There they halted, extending the coast road and laying down a water pipe from Sollum. The justification for not pushing on was clear, but it was one Mussolini preferred to avoid thinking about too much. The troops Graziani commanded were of poor quality. Their equipment, even by the standards of 1940, was derisory. Those two factors combined made Italian inadequacy only too painfully obvious.

The British, based on Egypt, had problems of their own. General Wavell, the Commander-in-Chief, had been saddled with far-reaching responsibilities in Africa as far south and east as Kenya and the Somalilands, and he had a contingent liability to send troops to Greece or elsewhere in the Balkans. He could spare, for an offensive in the Western Desert of Egypt, only about two divisions. Graziani had eight or nine.

Early in August 1940 the British forces covering the western frontier of Egypt, and which later became the Eighth Army, comprised the 7th Armoured Division and its Support Group made up of the 3rd Coldstream Guards, the 1st/60th Rifles, the 2nd Rifle Brigade, the 11th Hussars, one squadron of the 6th Royal Tank Battalion, and two mechanized batteries R.H.A., one of which was anti-tank.

This small force had to be distributed over a front of sixty miles. Nevertheless its effectiveness shows up in the casualty figures for the first three months of the Desert War. The Italians lost 3,500 men of whom 700 became prisoners. British casualties amounted to just over 150.

General Wavell had a hotch-potch of military, political, diplomatic and administrative problems of extreme complexity to face. Among these the effects of diverting shipping to Egypt round the Cape, the adoption of the Takoradi route and the need to make vehicles and aircraft desert-worthy loomed very large. During the autumn of 1940

reinforcements from India, South Africa and Australia were ordered to Egypt and by 9 December the British felt strong enough to counter-attack.

On that date a cataclysm broke around Marshal Graziani's head, which resulted in a smashing British victory. Sollum fell on 16 December and by the 21st Tobruk had been taken. A week later Derna was also in British hands. On 6 February 1941 Benghazi fell and the Italian situation in neighbouring Tripolitania now became precarious. This classic offensive brought Wavell and his subordinate commanders 130,000 prisoners in two months at a cost of fewer than 2,000 of their own side killed, wounded or missing. This was the dire state of affairs – from the Axis point of view – which brought the German Afrika Korps into being.

Hitler reacted at once. He dispatched Major-General von Funck to review the situation on the spot. This officer turned in so pessimistic a report, implying that one more push by the British and the whole of North Africa would be lost, that Hitler increased the proposed German force to two Panzer divisions and he also decided that a more aggressive general would be needed than the elderly von Funck. For this an officer who had once been commandant of the Fuehrer's own headquarters and who had later commanded a most successful Panzer division in France was chosen. Thus it was that in February 1941 Lieutenant-General Erwin Rommel entered the scene.

Rommel stands out from the bas-relief of Second World War generals as a tremendous personality, possibly the greatest of them all. Although he was defeated in Africa and later in France, his extraordinary achievements were all the time growing, only to be cut short by his enforced suicide on 14 October 1944 as a delayed result of the plot on Hitler's life the previous July. British and American historians naturally laud Eisenhower, Alexander, Montgomery and Patton, together with other generals whose talents helped the Allies to win this gruelling Second World War. On the German side Rommel remains unique. What sort of man was he who now reversed the situation, in a matter of weeks, after the first German troops began landing in Tripoli on 11 February 1941?

Churchill was to pay tribute to him in the

House of Commons at the beginning of those disastrous first nine months of 1942. 'We have a very daring and skilful opponent against us in Africa and may I say, across the havoc of war, a great general.' His effect on the chaotic state of affairs which met him was instant and immense. 'Finally, and beyond all other qualities that mark a great commander,' wrote Liddell Hart, 'comes the actual power of leadership. That is the dynamo of the battle-car and no skill in driving will avail if it is defective. It is through the current of great leadership that troops are inspired to do more than seems possible, and thus upset an opponent's "normal" calculations. There is no doubt on this score of Rommel's qualifications as a "Great Captain". Exasperating to staff officers, he was worshipped by the fighting troops, and what he got out of them in performance was far beyond any rational calculation.'[1] For nearly eighteen months there was no general on the British side who could in any degree approach the genius of

the Desert Fox. General von Mellenthin, who served him in Africa, describes him as 'perhaps the most daring and thrustful commander in German military history'.[2] It is not an exaggerated assessment.

When Rommel arrived in Africa to undertake the hardest task of his life so far, he had already become a controversial figure and was, in one sense, lucky to be still in the main stream. Back in 1938 he had already had a brush with the Nazi hierarchy. A stocky, alert colonel with the coveted *Pour le Mérite* medal – the German equivalent of the Victoria Cross in the First World War – he had been put in charge of the military training of the Hitler Youth, having recently attracted the Fuehrer's attention by publishing a valuable textbook on infantry tactics.

There he came up against the Reich's Youth Leader Baldur von Schirach who, in spite of the 'von', had never been a soldier himself and who held to the brash idea that 'youth should be led by

youth'. This resulted in *Schnoesels* of sixteen commanding their *Standarten* from big, shining Mercedes as though they were corps commanders. Rommel soon put an end to that. He also put the chopper to his own appointment and from that time on became quietly but definitely *persona non grata* with the Nazi Mafia.

Rommel never minced his words. He possessed great moral courage – a fairly unusual quality in pre-war Germany and not one to commend him to the inner Hitler clique. Once established in Tripoli, Rommel found himself instantly at variance with the Italian Supreme Command of the armed forces in North Africa in the person of General Gariboldi, a conventional officer who thought in terms of defence. This was scarcely surprising. Such Italian forces as were still in being were in no condition to attack. The views of 'Marshal Forwards' as Rommel was soon nick-named were, however, firm and to the point. Pure defence – as in the El Agheila position – would

lead to nothing more than a prolongation of the disease with no hope of a lasting cure.

Rommel therefore decided on an offensive probe, the idea being to advance as far forward as possible before the British could consolidate their gains. Gariboldi said no. Rommel ignored this reaction and, from then on, the Italian Calvary resulting from Rommel's impetuousness had begun. The first instance of this was for Rommel to remove himself smartly from Italian company and to visit the front line in person. Such action was not to the taste of the Commando Supremo whose outlook was more leisurely in such matters. Having had a good look round, Rommel then proceeded to act in whatever manner he thought the situation warranted.

Back in Tripoli he speeded up disembarkation of the German troops not only during the sunny February days but also at night with the use of searchlights. The high risk of air attack was brushed aside and the gamble paid off. By the end

Gloster Gladiator fighters arrive at a forward landing ground. No German troops had yet appeared in North Africa, but the Italians in Libya were preparing for a cautious advance across the Egyptian frontier

of March, 2 machine-gun battalions, 1 complete armoured regiment and 2 anti-tank units were on African soil. They had a somewhat mixed welcome.

'Singly and at regular intervals', wrote Heinz Werner Schmidt, who was on Rommel's staff,

the Panzers clattered and rattled by . . . the Italians stared with wide open eyes but were otherwise dumb. Where, I wondered, was their proverbial animation and enthusiasm? But I soon understood. After the Panzers had passed the saluting base, there was a gap in the column. Then followed, not quite so fast, not quite so noisily, a long line of Italian tanks. The tank commanders showed themselves as conspicuously as they could. Their expressions were bold, daring, audacious. There was an immediate cheer from all sides. The crowd waved and chattered wildly. There were cries of *Viva Italia*! With my staff comrades I pondered over the cool reception of the German troops who had come, after all, as allies to assist in the defence of the city. It seemed we were tolerated rather than popular. But their own dashing blades – they were heroes to the populace.[3]

The forces at Rommel's disposal were scarcely enough for a full-scale offensive. However, he was only too aware that every day that passed worked in favour of the British and against himself. Prompt action was needed. Boiling with energy and impatience, Rommel issued the order, 'On to

Agheila'. The newly arrived officers and men who had been hoping to explore the mysteries of the Orient in the alleyways of the Libyan capital were quickly disabused of the idea. To allay their disappointment Rommel sent them off into the desert on reconnaissance probes.

By 31 March all was ready. The British forces facing him had been widely dispersed in depth and were very vulnerable after their long advance. The reasons for this – at which, of course, Rommel could only guess – were that Wavell had been ordered to concentrate all available forces in Egypt, prepare them for dispatch to the Balkans at short notice and hold Cyrenaica with minimum forces. Taking a calculated risk, Wavell assumed that the newly arrived German contingent would not be ready for a major offensive before the summer and that meanwhile one infantry division and one armoured division (less one brigade) would provide a reasonable degree of security pending the arrival of more troops. Moreover, the infantry division was incompletely trained and only partially equipped, the armoured element of the armoured division being in need of re-equipment or, at least, a thorough overhaul.

Left: The British hit back. Italian troops surrender at Bardia in the course of an offensive which virtually destroyed the Italian Tank Army and cost the British fewer than 2,000 casualties
Right: The victors. Lieutenant-General R. N. O'Connor, commanding the Western Desert Force (left) confers outside Bardia with General Sir Archibald Wavell, Commander-in-Chief, Middle East, during the advance which took their forces in two months from the Egyptian frontier to El Agheila

Wavell counted on being able to remedy these shortcomings before the enemy arrived in strength.

Furthermore, a scarcity of transport made the infantry division so far from mobile that it could not be risked in the forward area and had to be moved to the rear. Therefore, the Mersa Brega position was held only by the Support Group of the armoured division with one armoured brigade in echelon behind it. The infantry division was far away.

Taking a risk, Rommel attacked through the salt marshes between Marada and Mersa el Brega. This attack paid off and by that same evening the position lay in his hands. He at once ordered the advance to continue and no more resistance was encountered before Agedabia, fifty miles away.

On 4 April Rommel occupied Benghazi and he now planned, at very great risk, to cut off Cyrenaica. This entailed crossing nearly 200 miles of trackless and waterless desert. To make things more difficult, once they were under way, a dreaded Ghibli sandstorm blew up which made breathing an agony and navigation all but impossible. Chaos set in. Yet through it all the advance continued. Rommel's iron will drove them on relentlessly and he made sure that his presence in the front line was known, hovering over them all in his Storch aircraft. Whenever a unit halted for no apparent reason, a note would flutter down from the aircraft to the commander on the spot. It said simply: 'If you do not move on at once, I shall come down. Rommel.'

'The effect of this audacious thrust was magical,' Liddell Hart has written. 'The British forces hastily fell back in confusion . . . the one British armoured brigade had lost almost all its tanks in the long and hasty retreat and the commander of the 2nd Armoured Division, with a newly arrived motor brigade and other units, was surrounded at Mechili and had to surrender . . . by April 11th the British were swept out of Cyrenaica and over the Egyptian frontier, except for a small force shut up in Tobruk.'[4]

Thus Rommel had regained in twelve days all that it had taken Wavell fifty to capture.

The sole remaining obstruction appeared to be Tobruk. This well-designed fortress now became the object of hot attention both by the British, who wished to relieve it, and by Rommel who knew he

must destroy this enemy strong-point in his rear before its relief could be organized.

Logistics – and more particularly the supply of petrol and ammunition as far as the Axis forces were concerned – now emerged as the dominant factor in the campaign. In the early summer of 1941 the problem was not yet acute since Rommel's rapid advance had gained him a rich booty in the form of British vehicles and the petrol dumps which fed them. At one stage Rommel was operating with eighty-five per cent British transport. Later, however, the supply position was to become crucial and in the end could be said to have been the basic cause of Rommel's final retreat.

Heat, sandstorms, bugs and inadequate supplies plagued Rommel's Panzer force as they did the British waiting to counter-attack. To these common factors in the desert must be added two which Rommel had to cope with alone. One was that the Luftwaffe in Africa was not subordinate to the Afrika Korps. As a result fighter and ground-strafing groups were used strategically rather than in tactical support of Rommel's ground forces. The second and far more difficult problem was

that Libya, being then Italian territory, was under the direct control of the Italian High Command. In theory the Germans were there only to assist and not to run the campaign. This did not suit Rommel at all. The German and Italian military outlook, to put it mildly, differed in intensity.

It seemed to the Germans that the Italians were always late or sometimes entirely missing whenever they were wanted. Yet Rommel and his subordinate commanders were uncomfortably aware that the British could only be defeated with Italian co-operation. 'Where is Gambara?' one of Rommel's generals repeatedly wirelessed from the front. But General Gambara did not appear on the battlefield and this phrase 'Where is Gambara?' became a stock witticism with the German troops in Africa.

Rommel himself wrote: 'The Italians had acquired a very considerable inferiority complex, as was not surprising in the circumstances. Their infantry were practically without anti-tank weapons and their artillery completely obsolete. Their training was also a long way short of modern standards so that we were continually being faced by serious breakdowns. Many Italian officers had

thought of war as little more than a pleasant adventure and were, perforce, having to suffer a bitter disillusionment.'[5]

The Desert War amply demonstrated the truth of the saying that there are no bad troops but only incompetent officers. In retrospect Rommel was generous to the Italian soldier and damning of his officers. 'The duties of comradeship,' he wrote, 'compel me to state unequivocally that the defects which the Italian formations suffered . . . were not the fault of the Italian soldier. The Italian was willing, unselfish and a good comrade, and, considering the conditions under which he served, had always given far better than average. . . .'[6]

In a later analysis of the Italian defeat, he went on:

The Italian command was, for the most part, not equal to the task of carrying on war in the desert, where the requirement was lightning decision followed by immediate action. The training of the Italian infantryman fell far short of the standard required by modern warfare. His equipment was so utterly bad that for that reason alone he was unable to stand his ground without German help. Perhaps the best example of the inferior quality of the Italian armament – apart from the grave technical defects of their tanks with their short-range guns and under-powered engines – was

to be found in the artillery with its low mobility and short range. Their supply of anti-tank weapons was totally inadequate. Rations were so bad that the Italian soldier frequently had to ask his German comrade for food. Particularly harmful was the all-pervading differentiation between officers and men. While the men had to make shift without field kitchens, the officers or many of them refused adamantly to forgo their several course meals. Many officers again considered it unnecessary to put in an appearance during battle and thus set the men an example.[7]

Rommel kept a running diary of events and, however exhausted he might be, managed to write a short letter almost every day to his wife. Although these little notes to his 'Dearest Lu' were mainly personal, the existence of such invaluable material written at the time and on the spot makes his considered opinions in retrospect the more valuable. 'Of all theatres of operations,' he wrote later,

it was probably in North Africa that the war took on its most advanced form. The protagonists on both sides were fully motorized formations, for whose employment the flat and obstruction-free desert offered hitherto undreamed-of possibilities. It was the only theatre where the principles of motorized and tank warfare, as they had been taught theoretically before the war, could be applied to the full – and further developed. It was the only theatre where the pure tank battle between major formations was fought . . . based on the principle of complete mobility.[8]

Commenting on his attempt to invest Tobruk, Rommel remarked:

In this assault we lost more than 1,200 men and this shows how sharply the curve of casualties rises when one reverts from mobile to position warfare. In a mobile action what counts is material, as the essential complement to the soldier. The finest fighting man has no value in mobile warfare without tanks, guns and vehicles. Thus a mobile force can be rendered unfit for action by the destruction of its tanks, without having suffered any serious casualties in manpower.[9]

In this connection – and in spite of the great use Rommel made of captured British equipment – von Mellenthin remarks: 'At no time did I hear Rommel express any interest in the Supply Dumps of the Eighth Army. We knew of their location but Rommel's aim was not to attack the British supplies, but to destroy their field army.'[10]

In June 1941, the British again turned to the offensive. This was immediately before Hitler's attack on Russia and was made possible, largely on Churchill's initiative, by the dispatch through the Mediterranean of a convoy to Alexandria containing a large reinforcement of tanks. This convoy, which had been assembled in April, was originally routed round the Cape.

On receipt of a telegram from Wavell, however, stressing the gravity of the situation and the urgency of his need for more armour, Churchill, with the approval of the Chiefs of Staff, ordered the five fast ships of the convoy to turn east at Gibraltar and make the Mediterranean dash.

'The fate of the war in the Middle East,' his minute read, 'the loss of the Suez Canal, the frustration or confusion of the enormous forces we have built up in Egypt, the closing of all prospects of American co-operation through the Red Sea – all may turn on a few hundred armoured vehicles. They must, if possible, be carried there at all costs.'[11]

One of these ships was sunk by a mine in the Sicilian Narrows but four got through with 238 invaluable tanks on board, and enabled Wavell to reconstitute two armoured brigades for the new offensive, to be code-named 'Battleaxe'.

The target of Operation Battleaxe as set by Churchill was to gain a decisive victory in North Africa, destroying Rommel's forces in the process. Wavell expressed a doubt but 'hoped the attack

The tide turns for the Axis powers. In the spring of 1941 Rommel's first offensive, launched when the British were preoccupied with developments in Greece, took him to the Egyptian frontier area but left his communications dangerously stretched. German troops refresh themselves at a cistern in the desert

would succeed in driving the enemy back west of Tobruk'.[12] In the event it failed and proved to be a sorry setback for the British. By nightfall on the first day half the British tanks had been lost, mainly in two of Rommel's anti-tank traps, whereas the German tank force remained almost intact, and, with the arrival of Rommel's other Panzer regiment from Tobruk, the balance shifted in his favour.

On 18 June 1941 Rommel was writing to his 'Dearest Lu':

> The three-day battle has ended in complete victory . . . the joy of the Afrika troops over this latest victory is tremendous. The British thought they could overwhelm us with their 400 tanks. We couldn't put that amount of armour against them. But our grouping and the stubborn resistance of German and Italian troops who were surrounded for days together enabled us to make the decisive operation with all the forces we still had mobile. Now the enemy can come, he'll get an even bigger beating.[13]

Almost the only bright spot for the British at that time was the continued possession of Tobruk. But in general the atmosphere was one of slightly incomprehensible dismay and disappointment. This now centred on the appointment of Wavell. Popular – very popular – though he was with the front-line troops, he was felt by the Chiefs of Staff to be tired out. He was also accused of being slow off the mark in Iraq and Syria. Perhaps Churchill and the Chiefs of Staff were in danger of overworking a willing horse. Perhaps it was time for a change.

Wavell's achievements in Eritrea, Abyssinia and the Somalilands had been considerable (and, incidentally, had had a useful effect on American public opinion and therefore on the supply of war material) but these had been offset by the disasters in Greece and Crete and now Operation Battleaxe was to be his *coup de grâce*. The War Cabinet ordered his replacement as Commander-in-Chief by General Auchinleck – equally distinguished as a general but a more remote, less accessible man with, perhaps, a diminished personal appeal. There was little joy in what was soon to be known as the Eighth Army at this change of command.

With hindsight it would be fair to say that the defeat at Sollum Halfaya which brought about this replacement in the high command was caused not by bad generalship but by the inadequacies of the British tanks. Rommel confirms this, in the process being generous, as he always was, to his

adversary: 'Wavell's strategic planning,' he wrote,

had been excellent. What distinguished him from other British Army commanders was his great and well-balanced strategic courage, which permitted him to concentrate his forces regardless of his opponent's possible moves. He knew very well the necessity of avoiding any operation which would enable his opponent to fight on interior lines and destroy his formations one by one with locally superior concentrations. But he was put at a great disadvantage by the slow speed of his heavy infantry tanks, which prevented him from reacting quickly enough to the moves of our faster vehicles. Hence the slow speed of the bulk of his armour was his soft spot, which we could seek to exploit tactically.[14]

In this connection it has to be borne in mind that after Dunkirk the British had no time to redesign their tanks embodying recent experience, since they were forced to produce at the utmost speed replacements of existing tanks as an essential first measure. Thus inevitably in the early stages of the Desert War German material had the edge on the British.

'In this battle,' Rommel continued,

the British used large numbers of their Mark II (Matilda) tanks which were too heavily armoured to be penetrated by most of our anti-tank weapons. However the gun which they carried was far too small and its range too short. They were also only supplied with solid, armour piercing shell. It would be interesting to know why the Mark II was called an infantry tank, when it had no H.E. ammunition with which to engage the opposing infantry.

The crucial position in this battle was the Halfaya Pass, which Captain Bach and his men held through the heaviest fighting. Major Pardi's artillery battalion also rendered distinguished service in this action, thus showing that Italian troops could give a good account of themselves when they were well officered. Had the British been able to take Halfaya Pass as they had planned, the situation would have been very different . . . when the German attack was launched from north of Sidi Omar, Wavell was prevented by the slowness of his infantry tanks from shifting his main weight at that moment from Capuzzo to the point of the Axis attack. There was nothing for him but a quick retreat, which he executed with the minimum of casualties to the British forces.[15]

This battle made a great impression on the German and Italian High Commands. It must be remembered that Hitler had attacked Russia on 22 June and his mind was therefore only partially on the North African campaign. General Roatta, who arrived in Africa some time later, informed Rommel that the Italian High Command realized the necessity of considerably reinforcing the Axis forces in North Africa. The German element was to be brought up to four mechanized divisions and

the Italian to an armoured corps of three divisions, with a further two to three motorized divisions. 'Their zeal,' Rommel comments, 'unfortunately did not last long.'

Rommel further considered that, had he been reinforced as was then planned, he could have beaten off the forthcoming British offensive in the winter of 1941 and he would then have been strong enough to destroy the British in Egypt in the spring of 1942. This could have led to an advance into Iraq and a cutting off of the Russians from Basra. Such a strategic blow might well have affected the whole timing of the war.

However, a pause now ensued. The channels of command were 'tidied up' as General Westphal, later to be Rommel's chief of staff, succinctly put it, and Rommel himself was promoted to Panzer General. On 21 August 1941 he wrote to his wife:

Had another visit from the Italian C.-in-C. yesterday; purely 'comradely' however. On the official level I've been disagreeing with a number of things which have been done and have said so through Calvi, so this visit was probably a goodwill gesture. I've got a number of visitors today. We're having chicken and I'm not going to miss it in spite of my diet. This perpetual mush loses its fascination after a time. I'm very pleased about my new appointment

(Commander of the Panzer Group, Afrika). Everybody else in that position is a Colonel-General. If things here go as I should like them, I, too, will probably get that rank after the war's over . . . the heat's frightful, night time as well as day time. Liquidated four bugs. My bed is now standing in tins filled with water and I hope the nights will be a little more restful from now on. Some of the others are having a bad time with fleas. They've left me alone so far. . . .[16]

Rommel had intended to visit Hitler's headquarters soon after the battle of Sollum but 'it's no good going until the Russian affair is more or less over, otherwise there'll be scant regard for my interests'. However, influential men did come to Africa to see the victorious Panzer General. On 10 September he wrote: 'We have a distinguished visitor coming today – Major Melchiori, a close confidant of the Duce. I'm hoping for a lot from this visit, as the feeling towards us is not particularly friendly at the moment. Things have changed!' No doubt this visit was a success, since Rommel wrote on 29 September: 'The last few days have been exciting. A large shipment arrived for us at Benghazi. It took fifty hours to unload. All went well. You can imagine how pleased I was. With things as they are in the Mediterranean it's

not easy to get anything across. For the moment we're only step-children and must make the best of it.'[17]

During the autumn the Italian Commander-in-Chief Gariboldi was to be replaced by General Cavallero. To Rommel this seemed a step in the right direction, though Cavallero soon proved himself to be just as obstructive and hesitant as his predecessor. An instance of what was meant in practice was reported by Rommel after inspecting the Bardia defence area:

> I found vast quantities of material lying in the defences where it had been left by Graziani's army. This material was just waiting to be used, and I therefore gave immediate instructions for all unclaimed Italian guns to be collected up and used to strengthen the Sollum Halfaya-Sidi Omar front. A substantial number of these guns was put in order by one or two of our German workshops and then installed in the strong points. But the Italian High Command did not agree at all, and General Gariboldi had me informed, through Heggenreinen, that the guns were Italian property and were only to be used by Italians. They had been perfectly content up till then to stand by and watch this material go to wrack and ruin, but the moment the guns had been made serviceable on our initiative, they began to take notice. However, I was not to be put off.[18]

By the end of September 1941 approximately one-third of the troops and no more than a seventh of the essential supplies Rommel needed had actually arrived in Cyrenaica. He was therefore compelled to postpone the attack he planned, and early in November went to Rome for a short period of leave with his wife and son. As a result of his August promotion when his command was raised to the status of a Panzer Group, Lieutenant-General Cruewell was appointed Commander of the Afrika Korps with Colonel Bayerlein (later to be promoted Lieutenant-General) as his chief of staff. The British kept a sharp eye on these changes in command and before launching their own winter offensive – Operation Crusader – made a daring attempt to capture Rommel 'dead or alive'.

This took the form of a raid by the Commandos on Beda Littoria during the night of 17–18 November when they tried to wipe out what they supposed to be Army headquarters but which was currently in use by the quartermaster's staff. Rommel had, in fact, previously had his command post in this house which was two hundred miles behind the German front, using the first floor himself with his A.D.C.s on the ground floor. 'The British,' Colonel Bayerlein reported, 'must have received knowledge of this through their Intelligence Service.'

When challenged, the British Commandos answered the sentry in German. 'Although they did not know the password, the sentry did not fire, thinking they were Germans who had lost their way. The British were wearing no insignia which might have identified them as enemy. They quickly pressed into the house, fired a volley into the room on the left of the entrance door, killing two Germans, and tried to get up to the first floor. Here, however, they were met by German bullets. One British officer was killed and a German fatally wounded. The remainder of the British Commandos withdrew.'[19]

This type of deep penetration raid became a speciality of the British under Colonel David Stirling, whose Special Air Service and Long Range Desert Group brought guerilla-type warfare beyond and behind the front line to a fine art.

German Intelligence, in turn, had made the High Command fully aware of the extent of the British build-up of troops and material in Egypt which had been set in motion the previous autumn and, although Rommel felt gravely handicapped by the Axis failure to equip him with anything like what he needed, time pressed and Rommel told the O.K.W. that he must attack in the second half of November. Any further postponement would only result in the balance of strength being even less favourable to the Axis powers.

In the event the British struck first and Operation Crusader began on 18 November 1941 with a long flanking march round Sollum. The attacking force comprised the equivalent of seven divisions, including the Tobruk garrison. It was opposed by three German and seven Italian divisions. 'But such figures give a false impression,' Liddell Hart wrote, 'because the issue mainly turned on armour and air-power. The British had five brigades of armour, while Rommel had the equivalent of two German and one Italian.'[20]

The number of British tanks totalled over 700 with some 200 in reserve, which were sent up at the rate of about 40 a day. Rommel's strength at the start was just over 500 (including 150 Italian). He had some 50 under repair but could call on no reserve of new tanks. In the air British predominance was much greater. In aircraft fit for action

they had over 700 against 120 German and about 200 Italian. The initial advantage could thus be multiplied by surprise.

Rommel himself was still in Rome in the first half of November. He had gone there to win sanction for an early attack on Tobruk and stayed on to spend his birthday, the 15th, with his wife – flying back to Africa just before the British advance began.

Operation Crusader brought on by far the biggest tank battles fought up to that time in the North African theatre. By the end the tide of victory was flowing for the British but between mid-November 1941 when the battle opened and early January 1942 when Rommel had been pushed back to Agedabia and the siege of Tobruk had been lifted, there were many moments when it was touch and go.

By now 13th Corps and 30th (Armoured) Corps had been duly constituted as the Eighth Army under Lieutenant-General Sir Alan Cunningham but to the irritation of Churchill in London the new Commander-in-Chief General Sir Claude Auchinleck proved equally firm in resisting pressure to renew an offensive until in his opinion

he was fully prepared and strong enough to stand a good chance of success. One reason for Auchinleck's caution was that with the exception of the 30th Corps commander, Lieutenant-General C. W. M. Norrie, none of the new commanders had had experience of handling tanks and of operating against armoured forces.

The basis of the British plan of attack was that 13th Corps (which included the New Zealand and 4th Indian Divisions and a brigade of infantry tanks) should pin down German and Italian troops holding their frontier positions whilst 30th Corps would sweep round the flank to seek out and destroy Rommel's armoured force. They were then to link up with the Tobruk garrison, some seventy miles west of the frontier, which was to break out and meet the 30th Corps.

This plan had a serious defect which in the event nearly proved fatal. The armour of 13th and 30th Corps would be widely separated and the wide outflanking movement, whilst initially taking Rommel by surprise, resulted in the British attack becoming disjointed. Rommel is reported as commenting corrosively: 'What difference does it make if you have two tanks to my one, when you

spread them out and let me smash them in detail? You presented me with three brigades in succession.'[21]

By nightfall on the first day British armour was astride the Trigh el Abd but by next morning their 35-mile frontage had been stretched to 50 miles. In the centre, 7th Armoured Brigade had captured the enemy airfield at Sidi Rezegh only 12 miles from Tobruk, but the rest of the brigade and the division's support group were slow in coming up. By the time they did so, Rommel had blocked their path with a large number of anti-tank guns. Thus no reinforcements arrived to strengthen the British centre force and meanwhile the other two armoured brigades were in trouble – far apart on the western and eastern ends of the front.

Severe losses were inflicted on the British and on 23 November Rommel was writing to Lu: 'The battle seems to have passed its crisis . . . two hundred enemy tanks shot up so far. Our fronts have held.'[22] The twenty-third of November was Advent Sunday to the British and Totensonntag – the Sunday of the Dead – to the Germans, who subsequently gave this name to the battle.

Conditions of very considerable confusion existed, caused mainly by poor communications, and in essence neither side drew more than temporary advantage from this. One incident typifies the extraordinary conditions in which both sides had to operate in the Desert War. General Cruewell (and Rommel) both used captured British Mammoths (Armoured Vehicles) as their mobile headquarters up at the front. At one moment during this confused to-ing and fro-ing, Cruewell and his staff were suddenly ringed round by British tanks. 'The German crosses on the sides of the vehicles were not easy to identify,' Colonel Bayerlein reported,

and the hatches were shut. The British, who had fired off all their ammunition, had no idea whom they had met. A number of them left their tanks, walked across to the Mammoth and knocked on the armour plate, whereupon General Cruewell opened the hatch and found himself looking into the face of a British soldier, to the great astonishment of both. At that moment gunfire started to spray into the neighbourhood. The occupants of the Mammoth threw themselves flat on the thin wooden flooring and the vehicle escaped undamaged. A German 20 mm anti-aircraft gun had opened fire on the dismounted British tank crews, who promptly jumped back into their tanks and disappeared as fast as they could to the south,

Previous pages

Left: Rommel's failure to take Tobruk during his otherwise brilliantly successful first offensive ruled out any further advance until he could be substantially reinforced. British troops at Tobruk, 1941

Right: In the winter of 1941–2 Operation Crusader recaptured Cyrenaica for the British but left Auchinleck without the means of holding the positions he had won. South African troops search buildings at Sollum

Right: Early in 1942 Rommel's second offensive drove the British back to the Gazala-Bir Hacheim line, but left Tobruk still in their hands. The photograph shows gunners of the Free French contingent which manned the southern extremity of the line at Bir Hacheim

thus releasing the staff of the Afrika Korps from a highly precarious situation.[23]

On another occasion Rommel summoned Cruewell to meet him at Panzer Group's forward headquarters, said to be located near Gambut. After searching for a long time in the darkness, Cruewell eventually discovered a British lorry which he approached with great caution. Inside he found Rommel and his chief of staff unshaven, worn out with lack of sleep and caked with dust. In the lorry there was a heap of straw as a bed, a can of stale water to drink and a few tins of food. Close by were two wireless trucks and a few dispatch riders.

Operation Crusader revealed Rommel as a master tactician, but he was inevitably handicapped by an almost total lack of air reconnaissance and a consequent 'communication fog'. Moreover, the mobility on which his tactics relied caused a dangerously high consumption of fuel. Early in the battle the 21st Panzer Division had run out of fuel on its eastward lunge and had become temporarily stranded. As against this the British had good information about enemy movements but were slow to take advantage of this – at

one stage the 'I' tank brigade of 13th Corps found itself only seven miles from the armoured battle 'panting to advance and eager to help', but it was not called on to do so.

In the end, however, the superiority of the British in weight of armour available began to tell. After the battle of Totensonntag, some five days after the main operation had started, the Afrika Korps was down to some 90 effective tanks. Whilst the British had suffered heavier losses (30th Corps had only 70 tanks left out of the 500 with which it had begun), they also had a large reserve from which to replenish their resources. Rommel had none.

The day after Totensonntag, Rommel tried another daring thrust eastwards across the frontier and into the rear area of the Eighth Army. Liddell Hart describes this gamble by saying that, 'Rommel was striking at the mind of the opposing commander, as well as against the rear of opposing forces and their supplies'.[24] In the event he came nearer to success than he could possibly have guessed at the time, since Cunningham had wanted to retreat over the frontier the previous day and had only been stopped by the arrival in

person of Auchinleck who then replaced Cunningham as Commander of the Eighth Army with Neil Ritchie, his Deputy Chief of the General Staff.

However, a lack of fuel and the non-arrival of the Italian Ariete Division caused Rommel's threat to fail. This was compounded by misinterpreted orders due to poor communications and, reluctantly, Rommel ordered the withdrawal westwards of the Afrika Korps. The strategic counter-thrust had failed, and now it was a question of whether he could withdraw and still keep the upper hand.

The British now had a superiority of 5 to 1 in tanks (and 7 to 1 in gun-armed tanks) and, as Liddell Hart observes, 'if they had been used in the fully concentrated way the Afrika Korps would have had a poor prospect of survival, and the 7th Armoured Division alone should have been able to crush it'.[25] Astonishingly enough Rommel escaped after some brilliant rearguard actions in spite of the balance in armour against him. On 7 December, Rommel decided to withdraw to the Gazala line, and by the 11th he was safely there.

On 13 December the 13th Corps attacked the Gazala line and on the following day the 4th Armoured Brigade was sent to Halegh Eleba on a wide flanking movement to cut the Panzer retreat. Both these attacks were halted and failed although by the 15th the Afrika Korps had barely thirty tanks left as against nearly 200 operated by the British. However, attrition had won the day for the British, and Rommel decided he would retreat to the Mersa Brega line which had been the springboard for his first offensive and there build up his strength for the next time.

The year ended with the Germans driven back first to the Agedabia area, and then further to Agheila. The siege of Tobruk had been lifted, and on 2 January 1942 Bardia surrendered to the British. Total Axis casualties were 33,000, of which two-thirds were Italian, as against 18,000 on the British side, but, proportionately, the British had lost more front-line troops including many highly trained desert veterans whom it was difficult to replace.

Meanwhile, a month previously, the Japanese attack on Pearl Harbor had brought the Americans raging into the war. Thus the fateful year of 1942 began – a year of decision for both sides.

The primary aim of the British and their allies throughout the North African campaign was to reopen the central and eastern Mediterranean to their shipping by gaining undisputed control of the African shore and removing the threat to Malta. Right: Grand Harbour, Valletta, under air attack

2
THE
GRAND
STRATEGY

The strategic situation in the Mediterranean at the time the United States entered the war gave little comfort to the Allies. By the turn of the year Rommel had certainly been driven back. He had not been decisively beaten nor was he likely to be in the near future because setbacks suffered by the Royal Navy in the Mediterranean theatre coincided with the diversion of naval forces to the Far East to fight Japan.

The fortunes of the British Eighth Army with their extended lines of communications were to a very large extent dominated by the war at sea. Here again good fortune seemed to have deserted the British. On 19 December 1941, the Malta Squadron, Force K, had suffered a disaster in the minefields off Tripoli. The cruisers *Neptune* and *Aurora* had been sunk and crippled respectively and a destroyer had also been lost. This had enabled an Axis convoy to get through with 7,000 tons of vital supplies. Elsewhere in the Mediterranean the aircraft-carrier *Ark Royal* and the battleship *Barham* had been sunk and the battleships *Queen Elizabeth* and *Valiant* gravely damaged. In the Far East the numbing loss of two great capital ships the *Prince of Wales* and the *Repulse*

made matters worse.

Rommel had been strengthened at a critical moment. The British had been trying to tempt General Weygand in French North Africa to break with Vichy and declare for the Allies. To back up this proposed operation – code-named 'Gymnast' – one armoured and two infantry divisions were held at short notice to embark in England and it was hoped that an advance into Tripoli on the long road to Tunis, plus the defeat of Rommel, would encourage the pint-sized French General to take the plunge.

But French memories of the destruction of their Atlantic Fleet by the Royal Navy at Oran in July 1940 were too recent and too cruel for them to respond favourably to any strictly British overture. Churchill had gone to Washington shortly after Pearl Harbor, and a plan for Anglo-American intervention in French North Africa – code-named 'Super-Gymnast' – had received presidential support. 'The enemy's firm stand at Agedabia and his orderly withdrawal to Agheila,' Churchill wrote, 'was therefore of far greater significance to me and to all my thought than the mere arrest of our westward movement in the desert.'[1] Worse

was to come.

As other British generals had done before and were to do again, Auchinleck underestimated the German power of recuperation, and in any case difficulties of supply would have prevented him from doing much more than he did. The R.A.F. in Malta under the aggressive leadership of Air Vice-Marshal Lloyd had greatly contributed to the westward advance of the Eighth Army by its autumn attacks on Italian ports and shipping. The Germans were soon to adjust this matter. Under Field-Marshal Kesselring they moved a powerful Luftwaffe force into Sicily, temporarily knocking out the R.A.F. in Malta.

Further British misfortune at sea prevented Admiral Sir Andrew Cunningham, based on Alexandria, from intervening effectively on the sea route to Tripoli. None of these factors suggested to the French that now would be a good moment to come in again on the Allied side, especially as the Allies were doing so badly in Malaya and the Philippines.

To the west the rock, harbour and air strip of Gibraltar, controlling the entrance to the Mediterranean, comprised the sole British position in that part of the world. By means of a balance of threat – military occupation by the Axis versus starvation through Allied blockade – the Iberian peninsula was being maintained in a precarious state of neutrality. This was heavily loaded, so far as Spain was concerned, in favour of Germany and Italy. The guns of Algeciras, across the bay from Gibraltar, which had been mounted with expert German advice, could reduce the Rock's facilities to zero in a few short hours and this fact had to be taken into account in all strategic planning. Lisbon and Tangier – then an international free port – were humming centres of espionage and the whole southern coast of Andalusia swarmed with spies and agents preponderantly in the Axis cause.

In French North Africa the Vichy régime maintained itself uneasily, in the main relying upon the decayed messianic figure of Marshal Pétain. Metropolitan France had been divided, by the armistice with the Axis in June 1940, into an Occupied and an Unoccupied zone. In the latter, which of course included French North Africa, almost no German or Italian uniforms were apparent in everyday life but the grip of the Gestapo, working through its Vichy counterpart, became as all-pervading as that of the present-day K.G.B. in the Russian satellite countries. Britain and the United States, upon both of whom the thorny personality of de Gaulle had been foisted by the accident of war, never really understood the stricken French. Why was there so little support for de Gaulle? How was it that the ancient Marshal Pétain, aided by such figures as the detested politician Laval and the enigmatic Admiral Darlan, could still contrive, apparently without effort, to maintain the loyalty if not the respect of the vast majority of the French?

The short answer was that Pétain was the legal head of state and Darlan, who had rebuilt the French Navy, his trusted lieutenant. De Gaulle, on the other hand, was regarded by the majority of French people in France as an unknown adventurer, brave, certainly, but a usurper of the seat of power, to be trusted as little perhaps in their realist thinking as the Stuart pretenders to the British throne two centuries ago.

It must be remembered that until the Anglo-American landings in North Africa of November 1942, the United States maintained an embassy in Vichy and a roving ambassador in the person of Robert Murphy in French North Africa. The services of the American Admiral Leahy in Vichy and of the career diplomat Murphy in Algeria were unique and when the balance sheet is totted up, invaluable. But part of the problem was that other professional men with similar qualifications simply did not exist. When the United States came into the war, the American Departments of State, of War and of the Navy failed to produce one single American familiar with the Arab language and with conditions in Moslem countries. This made things tricky when later on American backing was sought for an attempt to overthrow the pro-German Bey of Tunisia. Moreover when it came to collecting intelligence of any military value, the situation could be summed up by Murphy's sardonic assessment that 'one or two of us with luck might be able to distinguish a battleship from a submarine on a particularly clear day'.[2]

Whatever their loyalties and however disguised their private feelings might be, the French remained realists. On 22 June 1941 when Hitler invaded Russia, General Weygand remarked to Ambassador Murphy in Algiers: 'When we discussed the war and you expressed your belief that Britain would win in the end, I asked you where the divisions would come from. Now I know where they will come from – Russia. Germany has lost the war.'[3]

But between such an opinion and any effective action lay a very large gap and, with hindsight, it is perhaps lucky that Hitler continued to have a blind spot so far as the Mediterranean was concerned. This enabled diplomacy to become, in certain circumstances, as powerful a weapon as a battle fleet. This was particularly true of Spain. The Spanish Ambassador to Vichy, Señor Jose Felix Lequerica, who was later to become his country's ambassador to the United States, remarked: 'If the Germans had been aggressive, Spain would not have resisted them. We had nothing with which to resist ten German divisions but we kept them out by diplomacy.'[4]

After the United States entered the war, a fundamental change in American thinking towards Africa had to take place. Until 1940 the United States had not rated Africa high on its list of vital interests. The United States had not participated in the nineteenth- and twentieth-century European scramble for African colonies, and thus after the First World War had not been concerned in their redistribution.

The Americans, however, did have a contingency plan. War Plan Rainbow made provision for the ultimate dispatch of U.S. forces to Africa or Europe in order to bring about the decisive defeat of Germany or Italy or both and had been approved by the President in 1939. The question now was whether it would still hold good in the circumstances created by the fall of France, the withdrawal from Europe of the B.E.F. and the subsequent British success in the Battle of Britain.

Ambassador Murphy's preliminary information on his large, sprawling domain had, perforce, to come from documents assembled in France, Britain, Italy and Germany – many of them not translated into English. It was a daunting task to which Murphy addressed a spry sense of humour and a charisma in which luckily all shades of French and North African opinion felt able to trust.

But in the end sea power was what really mattered in the Mediterranean. Territorial gains could only be achieved by land armies, assisted from the air. However, it was upon the Royal Navy that responsibility rested for getting the Army to the point where it could be used and for seeing that, thereafter, its necessary supplies were delivered. Whilst throughout the war the British maintained their control of either end of the Mediterranean, the central fortress of Malta stood within a few days of collapse in the summer of 1942. How did this come about?

South Street, Valletta, choked with rubble

Logistics, which had always been a dominant factor, now moved into the 'front thinking' of the British in January 1942 and again it was in the Western Desert that questions of supply became crucial. The Eighth Army had naturally hoped to repeat their success of the previous year when the Italian retreat southward from Benghazi had been cut off by a swift advance to Antelat and over 100,000 prisoners had been taken. Now, however, they were up against Rommel. The Germans had no intention of being caught in this way. They held the Antelat position firmly, prepared a strong defensive position at Agedabia and retired behind this line unmolested on 7 January 1942. The British advance petered out.

It is necessary to understand that Auchinleck could not advance beyond Agedabia until Benghazi was back into full working order, and his hopes of pushing on to Tripoli in the near future had been destroyed by naval setbacks in the Mediterranean and the dire events in the Far East. It was not so much a question of what the Germans intended but of what Auchinleck could do with the one and a half to two divisions which were all he could maintain in the forward area.

In essence the Eighth Army now found itself at the extreme end of its administrative tether. An unfortunate delay, ascribed to bad weather and enemy air interference, took place in bringing back into working order the port of Benghazi. Supplies for the forward troops had therefore to be brought by road from Tobruk and not enough got through to provide the necessary build-up. In mid-January the newly arrived 1st Armoured Division relieved the Guards Brigade and the 7th Armoured facing the Germans at Agheila. These troops were, for a time, neither strong enough to attack nor well enough prepared against a counter-attack by the Afrika Korps.

On 21 January Rommel launched a reconnaissance in force, consisting of three columns each of about 1,000 motorized infantry supported by tanks. These rapidly found their way through gaps in the British line. The series of disasters for the British in 1942 had begun.

By 26 January Rommel had pushed forward to Msus; he then had the option of striking north-west to Benghazi or north-east to Mechili. He did both. He made a feint towards Mechili and sent the 5th Light Division and the Italian 20th Corps

towards Benghazi. This provoked the evacuation of Benghazi and the whole 13th Corps then fell back to the Gazala–Bir Hacheim line. Here the position was to remain stabilized until the end of May when Rommel had become strong enough to strike again.

Rommel had once more proved himself a master of desert tactics, but the main blame for this setback to the British rests squarely upon indifferent leadership in the field. Sad incidents point this up. General Ritchie perhaps tried to do too much and also thought that the thrust towards Mechili was probably the enemy's main effort. The armoured element of the newly arrived 1st Armoured Division was composed of three converted cavalry regiments. These had no experience of desert warfare and little of armoured operations. This resulted in their losing over 100 of their tanks, but some of these had simply been abandoned in the desert. The Guards Brigade, withdrawing under orders, found large petrol supplies which they had to destroy as the enemy was near, but they soon took to bringing on as much petrol as they could in order to drive back these abandoned tanks. One company of the

Coldstream alone collected six and other companies emerged stronger than when they had set out, having acquired a few tanks to work with their motorized infantry in the German fashion.

As Churchill commented: 'When we remember the cost, time and labour the creation of an entity like an armoured division, with all its experts and trained men, involves, the effort required to transport it round the Cape, the many preparations made to bring it into battle, it is indeed grievous to see the result squandered through such mismanagement . . . nor should the British nation, in probing these matters, be misled into thinking that the technical inferiority of our tanks was the only reason for this considerable and far-reaching reverse.'[5]

It now seemed likely, especially in view of the renewed air attacks on Malta, that the German strength in the desert would grow more quickly than the British. Malta thus became crucial to the prolonged and desperate struggle for maintenance of the British position in Egypt and the Middle East, and the British also needed access to the airfields of western Cyrenaica.

In the Western Desert the outcome of each

phase began to be determined by the rate at which supplies could reach the combatants by sea. For the British this meant the use of high-class shipping for periods of two to three months. This shipping was subject to increasing U-boat attack for voyages to the Suez Canal round the Cape. For the Germans and Italians the two- to three-day passage from Italy to North Africa entailed the use of only a moderate number of smaller ships. The disparity in these two supply routes would have been extreme but for the presence of Malta right athwart the Axis route to Tripoli.

Yet Malta itself needed considerable supplies and as 1942 wore on its plight became increasingly acute. One reason for this was a change in Hitler's thinking provoked by Grand Admiral Raeder after the two battle-cruisers *Scharnhorst* and *Gneisenau* had successfully made their Channel dash from Brest to Norway in the middle of February. This naval feat put Hitler into a receptive mood when Raeder renewed his suggestion that the Axis should go over to the offensive in the Mediterranean.

German intervention in North Africa had so far been looked upon as a purely defensive measure to prevent an Italian collapse. 'However,' the Grand Admiral observed, 'the favourable situation in the Mediterranean, so pronounced at the present time, will probably never occur again. All reports confirm that the enemy is making tremendous efforts to pour all available reinforcements into Egypt . . . it is therefore imperative to take Malta as soon as possible and to launch an offensive against the Suez Canal.'[6]

But Hitler was a land animal. He continued to hesitate, hoping – as he had vainly done in the Battle of Britain – that relentless air assault would bring about a capitulation. Moreover he had only just authorized final cancellation of his long-term plans for the invasion of England which had lingered on since 1940. Instead the order to step up the air attacks went out.

In March 1942 the Admiralty decided to run four merchant ships to Malta from the east. On the 20th these ships left Alexandria escorted by 4 light cruisers and a destroyer flotilla, under the command of Admiral Vian. This time the Italians sent one of their most modern battleships, the *Littorio*, 2 heavy cruisers, a light cruiser and 10 destroyers to take care of the matter. The British

were 'somewhat out-gunned'.

Nevertheless on the 22nd Vian attacked and against heavy odds fought and won a successful action to protect the convoy which got through unscathed until within sight of Valletta. Then the inevitable heavy air attacks sank two of the ships with only eight miles to go. The two remaining ships reached Grand Harbour, only to be sunk whilst being unloaded. It was a heartbreaking blow and the decision was forced on the War Cabinet not to send through any more convoys until Malta could be reinforced with fighter aircraft. Thirty-four such aircraft had reached the island in March but these were not nearly enough.

On 1 April 1942 Churchill made a direct appeal to the American President:

> Air attack on Malta is very heavy. There are now in Sicily about 400 German and 200 Italian fighters and bombers. Malta can now muster only twenty or thirty serviceable fighters. We keep feeding Malta with Spitfires in packets of sixteen loosed from *Eagle* carrier from about six hundred miles west of Malta. This has worked a good many times quite well, but *Eagle* is now laid up for a month by defects in her steering gear. There are no Spitfires in Egypt. *Argus* is too small and too slow, and moreover she has to provide fighter cover for the carrier launching the Spitfires and for the escorting force. We would use *Victorious* but unfortunately her lifts are too small for Spitfires. Therefore there will be a whole month without any Spitfire reinforcements.
>
> 2. It seems likely, from extraordinary enemy concentrations on Malta, that they hope to exterminate our air defence in time to reinforce either Libya or their Russian offensive. This would mean that Malta would be at the best powerless to interfere with reinforcements of armour to Rommel, and our chances of resuming offensive against him at an early date ruined.
>
> 3. Would you be willing to allow your carrier *Wasp* to do one of these trips provided details are satisfactorily agreed between the Naval Staffs? With her broad lifts, capacity and length, we estimate that *Wasp* could take fifty or more Spitfires. Unless it were necessary for her to fuel, *Wasp* could proceed through the Straits at night without calling at Gibraltar until on the return journey, as the Spitfires would be embarked in the Clyde.
>
> 4. Thus, instead of not being able to give Malta any further Spitfires during April, a powerful Spitfire force could be flown into Malta at a stroke and give us a chance of inflicting a very severe and possibly decisive check on enemy. Operation might take place during third week of April.[7]

Roosevelt's response was generous and immediate. During April and May 126 aircraft were safely delivered to the Malta garrison from the *Wasp* and the *Eagle* with, as Churchill says, 'salutary results'. After the great air battles of 9 May daylight raiding abruptly ended.

Previous pages: Attempts to reinforce and supply Malta cost the Allies heavy losses. H.M.S. Ark Royal, *torpedoed by the submarines U.81 and U.205 on 13 November 1941, takes a heavy list. She sank the following day twenty-five miles from Gibraltar*

Left: H.M.S. Barham, also torpedoed by a German submarine, blows up with heavy loss of life on 25 November 1941

Following pages: Tobruk remained until the summer of 1942 a thorn in the flesh of the Axis powers. German troops outside the defensive perimeter, December 1941

'In June,' Churchill continued, 'the stage was at last set for another large-scale attempt to relieve the island, and this time it was intended to pass convoys through from the east and west simultaneously.'[8]

Past Gibraltar six ships entered the Mediterranean headed east for Malta. From Alexandria another convoy of eleven merchant ships set off in the other direction. Both convoys were as heavily protected as British resources allowed but were up against strong concentrations of German and Italian submarines, together with the whole Italian battle fleet. They would also have to endure overwhelming air attacks from Sicily.

In the event, so desperate were all these combined hazards that the eastern convoy looked in danger of becoming a complete loss. The cruiser *Hermione* had been sunk and the convoy was then turned back to Alexandria. Of the six western convoy ships four were sunk and thus out of a planned seventeen only two got through. The crisis deepened.

By this time Malta was expecting the worst – and with reason. Both the German and Italian High Commands were fully aware of the close interconnection between Malta and the desert operations. The moment Malta recuperated enough to strike back, Rommel's supplies failed to arrive. In March, in fact, only 18,000 tons out of a total requirement of 60,000 tons got through. It became essential, therefore, either to reduce Malta to impotence or, better still, to capture it.

The Axis plan to take Malta with parachute and airborne forces went by the code name of 'Hercules', and at the end of April Mussolini paid Hitler a visit at Berchtesgaden during which it was agreed that the attack on Malta should be launched early in July. It was further agreed that Rommel's offensive in Africa should be temporarily halted so that the full weight of the Luftwaffe could be switched to Malta.

What Rommel did not know – nor could anyone at the planning end of the operations in Africa – was that for all their fine words the two dictators were somewhat suspicious of each other when it came to matters of trust. No sooner had the Duce departed than Hitler renewed his doubts in discussions with his staff about the fighting qualities and general reliability of the Italian armed forces. They could not keep anything secret, Hitler

declared, and they had insufficient fighting spirit for success. Being Italian, they would not be punctual in supporting the German parachute troops, who would thus carry the brunt of the attack. Finally their Navy refused to face the British and this would be likely to leave the Germans stranded.

Sycophantic though they were, on this occasion Hitler's staff officers had no need of hypocrisy in the ready agreement they gave to the Fuehrer's analysis of the real state of affairs. Late in May, therefore, Hitler decided that preparations for 'Hercules' should continue only on paper and that the operation would, in any case, be dropped if Rommel were to capture Tobruk. The reason for this, Hitler argued, was that the supply ships could then be sent to Tobruk via Crete, thus by-passing Malta, which could be kept under by air attack and the denial of supplies. This argument begged the issue in that Tobruk might well prove to be unusable, but could be backed up by the narrowness of the margin by which German paratroops had escaped disaster in Crete. However, with Malta still in British hands, experience should have told the Fuehrer that crippled though the fortress might have become in the process,

sooner or later it would be relieved and would recover.

In the event Hitler's change of plan only became known when it was too late to do anything about it. Writing afterwards about the campaign, Rommel merely says: 'For some unaccountable reason the High Command abandoned this scheme. My request to have this pleasant task entrusted to my own army had unfortunately been refused in the previous spring.'[9]

In Malta itself the British armed forces and the Maltese population had long been living from hand to mouth and now, to many of them, the end was in sight. In March Governor-General Dobbie, 'that magnificent Cromwellian figure' as Churchill described him, had reported the situation as critical. On 20 April he signalled: 'It has now gone beyond that point, and it is obvious that the very worst may happen if we cannot replenish our vital needs, especially flour and ammunition, and that very soon . . . it is a question of survival.'[10] Bread consumption was cut by a further quarter and supplies would only last to the middle of June. In fact Malta was starving.

The ability to withstand terrible sieges is in the

A 25-pounder field gun in action at 'Knightsbridge', west of El Adem

Maltese blood and this was to be yet another heroic time. Starving people, however, can only just keep alive, they cannot work with anything like efficiency. There were a growing number of human casualties caused by the continuous bombing and in April the Governor himself became one of them. 'Disturbing news arrived about General Dobbie,' Churchill wrote. 'Up to this moment he had been magnificent . . . but the long strain had worn him down. I received this news with very deep regret and I did not at first accept what I was told. However a successor had to be chosen. I felt that in Lord Gort, the Governor of Gibraltar, would be found a warrior of the truest mettle. . . .'[11] So the change was made and Gort saw the island through until its relief in 1943.

By June the climax approached both in Malta and across the water in Cyrenaica. On 26 May 1942 Rommel began the dramatic offensive which was to carry him to within sixty miles of the Nile. That day he wrote to his wife: 'By the time you get this letter you will have long ago heard from the Wehrmacht communiqués about events here. We're launching a decisive attack today. It will be hard but I have full confidence that my army will win it. After all they all know what battle means. There is no need to tell you how I will go into it. I intend to demand of myself the same as I expect from each of my officers and men. My thoughts, especially in these hours of decision, are often with you.'[12]

In London Churchill's thoughts were on General Auchinleck and they were by no means as tender. There was a feeling in the War Cabinet, a feeling which had been building up since the reverse of February, that the Commander-in-Chief of the Middle East was not being nearly aggressive enough. 'During February,' Churchill wrote, 'it became apparent to us that General Auchinleck proposed to make another four months' pause in order to mount a second set-piece battle with Rommel. Neither the Chiefs of Staff nor I and my colleagues were convinced that another of these costly interludes was necessary.'[13]

Between then and May the anxiety had grown. Auchinleck had the huge total of 630,000 men on ration strength in February. Reinforcements were constantly arriving and the C.-in-C.'s apparent unwillingness to attack first puzzled and later exasperated London. The prodding which Auch-

inleck received became more and more insistent and by May Churchill was writing, 'It was decided to send General Auchinleck definite orders which he must obey or be relieved. This was a most unusual procedure on our part towards a high military commander.'[14]

In his replies to this waspish interference from Whitehall, Auchinleck made it clear that he did intend to go over to the offensive, but only when the moment was right. Churchill's fear was that he would leave it too late, and he summed it up succinctly in his own account of this time.

> I have often tried to set down the strategic truths I have comprehended in the form of simple anecdotes, and they rank this way in my mind. One of them is the celebrated tale of the man who gave the powder to the bear. He mixed the powder with the greatest care, making sure that not only the ingredients but the proportions were absolutely correct. He rolled it up in a large paper spill and was about to blow it down the bear's throat. *But the bear blew first.*[15]

The bear, in this case Rommel, blew with a devastating effect. On 26 May – a moonlit night – he moved quickly, turning the British flank of the fortified Gazala line with his 3 German divisions and 2 of the Italian mobile corps and leaving the 4 unmotorized Italian divisions to 'make faces' at the Gazala line.

The Gazala line was held by 13th Corps under Lieutenant-General 'Strafer Gott' – the 1st South African Division being on the right and the 50th on the left. 30th Corps with most of the armour was to cover the southern flank and would also counter any Panzer threat to the centre. Bir Hacheim was held by a French brigade supported by the armoured brigade of 7th Armoured Division, whilst ten miles to the north the 1st Armoured Division was stationed near Trigh Capuzzo. The British were, once again, dangerously dispersed and although Auchinleck had suggested to Ritchie, the Commander of the Eighth Army, that a closer concentration was desirable his suggestion was not put into effect.

Some 10,000 vehicles were involved in Rommel's outflanking movement and these were naturally spotted and reported before dark and again at dawn when they were sweeping round Bir Hacheim. The British, however, took this to be a feint and awaited the main attack they expected to be made on the centre of the line. When this attack failed to materialize, the British armoured brigades were slow to move, and, when they did so, came into action piecemeal and were thus disrupted.

H.Q. of 7th Armoured Division was overrun and its commander, Major-General F. W. Messervy, captured (although he later escaped). Rommel, however, did not succeed in cutting through to the sea and thus severing the Gazala line from its supplies. The Panzers came up against the American Grant tanks with their 75-mm guns for the first time and found themselves outranged.

On the second day Rommel renewed his effort to reach the sea and again failed. He was thus in a precarious position himself, his supplies having to make the long loop round Bir Hacheim, all the time suffering intensive R.A.F. bombing on his defensive position, now aptly called 'the Cauldron'. Indeed in the days which followed, the British thought Rommel had been trapped. He could be dealt with at leisure and, sooner or later, would be compelled to surrender. In fact, because Ritchie failed to concentrate the opposite happened. 'In spite of the precarious situation,' Rommel wrote, 'I looked forward full of hope to what the battle might bring. For Ritchie had thrown his armour into the battle piecemeal and had thus given us the chance of engaging them on each separate occasion with just enough of our own tanks . . . they should never have allowed themselves to be duped into dividing their forces. . . .'[16]

By the night of 13 June the whole balance had changed and on the following day Ritchie abandoned the Gazala line, retreating rapidly to the frontier. This left Tobruk isolated. Such a long step back had never been Auchinleck's intention and his orders were for the Eighth Army to rally and stand on a line west of Tobruk. But Ritchie failed to tell his Commander-in-Chief that the Gazala forces had been ordered back to the frontier and by the time Auchinleck discovered this fact it was too late to reverse the decision. By 15 June the battle of Gazala was over. The airfields at Gambut, east of Tobruk, were now in Rommel's hands and instead of pursuing the remnants of the British armoured brigades eastwards, Rommel promptly turned his attention to the capture of Tobruk. Some 400 British tanks had been put out of action and although the Commander of the Afrika Korps, General Cruewell, together with

his Storch aircraft, had fallen into British hands, German losses were, in Rommel's opinion, 'bearable'.

Tobruk remained the key to it all. In 1940 this had been one of the strongest fortresses in North Africa and although by 1942 the defences on the landward side had been allowed to run down, it was still a hard nut to crack. In 1941 it had presented Rommel with immense difficulties. 'Often the battle had raged round a square yard at a time,' Rommel had written, but in June 1942 'it could not be expected to put up such a stubborn and well-organized resistance, for the bulk of the troops had already given us battle and were tired and dispirited. The British Command, moreover, which was never very quick at reorganizing, had been given no time to build up its defensive machine.'[17]

In June 1942 the garrison was of approximately the same strength as in the previous year and consisted of:

2 Infantry Brigades of the South African Division
2 Battalions of the 201st Guards Brigade
11th Indian Brigade
2 Battalions of the 32nd Tank Brigade (Infantry tanks)
4th Anti-aircraft Brigade.

In addition to this force inside Tobruk, General Ritchie still had available five infantry divisions. Three of these had been very badly mauled; the other two had been freshly brought up. His two armoured divisions had been virtually wiped out in the recent fighting.

Tobruk was hemmed in on its eastern and western sides by rocky and trackless country which extended out to the south in a flat and sandy plain. It had been extremely well fortified by the Italians under Balbo, and a full account had been taken of the most modern weapons for the reduction of fortifications. The numerous defence positions running in a belt round the fortress were sunk in the ground in such a manner that they could only be located from the air.

In 1940, each defence position had consisted of an underground tunnel system leading into machine and anti-tank gun nests. These nests, of which most of the defence positions had a considerable number, could wait until the moment of greatest danger before throwing off their camouflage and pouring a murderous fire into the attacking troops. Artillery could not take them under direct fire because of the lack of apertures on which to take aim. Each separate position was surrounded by an anti-tank ditch and deep wire entanglements. In addition each fortified zone was surrounded at all points vulnerable to tanks by a deep anti-tank ditch. Behind the outer line or belt of fortifications, often in depth, stood powerful artillery concentrations, field positions and a number of forts. These impressive defence works were protected by deep minefields.

By June 1942 the Tobruk defences did not present nearly so formidable an aspect to an attacker but Rommel set about the problem with his usual strong determination, managing to write a mere four sentences to his wife: 'Only two hours' sleep last night. This is the really decisive day. Hope my luck holds. I'm very tired, though quite well otherwise.'[18]

At 0520 hours on 20 June 1942 the attack began. Several hundred aircraft hammered down their bombs on the break-in point south-east of the fortress. Great fountains of dust plumed up out of the Indian positions, whirling entanglements and weapons high into the air. Bomb after bomb tore through the British wire.

As soon as the aircraft left off, the infantry of the Afrika Korps (15th Rifle Brigade) and XX Italian Corps moved forward to the assault. Lanes had been cleared through the minefields the night before. Two hours later the German storming parties had succeeded in driving a wedge into the British defences. One position after another was captured in fierce hand-to-hand combat. Under very heavy fire German engineers had bridged the anti-tank ditch by 0800 hours. The way was now open to Rommel's armour.

At about the same time Rommel drove with his *Gefechtsstaffel* (small front-line staff) through the Italian Ariete Division's sector and into that of the 15th Panzer. Riding in an armoured troop-carrier, 'I went through as far as the lanes through the minefields, which lay under heavy British artillery fire. Considerable traffic jams were piling up as a result of this fire and I sent Lieutenant Berndt up immediately to organize a smooth flow of traffic. Half an hour later I crossed the anti-tank ditch with Bayerlein and examined two of the captured positions.'

Meanwhile the Afrika Korps had become the target of British tank attacks from outside the fortress. A violent tank battle flared up, in which the artillery on both sides joined. 'Towards 1100 hours I ordered the Ariete and Trieste who, after overcoming the anti-tank ditch, had come to a halt in the British defended zone, to follow up through the Afrika Korps' penetration. The German attack moved steadily on and the Afrika Korps, after a brief action in which some fifty British tanks were shot up, reached the crossroad Sidi Mahmud at about midday.'

At that moment Rommel held the fate of Tobruk in his hand. 'I now accompanied the Afrika Korps' advance onward from the cross-road. A furious fire beat into the attacking troops from the Fort Pilastrino area and several nests on the Jebel descent. Several British ships weighed anchor and made as if to leave harbour, apparently attempting to get their men away by sea. I at once directed the A.A. and artillery on to this target and six ships were sunk. Most of the men aboard them were picked up.'

The advance continued and they soon reached the descent into the town, where they came up against a British strong-point which fought back with extraordinary stubbornness. 'I sent Lieut. Schlippenbach with a summons to the garrison of fifty men to surrender. Their only answer was a withering fire on our vehicles. Eventually our out-rider, Corporal Huber, covered by six anti-aircraft men, succeeded in approaching the strong point and putting the garrison out of action with hand grenades.'

In the evening Pilastrino offered to capitulate and a Stuka attack on the fort was called off. Fort Solaro was stormed and another gunboat was sunk in the harbour. By nightfall two-thirds of the fortress lay in German hands, the town and harbour having been captured by the Afrika Korps in the afternoon.

'At 0500 hours on 21 June, I drove into the town of Tobruk. Practically every building of the dismal place was either flat or little more than a heap of rubble, mostly as the result of our siege in 1941. I drove along the Via Balbia to the west.' Some thirty tanks under repair but serviceable were surrendered, whilst vehicles on either side of the Via Balbia went up in flames. Everywhere chaos and destruction reigned. Then came the abrupt and astonishing end.

'At about 0940 hours on the Via Balbia about

Previous pages: *During the night of 26–27 May 1942, Rommel initiated a series of hard-fought battles by launching a turning movement round the southern flank of the Gazala-Bir Hacheim position*

Top left: *A British soldier seeks such cover as he can find during a dive-bomber attack on a stronghold at 'Knightsbridge'*

Bottom left: *French Foreign Legionnaires go into action wearing kepis instead of steel helmets*

Bottom right: *Out-fought in the battle of the Gazala-Bir Hacheim position, the British lost Tobruk and were forced to withdraw to the virtually unturnable El Alamein-Gattara position. A convoy on the move*

Top right: *Three Italian generals captured in the desert. Left to right: Brigadier-General Masina, Major-General Brunetti, Brigadier-General Bignani*

Right: *French gunners and infantry in action at Bir Hacheim*

four miles west of the town, I met General Klopper, G.O.C. 2nd South African Infantry Division and Garrison Commander of Tobruk. He announced the capitulation of the fortress of Tobruk. He had been unable to stave off defeat any longer, although he had done all he could to maintain control over his troops.' Rommel told the General, who was accompanied by his chief of staff, to follow him in his car back along the Via Balbia and into Tobruk. By now the road was lined with about 10,000 men about to become prisoners of war.

'On arrival at the Hotel Tobruk, I talked for a while with General Klopper. It seemed that he had no longer been in possession of the necessary communications to organize a break-out. It had all gone too quickly. I instructed the South African General to make himself and his officers responsible for order among the prisoners, and to organize their maintenance from the captured stores.'[19]

Subsequent military commentators maintain that 33,000 men, no matter how brave, could not have held Tobruk for more than a few days. No single-seat fighters were available to drive off the bombers and dive-bombers, working from air-

fields so close that they could make almost continuous sorties, to which the dispirited garrison was exposed. However, at the time, the fall of Tobruk struck British hopes an appalling blow. It found Churchill again in Washington, plugging hard for what was soon to be known as Operation Torch. In this matter he had the President on his side, but against both stood the powerful Pacific lobby which wanted first to defeat Japan before attending to Hitler. It took no military genius to see that this stunning defeat in the Western Desert opened the way to the Nile. If the Germans were about to take Egypt, then the future of both the British and the Russian war effort might well be at stake.

'This was one of the heaviest blows I can recall during the war,' Churchill wrote:

Not only were its military effects grievous, but it had affected the reputation of the British armies. At Singapore eighty-five thousand men had surrendered to inferior numbers of Japanese. Now in Tobruk a garrison of twenty-five thousand (actually thirty-three thousand) seasoned soldiers had laid down their arms to perhaps one-half of their number. If this was typical of the morale of the Desert Army, no measure could be put upon the disasters which impended in North East Africa. I did not attempt to hide

from the President the shock I had received. It was a bitter moment. Defeat is one thing; disgrace is another. Nothing could exceed the sympathy and chivalry of my two friends. There were no reproaches; not an unkind word was spoken. 'What can we do to help?' said Roosevelt. I replied at once, 'Give us as many Sherman tanks as you can spare, and ship them to the Middle East as quickly as possible.' The President sent for General Marshall, who arrived in a few minutes, and told him of my request. Marshall replied: 'Mr President, the Shermans are only just coming into production. The first few hundred have been issued to our own armoured divisions who have hitherto had to be content with obsolete equipment. It is a terrible thing to take the weapons out of a soldier's hands. Nevertheless if the British need is so great, they must have them; and we could let them have a hundred 105-mm self-propelled guns in addition.'[20]

The relationship between the British and American leaders compares well with that between Hitler and Mussolini. As Churchill remarked at the time, 'A friend in need is a friend indeed.'

The capture of Tobruk concluded the fighting in the Marmarica for a while. To the Afrika Korps this was the high point of the African war. Rommel issued the following Order of the Day:

Soldiers!

The great battle in the Marmarica has been crowned by your quick conquest of Tobruk. We have taken in all over 45,000 prisoners and destroyed or captured more than 1,000 armoured fighting vehicles and nearly 400 guns.

During the long and hard struggle of the last four weeks, you have through your incomparable courage and tenacity, dealt the enemy blow upon blow. Your spirit of attack has cost him the core of his field army, which was standing poised for an offensive. Above all he has lost his powerful armour. My special congratulations to officers and men for this superb achievement.

Soldiers of the Panzer Army Afrika!

Now for the complete destruction of the enemy. We will not rest until we have shattered the last remnants of the British Eighth Army. During the days to come I shall call on you for one more great effort to bring us to this final goal.
Rommel[21]

The next day Hitler made him a Field-Marshal. He was forty-nine. He became so busy in the days that followed that he forgot to change his shoulder badges to those of his new rank. It was only after he had reached El Alamein that Field-Marshal Kesselring pointed this out and gave him a pair of his own badges. Rommel received his actual baton when he saw Hitler in Berlin in September. Yet all the time he thought more of his troops and of the job in hand than of himself. As he remarked to his wife at the time, 'I would rather Hitler had given me one more division.'

A Valentine tank advancing through loose sand

3
THE ALLIES AT BAY

Whilst the North African campaign, Malta and the whole Middle Eastern theatre of war occupied the front of the stage, so to speak, during the first nine months of 1942, the American President and the British Prime Minister, together with their service advisers, had thrown themselves jointly and at once into the high strategic planning necessary to defeat first the Axis powers and then Japan at the earliest possible moment. This was no easy task. Once again the operative factor lay in control of the sea.

By great good fortune President Roosevelt had been a one-time Assistant Secretary of the U.S. Navy, and throughout his life retained a fascination for naval affairs. Churchill, who was a wily enough politician not to think twice about playing on susceptibilities for the benefit of national gain, worked on this and always described himself in his telegrams to Roosevelt as 'Former Naval Person'. Although no imperialist, Roosevelt was unashamedly and strongly pro-British. He was also firmly of the opinion, in contrast to the personal views of Admiral King, the head of the U.S. Navy, that Germany must be defeated before Japan.

The friendship and understanding between

Churchill and Roosevelt became an invaluable factor in the winning of the war. Prior to Pearl Harbor, Roosevelt had bent the United States constitution as far as he reasonably could to send aid to Great Britain during the eighteen months in which the British had fought on alone. He had done this despite his own Ambassador Kennedy's sour and negative recommendations from London. He had done it against considerable political opposition in the United States (which, however, died overnight after Pearl Harbor) and he continued to back British interests to the maximum possible during those crucial nine months in 1942 whilst America was fully engaged in gearing up her vast industrial potential to the war but was not yet in a position effectively to fight, and when it also seemed that disaster after disaster continued to assail the British.

The problems thus facing Churchill, Roosevelt and their Combined Chiefs of Staff (a newly set up organization unique in world history and very far removed from anything similar on the Axis side) were immense, vital and urgent. Time pressed and the timing of future agreed action became increasingly finer as the first nine months of 1942 went on

their way. In addition there was Stalin calling urgently for help, ready to take all and give nothing and, in the private opinion of both Roosevelt and Churchill, fully prepared, if things went too badly, to make another deal with Hitler as he had done in the Ribbentrop-Molotov non-aggression pact of 23 August 1939.

Yet however surly and incomprehensible 'Uncle Joe' might (and did) prove to be, the Russians were nevertheless draining away German resources in that terrible Russian winter. There was never any question but that the Russians had to be supported to the best of Allied ability. No matter how embarrassing his plea might be for a 'Second Front Now' – embarrassing in the sense that neither the United States nor Great Britain had the capability of obliging in the early part of 1942 – Stalin must somehow or other be kept going.

Of first importance, however, there remained the necessity of keeping the United Kingdom itself not only supplied but also increasingly stocked up as the Anglo-American arsenal from which a later attack into Europe would be sprung. This need was paramount. But how could such a vast build-up of men and material be organized

without diverting essential reinforcements from the Near and Middle East and thus risking the collapse of these vital areas in the way the Far East had gone?

Between 1 January and 30 June 1942 Allied losses in the Atlantic from U-boats alone amounted to over 3,000,000 tons of shipping. This figure cost the Germans no more than fourteen U-boats sunk throughout the Atlantic and Arctic oceans. After July the Allies did, in fact, regain the initiative and in that month alone a further eleven U-boats were sunk. But in the grim spring and early summer of 1942 it was a very near thing and Allied strategic planning was in no way helped by what had also been happening in the Western Desert.

The question of French North Africa – Morocco, Algeria and Tunisia – had been mooted at the Christmas 1941 meeting between Churchill and Roosevelt in Washington. Politically, Admiral Darlan in Vichy was thought to be on the crest of a wave and the situation with the French was that the British were lumbered with de Gaulle, whereas the Americans were in close and helpful touch with Vichy. Churchill's thinking at this time was set out in a minute to the First Sea Lord (who accompanied him to Washington) dated 13 December 1941:

> I hope we may make together a joint offer of blessing or cursing to Vichy or, failing Vichy, to French North Africa.
>
> We cannot tell yet how France will have been affected by the American entry. There are also hopes of favourable reactions from a Libyan victory. Above all, the growing disaster of the German armies in Russia will influence all minds.
>
> It may well be that an American offer to land an American Expeditionary Force at Casablanca, added to the aid we can give under 'Gymnast', would decide the action of French North Africa (and incidentally Madagascar). At any rate it is worth trying. I don't want any changes in our dispositions about 'Gymnast' or 'Truncheon' [a combined raid on Leghorn] until we know what the reply of Vichy will be.
>
> It must be borne in mind that the United States would be generally in favour of North and West Africa as a major theatre for Anglo-American operations.[1]

Churchill further analysed and developed this idea in a memorandum to the American President which began:

> Hitler's failure and losses in Russia are the prime fact of war at this time. We cannot tell how great the disaster to the German army and Nazi régime will be. The régime has hitherto lived upon easily and cheaply won successes. Instead of what was imagined to be a swift and easy victory, it has now to face the shock of a winter of slaughter and

expenditure of fuel and equipment on the largest scale . . . we ought, therefore, to try hard to win over French North Africa and now is the moment to use every inducement and form of pressure at our disposal upon the Government of Vichy and the French authorities in North Africa . . . if we can obtain even the connivance of Vichy to French North Africa coming over to our side we must be ready to send considerable forces as soon as possible.

Churchill then went on to say that, apart from anything which General Auchinleck could bring in from the east, should he be successful in Tripolitania (this was, of course, before the February setback) two divisions and one armoured unit were held ready in Britain (Operation Gymnast) comprising about 55,000 men together with the necessary shipping. If invited, these forces could enter French North Africa on the twenty-third day after the order to embark them was given. Leading elements and air forces from Malta could also reach Bizerta at very short notice.

It is desired that the United States should at the same time promise to bring in via Casablanca and other African Atlantic ports, not less than 150,000 men during the next six months. It is essential that some American elements, say 25,000 men, should go at the earliest moment after French agreement, either Vichy or North African had been obtained.

However, Churchill continued, the Allies must reckon with a refusal by Vichy to act as desired. On the contrary, they might well rouse French North Africa to active resistance. They might even help German troops to enter North Africa; the Germans might force their way or be granted passage through Spain; the French Fleet at Toulon might pass under German control and France and the French Empire thus be made by Vichy to collaborate actively with Germany against the Allied cause, although it was not likely that this would go through effectively.

The overwhelming majority of the French are ranged with Great Britain, and now, still more, with the United States. It is by no means certain that Admiral Darlan can deliver the Toulon fleet over intact to Germany. It is most improbable that French soldiers and sailors would fight effectively against the United States and Great Britain. Nevertheless we must not exclude the possibility of a half hearted association of the defeatist elements in France and North Africa with Germany. In this case our task in North Africa will become much harder. . . .

Churchill then went on to conclude that a campaign must be fought in 1942 to gain possession of, or conquer, the whole of the North African shore. This, of course, included the Atlantic ports

of Morocco, Dakar and other French West African ports which would need to be captured before the end of the year. Whereas, however, entry into French North Africa would be urgent to prevent a German penetration, some eight or nine months' preparation might well be afforded for the mastering of Dakar and the West African establishments. Plans should be set on foot forthwith. If sufficient time and preparation were allowed and the proper apparatus provided, these latter operations would present no insuperable difficulty.

Churchill then went on to suggest that relations with General de Gaulle and the Free French movement would need to be reviewed. He pointed out that the United States had entered into no undertakings such as the British perforce had acquired with de Gaulle.

> Through no particular fault of his own, his movement has created new antagonisms in French minds. Any action which the United States may now feel able to take in regard to him should have the effect, *inter alia*, of redefining our obligations to him and France, so as to make these obligations more closely dependent upon the eventual effort by him and the French nation to rehabilitate themselves.

He went on to say that if Vichy came in on the Allied side then the United States and Great Britain must try to bring about a reconciliation between de Gaulle and the rest of the French. If on the other hand they had to fight their way into French North Africa then de Gaulle must be supported to the full.

> We cannot tell what will happen in Spain. It seems probable that the Spaniards will not give the Germans a free passage through Spain to attack Gibraltar and invade North Africa. There may be infiltration but the formal demand for the passage of an army would be resisted. If so the winter would be the worst time for the Germans to attempt to force their way through Spain. Moreover Hitler with nearly all Europe to hold down by armed force in the face of defeat and semi-starvation, may well be chary of taking over unoccupied France and involving himself in bitter guerilla warfare with the morose, fierce, hungry people of the Iberian peninsula. Everything possible must be done by Britain and the United States to strengthen their will to resist. The present policy of limited supplies should be pursued.

Churchill ended by again stressing that the main offensive action in the West by the United States and Great Britain should, in 1942, be the occupation and control of the North and West African possessions of France and the further control by Britain of the whole North African shore from Tunis to Egypt. This would allow free passage through the Mediterranean to the Levant and the Suez Canal.

> These great objectives can only be achieved if British and American naval and air superiority in the Atlantic is maintained, if supply lines continue uninterrupted and if the British Isles are effectively safeguarded against invasion.[2]

This document which Churchill put in front of Roosevelt and which Roosevelt in essence approved, turned out to be an accurate prognosis of events in almost every respect except that of timing. Because of events which were then about to happen in the Mediterranean, control of the whole North African shore was not obtained until May 1943. Otherwise everything Churchill had foreseen – or very nearly everything – came about. Thus began the vast operation later to be given the code name of 'Torch'.

The British War Cabinet appointed the first three Commanders-in-Chief in the early spring of 1942 and they were set to work in clammy bomb-proof concrete boxes deep under the War Office in Whitehall. These were the British Commanders-in-Chief designate of the Expeditionary Force, an embryo organization generated for purposes of 'the ultimate offensive' which was to reach its full maturity in Normandy over two years later. Early in 1942, however, the Expeditionary Force consisted only of Vice-Admiral Sir Bertram Ramsay, General Sir Bernard Paget and Air Chief-Marshal Sir Sholto Douglas, together with a small handful of staff officers, of which I was one.

This tiny planning unit was initially a part of the burgeoning Combined Operations organization which had been recently and basically revitalized by the appointment the previous November of Lord Louis Montbatten as its chief. This had been effected before Pearl Harbor and therefore preceded direct American involvement in the war. Mountbatten had replaced the veteran Admiral of the Fleet Lord Keyes. Mountbatten had accepted the post with reluctance, having only just taken command of the aircraft-carrier *Illustrious* in the Mediterranean. This command, in turn, had followed after he had been sunk in his destroyer flotilla leader *Kelly* during the battle of Crete. Mountbatten's preference to go back to sea had provoked a celebrated brush with Churchill who tersely inquired what he hoped to achieve other than again being sunk in a bigger and more expensive ship. Churchill had then given Mountbatten his directive in more or less these words:

> You will continue with the Commando raids in order to keep up the offensive spirit and gain essential experience of landing on enemy occupied coasts, and to harass the enemy. But above all I want you to start the preparations for our great counter-invasion of Europe . . . I want you to work out the philosophy of invasion, to land and advance against the enemy. You must collect the most brilliant planners in the three services to help you. You must devise and design new landing craft, appurtenances and appliances and train the three services to act together as a single force in combined operation.[3]

Mountbatten set to work with a will. On taking over Combined Operations headquarters he found it composed only of twenty-six officers and men, not one of whom was regular active service. This soon changed in a dramatic way. It must be remembered that in those days there was no such thing as a Ministry of Defence. Each of the three British services looked on itself as a sovereign power in its own right. New ideas were, therefore, urgently required and these Mountbatten amply and effectively supplied, in the process breaking down old prejudices and barriers and making himself unpopular in certain quarters. The appointment of Ramsay, Paget and Sholto Douglas marked the hiving off of the planning side of this assignment.

On 8 April 1942 Roosevelt sent his personal representative, Harry Hopkins, and the U.S. Army Chief of Staff General Marshall to London with proposals to invade France across the English Channel in the spring of 1943 (Operation 'Round-up'). The Americans also suggested that a small bridgehead should be established on the French coast in the autumn of 1942 as a foothold for the major offensive. There was no mention of 'Gymnast' or of any operation to take control of French North Africa.

This visit crystallized the already serious divergence in strategic thinking between the United States and Great Britain. The British were wholly in favour of building up Allied forces in the United Kingdom for an invasion of France when – but only when – the time was ripe. The Americans observed that while they might themselves lack war experience, they were confident that their enthusiasm and weight of numbers would carry them straight away into the heart of France. They considered that British defeats in Norway, Dunkirk and the Mediterranean and the consequent

dispiriting withdrawals had made their ally over-cautious. It became clear to the British that the strategic importance of the Mediterranean left the Americans unmoved.

The British had already prepared a plan (Operation 'Sledgehammer') for a seaborne assault across the Channel to capture the Cherbourg peninsula. This was predicated for the autumn of 1942, but was visualized only as a desperate measure to bring relief to the Russians. The British had no wish for a second Dunkirk, and pointed out that an assault across the Channel so late in the year might well end in disaster.

On the night of 14 April the British Chiefs of Staff saw their American visitors at a memorable meeting at 10 Downing Street. Here the differing points of view were fully hammered out and, subject to the qualification that the defence of India and the Middle East must be assured, the American plan for 'Round-up' in 1943 was agreed. Again no mention was made of a venture into French North Africa.

Meanwhile, the naval situation in the Mediterranean continued to go from bad to worse. The rot had begun in November 1941 with the loss of

the famous aircraft-carrier *Ark Royal* and the battleship *Barham*. This had been followed in December by the daring Italian human-torpedo attacks in Alexandria harbour on the battleships *Queen Elizabeth* and *Valiant*. These combined losses left the Mediterranean Fleet without any capital ships to face the Italians.

In the same month of December 1941 Force K, the cruiser force based on Malta, was virtually annihilated as a fighting unit following the sinking of the *Neptune* off Tripoli and the damaging of the other cruisers *Aurora* and *Penelope*. Mediterranean naval forces had further to be depleted in order to bolster up the situation in the Far East consequent on the destruction of the *Prince of Wales* and the *Repulse* a few days after Pearl Harbor.

In January 1942 attacks by air on Malta were intensified. A letter from Vice-Admiral Ford, the admiral in command, to his commander-in-chief Admiral Cunningham in Alexandria, gives a gloomy picture of the then current state of affairs (Admiral Ford had been five years in Malta and was long overdue for another appointment):

> I've given up counting the number of air raids we are getting. At the time of writing, 4 p.m., we have had exactly seven bombing raids since 9 a.m. quite apart from over a month of all-night efforts. The enemy is definitely trying to neutralize Malta's effort, and, I hate to say so, is gradually doing so. They've bust a sad number of our bombers and fighters, etc. and must continue to do so . . . now we have Libya and soon, I trust, Tripoli, I consider Malta must be made stiff with *modern* fighters, Mosquitoes which can fly out from the U.K. on their own and Spitfires from Takoradi if a carrier cannot buzz them off. Guns and stores must come in a submarine beforehand . . . the powers at home must give up safety first and send us out the latest if they want to hold Malta and use it as a base . . . minesweeping is now difficult and they appear to be laying them everywhere. Poor *Abingdon*, the only sweeper, and in daylight she got machine-gunned, eight casualties in *Abingdon* alone. I am trying to sweep during the dark hours . . . work in the Yard is naturally very much slowed up at present as the result of the constant raids . . . until we get net defence I shall continue to be worried, especially for Marsamuscetto and the submarines. Nothing really to stop 'em. Why oh! why did not . . . press for my scheme of underground shelters. They would have been finished by now. As I write another bombing raid is just over and at least two more of ours burnt out – damnable to be quite useless. Something must be done at once. How I can unload convoys I cannot think. . . .[4]

It was to get very much worse. On 17 January 1942 only one out of four merchant ships convoyed to Malta got through, one of the destroyer escorts, H.M.S. *Ghurka*, also being sunk and after

Benghazi had been evacuated by the retreating Eighth Army on the 25th (just after the Royal Navy had unloaded 3,000 tons of petrol in the port) the convoy route to Malta from the east had now to pass through the 200-mile gap between Crete to the north and the bulge of Cyrenaica to the south. Enemy aerodromes thus lined each flank of the convoy route and the future of Malta looked very black indeed.

In mid-February all four ships in a convoy from Alexandria were sunk and in March, in spite of the successful naval outcome of the battle of Sirte, only 5,000 tons out of a total of 26,000 in the convoy got through.

The point had now been reached at which it was too hazardous to maintain any surface forces in Malta. All ships that remained, therefore, sailed. The cruiser *Carlisle* and four destroyers went to Alexandria, the *Aurora* and a destroyer to Gibraltar and later the sorely battered *Penelope* which had been constantly damaged in dry dock was at last got clear and made a safe passage to Gibraltar. For a few more weeks submarine patrols were maintained but these formed the only remaining hindrance in the central Mediterranean to the essential and dangerous reinforcement of Rommel.

April saw the arrival of forty-seven Spitfires flown in from H.M.S. *Eagle* and the U.S.S. *Wasp*, but within a few days the great majority of these had been destroyed, the defence of the fortress now depending on guns severely rationed for ammunition. So bad now was the bombing and so intense the minelaying (by aircraft and motor torpedo boats from Sicily) that even the submarines could not be operated and at the end of the month they were withdrawn to Alexandria. Three had been sunk by bombs and another, the last to leave, was destroyed by a mine off the harbour mouth.

In June the final attempts to run convoys through to Malta from the west and from the east resulted, as previously described, in almost total disaster, only two out of seventeen ships reaching Valletta. By now although Malta was still just hanging on, Rommel had renewed his offensive.

By 17 June the Eighth Army had virtually collapsed; although the 50th Division and the 1st South African Division were intact, Ritchie's armour had taken a beating. By 21 June Tobruk had fallen into enemy hands, and it was only in

Previous pages: Anti-aircraft gunners stand to as a destroyer enters Grand Harbour, Malta

Left: The desert was by no means flat. A ridge and peak photographed through the windscreen of a patrolling vehicle

Following pages: German troops in action at First Alamein

July that Rommel was eventually brought to a halt by the big battle of First Alamein (sixty miles from Alexandria), which is now seen as a turning point of the Desert War. The strategic planners in London and Washington, therefore, could detect no gleam of hope so far as the naval situation was concerned in the eastern Mediterranean. Indeed it was now to be a question of moving such valuable units as remained in Alexandria south through the Suez Canal. The threat to Egypt and the whole of the Near East rose to its peak in August 1942.

Meanwhile, out of the limelight and under conditions of rasping difficulty, the French Navy – or what was left of it after Mers-el-Kebir – contrived somehow or other to remain in being. Under the armistice decrees it did not – could not, of course – fight but its ships remained under the French flag and partially manned. The French Navy and the merchant ships it controlled were still – just – alive.

With metropolitan France two-thirds occupied by the Germans and one-third nominally 'free', the conditions under which any movement at all proved possible were bizarre, and yet movement

there was. Between September 1940 and 8 November 1942, some 540 French convoys comprising 1,750 merchant ships traversed the Straits of Gibraltar in one direction or the other, bringing an estimated 3,000,000 tons of vital food and supplies to metropolitan France. Without them France would undoubtedly have starved. Sixty-five to eighty ships a week made the crossing between French North Africa and the ports of southern France, bringing across some 4,500,000 tons and keeping open a lifeline of Empire.

This was achieved, despite mounting German fury, by Gallic guile, by the *esprit de corps* of French naval officers and men, and perhaps most of all by the machinations of the shrewd Admiral Darlan. As Admiral Auphan, second-in-command to Darlan, afterwards wrote: 'The German and Italian "control" which so disquieted the English existed only on paper or in the shore establishments. No lies were told to the "controllers". Their questions were answered and they were shown what they asked to see – but no more than that. In turn they had the good sense never to go on board an armed ship where the service continued to function as before.'[5]

Ceaseless wrangling went on with the Armistice Commission in Wiesbaden and with the German authorities in Paris. Concessions were constantly bartered. One result of this was that the naval establishment of 3,000 or 4,000 sailors permitted by the Armistice grew to 75,000 by November 1942 and this did not take into account numbers of naval personnel disguised as civilians. Undoubtedly the lion's share of the credit for this must be given to Darlan, the first Admiral in the history of France to become virtually its Head of State, and that at the height of one of the worst storms in the country's history. This had come about as follows.

In May 1940 Marshal Pétain, at that time still merely the French Ambassador to Spain, had paid a visit to Maintenon, south of Paris, where Darlan with psychological insight had set up the French Admiralty in order to remove it from the political and social temptations of Paris on the outbreak of war. Darlan's principle was always to keep the French Navy distinct and apart. This was one of the keys to his power. Certainly the order and discipline of the Navy impressed the elderly Marshal and so, naturally, he chose Darlan as his

Minister of Marine when a few weeks later he himself took over as Head of State.

From June to December 1940 Darlan's only responsibility was the French Navy. He delegated the day-to-day running of the Fleet to Admiral Auphan and devoted his energies to securing the release of the 12,000 sailors who had become prisoners in German hands, to the maintenance of the Navy itself and to the defence of the French Empire.

On 13 December 1940 a curious incident took place. Marshal Pétain demanded and received the written resignations of every single member of his government. A few moments later he announced 'in the sovereign and glacial tone which was his alone' that he had refused every resignation except that of Pierre Laval and of one other minister who was to keep him company. This became known as 'the coup of 13 December,'[6] designed by Pétain to save France from the dangerous course on which Laval had managed to set her.

An unpleasant assignment was given the very next day to Darlan. Just before he had been dismissed, Laval had agreed with the Germans that

he would get Marshal Pétain to Paris to receive back – at Hitler's express edict – the coffin of Napoleon's son who had died in Vienna. Pétain refused to go to Paris and be honoured by German troops. However, if the rupture which Laval's dismissal had caused was not to be worsened, then someone from the government must go instead. Darlan was 'told off' for this and thus had his first contact with the top echelon of the Reich. It was to serve his purposes very well indeed.

In February 1941 Darlan became Vice-President of the Council and Minister of Foreign Affairs in addition to his naval responsibilities. A few weeks later he had also acquired the portfolios of the Interior, of War and of Information. No politician in France had ever before concentrated such powers upon himself. A malicious comment was that two-thirds of France was now run by the Germans and the remainder by the Navy. Collaborate though he naturally did – and had to – Darlan remained an intense patriot, and in his period of office he saved countless French lives.

Darlan met Hitler twice. At the first meeting on Christmas Day 1940 he found himself at the receiving end of one of the Fuehrer's well-known

tirades. According to Hitler's interpreter Schmidt, it had no more effect on Darlan than a bucket of salt spray on an ancient mariner. Darlan invariably asked for a quid pro quo in return for the many concessions demanded by the Germans, and this interminable process led to another meeting with Hitler in May at Berchtesgaden when the Germans were at the height of their power. The Balkan campaign had ended in triumph and now Hitler wanted Tunisia – nominally for his Italian ally. Darlan appeared to bend to the wind and a tough bargaining session then opened in Paris.

The realities of the situation were only too obvious. If the Germans really wanted Bizerta, they could take it without too much difficulty. Darlan, however, played for time. He agreed to German use of the North African ports – or at least he appeared to – but subordinated this, at the last moment, to a clause giving France considerable concessions with the object of turning French opinion in favour of the Germans. On this, of course, the whole idea foundered and in the end all that Darlan had to give away were a few French transports for Axis use.

Then came the German invasion of Russia, advance news of which Darlan had received from his Military Attaché in Bucharest. Thereafter by continued shifting, shuffling, delays and prevarication the French Admiral contrived to ensure that no uniformed Germans set foot in French North Africa throughout 1941. Indeed 'the African void' was never filled until November 1942 and then only by the Americans. By this time, however, German pressure had caused Laval, the eager henchman, to regain his position of control. Darlan was stripped of his political powers – though still left as overall Commander-in-Chief of the armed forces – in April 1942.

Considering what was to happen in November 1942 this was, perhaps, on balance fortunate for the Allies since, with the distrusted Laval (whom Darlan personally despised) in the political hot seat, Darlan found himself able to devote more time to naval affairs in general and to the maintenance of French sovereignty in Morocco, Algeria and Tunisia in particular during the crucial summer and autumn of 1942.

So much for the western side – over in the east, 'After the temporary cessation of our attack on the Alamein line,' Rommel wrote in August, 'a calm

set in over the front. Both sides sought to use the breathing space to refit their forces and bring up fresh troops. Once again we were in a race to reorganize.'[7]

Thus it seemed to the men on the spot. On the German and Italian side the problem was basically one of supplies. On the British, with General Ritchie relieved of his command after the fall of Tobruk, there were also pressing personality questions. Rommel, Kesselring and the nominal Supreme Commander-in-Chief, the Italian General Bastico, were up against Hitler's absorption in the Russian campaign and the consequent deflationary fact that, however successful the Afrika Korps might be, strategically the African campaign rated as no more than a diversion. The Russian front was what mattered. Everything else must be subordinate to that.

'Trouble with supplies,' Rommel wrote to his wife on 5 August, 'Rintelen does little in Rome and constantly lets himself be done in the eye, for the Italian supplies are working excellently.'[8]

A German officer going on leave to Germany via Rome pointed up a striking contrast between the war effort of the two Axis nations:

Within days of being in a bloody and historic action, I found myself walking the peaceful streets of the Eternal City with elegant women and debonair men frequenting restaurants where life was suave and luxurious . . . then through the Alps to Munich. Civilian life was far more straitened than it was in Italy. There was none of the elegance of the Roman promenade. Men and women were all working, all in a hurry, all in uniform or in factory clothes. In Rome swarms of porters had almost fought to carry my bags. Here in Munich I had to carry my own and like it . . . at Bonn one saw relatively few in army uniform. Those who were in uniform were usually in the grey of the East Front soldier – the man who was fighting Russia. A number wore the light blue of the 'Anti-Flak' chaps from Sicily. The khaki of the Afrika Korps was a rarity. Wearing civilian clothes, I several times received a white feather.[9]

On the British side no white feathers were being handed out, but a vote of censure was moved in the House of Commons on the conduct of the war. After one of Churchill's more memorable speeches the motion of 'no confidence' was defeated by 475 votes to 25. However, it seemed then in London that something was very badly wrong with the Middle East command and changes were going to have to be made. One member of Parliament had tartly remarked that 'if Rommel had been in the British Army, he

Top left: Directing desert traffic. Above: Rommel, September 1942

would still be a sergeant' and another had observed that we had lost our empire in the Far East in a hundred days. What would happen in the next hundred days?

At Churchill's request, therefore, Sir Stafford Cripps had investigated the matter in depth and had come up with a lengthy report, the gist of which was that:

(1) There was over-optimism in Cairo.
(2) Better generalship was needed.
(3) The supreme military command was out of date.
(4) Our tanks and weapons were inferior even after three years of war.
(5) We were behind in research and invention.
(6) Finally, it was pointless and dangerous to claim 'moral superiority in the air' and yet fail to stop Rommel's advance.

Chapter and verse were given for each of these grave criticisms and since, as Admiral Keyes who supported the motion of censure was quick to point out, 'We look to the Prime Minister to put his house in order, and to rally the country once again for its immense task', it was necessary to take drastic and urgent action. As a result Churchill decided to fly to Cairo and settle matters on the spot.

Australians in Bren-gun carriers, moving up to the assault in battle formation

4
THE DECISION FOR 'TORCH'

During the six months elapsing between the first and second Washington conferences, from January to June 1942 the long tally of disasters which afflicted the western Allies grew in a sinister way. The net result threatened to drive a wedge between Britain and America on the one hand and the U.S.S.R. on the other. The clamour for a 'Second Front Now' grew more strident as the year progressed and, as an embarrassing corollary, it became undeniably evident to the planners that any effective lunge across the Channel into France could never succeed in 1942. All must be put into Operation 'Round-up' – the great assault on France now scheduled for 1943.

Stalin neither understood nor agreed with this and he did not hesitate to say so bluntly and frequently. Communist subversives in both the United Kingdom and the United States seized upon this with relish, daubing slogans on walls and taking full advantage of the many, almost daily, opportunities for dissension which this situation provided. This served only to irritate the British, whose feelings were well reflected in a contemporary verse by A. P. Herbert:

Let's have less nonsense from the Friends of Joe,
We laud, we love him; but the nonsense – no.
In 1940 when we bore the brunt,
We could have done, boys, with a Second Front.
A continent went down a cataract,
But Russia did not think it right to act.

A. P. Herbert went on to observe that it was not our way to make treaties of friendship with the man we hate, as Stalin had done, although

. . . alas, these sly manoeuvres had to end
When Hitler leaped upon his largest friend.

and who was it then who came to Stalin's aid?

This tiny island, antiquated, tired,
Effete, capitalist and uninspired . . .
This tiny isle of muddles and mistakes,
Having a Front on every wave that breaks.

Not only did we come to Russia's aid – we took the tanks they needed to the door via perilous Arctic convoys. For this we received no thanks, but only renewed nagging from the Soviet dictator. A. P. Herbert concluded:

Honour the Kremlin, boys, but now and then
Admit some signs of grace at Number Ten.

What, in fact, was going on at Number 10 during this critical period? 'In planning the gigantic enterprise of 1943', Churchill wrote,

it was not possible for us to lay aside all other duties . . . I

was in complete accord with what Hopkins called 'a frontal assault upon the enemy in Northern France in 1943' but what was to be done in the interval? The main armies could not simply be preparing all that time. Here there was a wide diversity of opinion. General Marshall had advanced the proposal that we should attempt to seize Brest or Cherbourg, preferably the latter, or even both, during the autumn of 1942. The operation would have to be almost entirely British. The Navy, the Air, two-thirds of the troops, and such landing craft as were available must be provided by us.

Only two or three American divisions could be found. These it must be remembered were very newly raised. It takes at least two years and a very strong professional cadre to form first-class troops. The enterprise was therefore one on which British Staff opinion would naturally prevail. Clearly there must be an intensive technical study of the problem.

Whilst not rejecting the idea from the outset, there were other alternatives to be considered. The first was the capture of French North-West Africa, but there was a second alternative,

for which I always hankered and which I thought could be undertaken as well as the invasion of French North Africa. This was 'Jupiter' – the liberation of Northern Norway. Here was direct aid to Russia. Here was the only method of direct combined military action with Russian troops, ships and air. Here was the means by securing the northern tip of Europe, of opening the broadest flood of supplies to Russia. Here was an enterprise which, as it had to be fought in Arctic regions, involved neither large numbers of men nor heavy expenditure of supplies and munitions.

The Germans had taken those vital strategic areas by the North Cape very cheaply. Churchill considered they could be regained at a small cost compared with the scale on which the war was now being waged.

My own choice was for 'Torch' and if I could have had my full way, I should have tried 'Jupiter' also in 1942. The attempt to form a bridgehead at Cherbourg seemed to me more difficult, less attractive, less immediately helpful or ultimately fruitful. It would be better to lay our right claw on French North Africa, tear with our left at the North Cape, and wait a year without risking our teeth upon the German fortified front across the Channel . . . if it had been in my power to give orders I would have settled upon 'Torch' and 'Jupiter' properly synchronized for the autumn, and would have let 'Sledgehammer' (the Cherbourg assault) leak out as a feint through rumour and ostentatious preparation. But I had to work by influence and diplomacy in order to secure agreed and harmonious action with our cherished ally, without whose aid nothing but ruin faced the world.[1]

These ideas were not conveyed – or at least were only partially revealed – to the Russians, whose

impatience grew as spring wore on into summer. In May Molotov, Stalin's Foreign Minister, was invited by Roosevelt to visit Washington and did so via London 'since it was upon Great Britain that the main task of organizing the Second Front would initially fall'. The object of Molotov's visit, as declared at a formal meeting with Churchill on 22 May (four days before Rommel resumed his attack eastwards in Libya) was 'to learn how the British Government viewed the prospects of drawing off in 1942 at least forty divisions from the U.S.S.R., where it seemed that at the present time the balance of advantage in armed strength lay with the Germans. Could the Allies do it?'[2]

Churchill replied with a detailed analysis and evaluation of any cross-Channel operation which could be undertaken that year. No mention was made of 'Gymnast' or the possibility of such an operation. As Molotov appeared to be very little impressed with Churchill's reasoning, the Prime Minister ended by asking the Russian to bear in mind the difficulties of overseas invasions. 'After France fell out of the war, we in Great Britain

were almost naked – a few ill-equipped divisions, less than a hundred tanks and less than two hundred field guns. And yet Hitler had not attempted an invasion, by reason of the fact that he could not get command of the air. The same sort of difficulties confronted us at the present time.'[3]

Molotov went on to Washington. There he had a generally satisfactory meeting with the President and on his return, again via London, a communiqué was issued saying that 'in the course of the conversations full understanding was reached with regard to the urgent tasks of creating a Second Front in Europe in 1942'.

However, Churchill felt it important not to mislead 'Uncle Joe' in the process of trying to mislead the enemy. He therefore pressed into Molotov's hand the following *aide-mémoire*, in which the clause in italics – to which much future reference would be made – reserved the Anglo-American position.

We are making preparations for a landing on the Continent in August or September 1942. As already explained, the main limiting factor to the size of the landing force is the availability of special landing craft. Clearly, however, it would not further either the Russian cause or that of the Allies as a whole if, for the sake of action at any price, we embarked on some operation which ended in disaster and gave the enemy an opportunity for glorification at our discomfiture. It is impossible to say in advance whether the situation will be such as to make this operation feasible when the time comes. *We can therefore give no promise in the matter,* but provided that it appears sound and sensible we shall not hesitate to put our plans into effect.[4]

During the weeks following Molotov's visit, intensive staff work took place on each and every scheme which had been mooted. This was a process aptly described by Churchill as 'strategic natural selection' and from it came a watertight veto by the British on any *major* cross-Channel expedition in 1942. Churchill's pet Norwegian project also fell by the wayside. All were agreed on the vast invasion of France scheduled for 1943, but what was to be done in the interval? Churchill summed it up by saying: 'It was impossible for the United States and Britain to stand idle all that time without fighting, except in the desert. The President was determined that Americans should fight Germans on the largest possible

Far left: Second-Fronters. Generalissimo Stalin (in uniform) with his Foreign Minister, Vygadieslav Molotov
Left: General George C. Marshall, Chief of Staff, United States Army. He, too, was a keen advocate of a 'second front in Europe'

scale *during* 1942. Where then could this be achieved? Where else but in French North Africa, upon which the President had always smiled? Out of the many plans the fittest might survive. I was content to wait for the answer.'[5]

A month after Molotov's visit, Churchill went to Washington himself. No final decision had yet been agreed on the European operations to be undertaken in 1942–3 and there was now a danger that the American Chiefs of Staff would succumb to pressure from their own Pacific lobby and thus throw out the agreed strategy of defeating Germany first.

In a definitive note dated 20 June 1942 which Churchill prepared for Roosevelt before these meetings, the British Prime Minister stressed that the continued heavy sinkings at sea (which reached their climax that month) constituted the Allies' greatest and most immediate danger. Further urgent measures must be taken to reduce these losses. Without a build-up of supplies in the United Kingdom, nothing could be achieved at all.

On the question of an invasion of France, he was even more forthright. 'We hold strongly to the view that there should be no substantial landing in France this year unless we are going to stay. No responsible British military authority has so far been able to make a plan for September 1942 which had any chance of success unless the Germans became utterly demoralized, of which there is no likelihood.'

He went on to ask if the American staff had a plan and then came to the point:

But in case no plan can be made in which any responsible authority has good confidence, and consequently no engagement on a substantial scale in France is possible in September 1942, what else are we going to do? Can we afford to stand idle in the Atlantic theatre during the whole of 1942? Ought we not to be preparing within the general structure some other operation by which we may gain positions of advantage, and also directly or indirectly to take some of the weight off Russia? It is in this setting and on this background that the French North-West Africa operation should be studied.[6]

The following day, 21 June, was perhaps the nadir of the war so far as Great Britain was concerned, the point of maximum danger, the stage beyond which there had to be either collapse or a slow crawl back to recovery. Churchill was with Roosevelt in his study at the White House when a telegram was put into the President's

hands. 'He passed it to me without a word. It said "Tobruk has surrendered, with twenty-five thousand men taken prisoners." This was so surprising that I could not believe it. I therefore asked Ismay to inquire of London by telephone. In a few minutes he brought the following message which had just arrived from Admiral Harwood [the C.inC. of the British Mediterranean Fleet] at Alexandria:

> Tobruk has fallen and situation deteriorated so much that there is a possibility of heavy air attack on Alexandria in near future, and in view of approaching full moon period I am sending all Eastern Fleet units south of the Canal to await events. I hope to get H.M.S. *Queen Elizabeth* out of dock towards the end of this week.

This was one of the heaviest blows I can recall during the war.'[7]

In this deeply depressing atmosphere the British and American High Commands then sat down to confer about future strategy. It was agreed that operations in France or the Low Countries in 1942 would, if successful, yield greater political and strategic gains than in any other theatre and that plans to this effect should be pushed forward with all possible speed, energy and ingenuity. If, on the other hand, detailed examination were to show that success would be improbable, then 'we must be ready with an alternative'. What was to become 'Torch' moved a step nearer.

> The possibilities of French North Africa (Operation 'Gymnast') will be explored carefully and conscientiously, and plans will be completed in all details as soon as possible.[8]

It was further agreed that the planning for the cross-Channel operation should continue in London. 'Gymnast' would be centred on Washington.

That same day Harry Hopkins said to Churchill, 'There are a couple of American officers the President would like you to meet, as they are very highly thought of in the Army, by Marshall and by him.' These were Major-Generals Eisenhower and Clark, who came on to see Churchill after a briefing by the President. 'I was immediately impressed by these remarkable but hitherto unknown men . . . we talked almost entirely about the major cross-Channel invasion in 1943 . . . I felt sure these officers were intended to play a great part in it, and that was the reason why they had been sent to make my acquaintance . . . thus began a friendship which across all the ups and downs of war I have preserved with deep satisfaction. . . .'[9]

Churchill flew back to London to face a vote of censure and the appalling state of affairs consequent on Rommel's advance to El Alamein. Between 26 June, when he arrived back in London, and 2 August when he set off again for Cairo and then on for the first meeting with Stalin in Moscow, Churchill's time was in large measure taken up with the grave and deepening dissensions between the British and American planning staffs as they came to grips with the problems they had been ordered to solve. Time was short and tempers increasingly frayed. Moreover, unlike the Axis dictators, the Allies had to base their major decisions on the consent of their naval, military and air force experts. This was a sounder way to proceed but the process was lengthier and more wearing on the nerves.

'During this month of July,' Churchill wrote, 'when I was politically at my weakest and without a gleam of military success, I had to procure from the United States the decision which, for good or ill, dominated the next two years of the war. This was the abandonment of all plans for crossing the Channel in 1942 and the occupation of French North Africa in the autumn or winter by a large Anglo-American expedition.'[10] Perhaps Churchill was being over gloomy: the situation had at least been stabilized in July at First Alamein.

On 8 July the Former Naval Person was cabling the President giving detailed objections to a cross-Channel operation and arguing, almost pleading, for 'Gymnast'.

I am sure myself that French North Africa is by far the best chance for effecting relief to the Russian front in 1942. This has all along been in harmony with your ideas. In fact it is your commanding idea. Here is the true Second Front of 1942. I have consulted the Cabinet and Defence Committee, and we all agree. Here is the safest and most fruitful stroke that can be delivered this autumn.

It must be clearly understood that we cannot count upon an invitation or a guarantee from Vichy. But any resistance would not be comparable to that which would be offered by the German army in the Pas de Calais. Indeed it might be only token resistance. The stronger you are, the less resistance there would be and the more to overcome it. This is a political more than a military issue. It seems to me that we ought not to throw away the sole great strategic stroke open to us in the Western theatre during this cardinal year.[11]

But strong tensions were building up in the American High Command. General Marshall

was divided from Admiral King as between Europe and the Pacific. Neither favoured the North African venture. On 14 July, Churchill pressed his ideas on the President more sharply and shortly.

> I am most anxious for you to know where I stand myself at the present time. I have found no one who regards 'Sledgehammer' as possible. I should like to see you do 'Gymnast' as soon as possible and that we, in concert with the Russians, should try for 'Jupiter'. Meanwhile all preparations for 'Round-up' in 1943 should proceed at full blast, thus holding the maximum enemy forces opposite England. All this seems to me as clear as noonday.[12]

But deadlock approached. Roosevelt's liking for North Africa grew steadily stronger but he, like Churchill, had to carry his Chiefs of Staff with him. In this he was aided by the British Field-Marshal Dill in Washington, whose qualities and experience (he was an ex-Chief of the Imperial General Staff) had won him the confidence of all the rival schools of thought and whose tact preserved their goodwill. On 12 July Churchill had cabled Dill pointing out forcefully that

> 'Gymnast' affords the sole means by which United States forces can strike at Hitler in 1942 . . . however if the President decides against 'Gymnast' the matter is settled. It can only be done by troops under the American flag. The opportunity will have been definitely rejected. Both countries will remain motionless in 1942 and all will be concentrated on 'Round-up' in 1943.
>
> There could be no excuse in these circumstances for the switch of United States effort to the Pacific and I cannot think that such an attitude would be adopted.[13]

However, 15 July proved to be a crucial day. Churchill was battling the vote of censure in the House of Commons, Auchinleck's defence of Cairo seemed to hang in the balance and there was also 'a very tense day in the White House'. Strong pressure in the second line of the American staff was manifested for abandoning the European theatre of war and concentrating on Japan. In spite of Admiral King's anti-British feelings, there was no evidence that he and General Marshall shared this extreme position, and the President 'withstood and brushed aside this fatal trend of thought'.[14]

One result of this standstill in strategic planning, however, was Roosevelt's decision to send his most trusted friends to London to try to reach an accord. General Marshall, Admiral King and Harry Hopkins flew the Atlantic, arriving in London on 18 July and immediately went into

conference with the American service chiefs who were already there for 'Round-up' and 'Sledgehammer' purposes. These were Generals Eisenhower and Clark for the U.S. Army, Admiral Stark for the U.S. Navy and General Spaatz for the U.S. Army Air Force. Up to this moment all these officers held firm 'cross-Channel' views and were not impressed with any North African ideas.

The President, however, had sent Marshall, King and Hopkins across with clear instructions to get an agreement within one week of their arrival. Churchill described these instructions and the analysis on which they were based as 'the most massive and masterly document on war policy that I ever saw from his [Roosevelt's] hand'.[15] These instructions made it unmistakably plain that if 'Sledgehammer' proved to be impossible of execution, then there should be an operation in Morocco and Algeria against the back door of Rommel's armies. However, 'Sledgehammer' was considered to be of such grave importance that every reason called for the accomplishment of it. So the in-fighting began on the morning of Monday 20 July in the Cabinet Room at 10 Downing Street. Neither side would yield,

and by the afternoon of 22 July General Marshall declared that a complete deadlock had been reached and that he would have to ask the President for further instructions.

President Roosevelt replied at once that he was not surprised at the disappointing outcome of the London talks. He agreed that it was no use continuing to press for 'Sledgehammer' in the face of British opposition and instructed his delegation to reach a decision on some other operation which would involve American land forces being brought into action against the enemy in 1942.

Thus 'Sledgehammer' fell by the wayside and 'Gymnast' came into its own. Marshall and King, though naturally disappointed, bowed to the decision of their Commander-in-Chief and the greatest goodwill between us all again prevailed.

I now hastened to rechristen my favourite. 'Gymnast', 'Super-Gymnast' and 'Semi-Gymnast' vanished from our code names. On July 24th in an instruction from me to the Chiefs of Staff 'Torch' became the new and master term. On July 25th the President cabled to Hopkins that plans for landings in North Africa to take place 'not later than 30th October' should go ahead at once. That evening our friends set off on their journey back to Washington.[16]

The British Prime Minister and the American President exchanged messages of congratulations on this outcome, Roosevelt saying: 'I cannot help feeling that the past week represented a

turning-point in the whole war and that now we are on our way shoulder to shoulder.'

The appointment of suitable commanders had now to be settled. Churchill and the British Chiefs of Staff wanted General Marshall for the job and Field-Marshal Dill in Washington cabled that he believed Marshall would accept, but that equally he could not be spared from Washington at present, 'but Eisenhower could well act with his authority . . . and the Eisenhower deputy idea may be welcome'. In fact General Marshall had already taken this decision during his London visit. 'In his headquarters at Claridges Hotel on 26 July,' Eisenhower recorded, 'General Marshall informed me that I was to be Allied Commander-in-Chief of the expedition. He stated that while this decision was definite some little time would be necessary to accomplish all the routine of official designation.'[17] On 14 August Eisenhower was formally appointed as Commander-in-Chief in a directive from the Combined Chiefs of Staff. So 'Torch' began.

Meanwhile the peripatetic Former Naval Person set off east in an American Liberator aircraft, from which the bomb racks had been removed and which was piloted by a young American pilot of a mere million miles' flying experience, first to Gibraltar in one hop and thence after a sharp turn southwards over French North Africa in another single hop to Cairo. The last message he had received at Lyneham airfield before setting off was from Field-Marshal Dill in Washington and said enigmatically, 'May what you are at have the success which courage and imagination deserve.' In fact neither his self-assumed task in Cairo nor his visit to Moscow would be likely to yield anything but 'blood, sweat and tears' on a personal level, yet no such journey had become more necessary at any period of the war.

There were two basic reasons for Churchill to absent himself yet again from London at such a crucial time. One was that an urgent requirement had now arisen to settle vital questions about the High Command in the Middle East out there and on the spot: the other was that 'we were all anxious about the reaction of the Soviet Government to the unpleasant though inevitable news that there would be no crossing of the Channel in 1942'. A personal visit by the British Prime

Minister to Moscow might help to sugar the pill.

It happened that on the night of 28th July I had the honour of entertaining the King to dinner with the War Cabinet in the propped-up garden room at Number 10, which we used for dining. I obtained his Majesty's approval for my journey, and immediately he had gone, brought the Ministers, who were in a good frame of mind, into the Cabinet Room and clinched matters.

Churchill had then telegraphed to Stalin:

... I am willing, if you invite me, to come myself to meet you in Astrakhan, the Caucasus, or similar convenient meeting place. We could then survey the war together and take decisions hand in hand. I could then tell you plans we have made with President Roosevelt for offensive action in 1942. I would bring the Chief of the Imperial General Staff with me.

I am starting for Cairo forthwith. I have serious business there, as you may imagine. From there I will if you so desire it fix a convenient date for our meeting. ...

Stalin replied with an invitation to Moscow as neither he nor the members of his government could leave the capital 'at the moment of such an intense struggle against the Germans'.

So, on the morning of 4 August 1942, 'there in the pale, glimmering dawn the endless winding silver ribbon of the Nile stretched joyously before us ... never had the glint of daylight on its waters been so welcome to me'. Now for a short spell Churchill became the man on the spot. Instead of sitting at home waiting for news from the front, he could send it himself. He found this 'exhilarating'.[18]

The 'serious business' which the Prime Minister had to attend to could be put in two complementary but uncomplimentary questions. Had General Auchinleck and his staff lost the confidence of the Desert Army? If so, should they be relieved and who would succeed them? However simple a job of hiring and firing this may seem now that thirty years have passed, it was far from uncomplicated at the time. We know now the outcome both of the desert campaign and of the war itself, but matters were far from certain in August 1942. 'In dealing with a commander of the highest character and quality, of proved ability and resolution, such decisions are painful,' Churchill wrote.[19] He might well have added that there could be no guarantee that replacements would do any better.

But the situation remained crucial and time was of the essence. The Sherman tanks which Roosevelt had so generously diverted to British use were about to arrive and Churchill was forti-

Previous pages: German assault troops outside Tobruk

Right: Some of the 35,000 troops captured by the Axis forces

fied in the knowledge that 'Torch' had been agreed and in two to three months would alter the balance, it was hoped in an irreversible way. But now at this very moment Rommel was breathing down their necks, control of the sea had been lost and at any moment an airborne force might descend on Malta, as it had done on Crete. Civilian Egypt tolerated the British presence, but neither liked it nor wanted the occupation of their country to continue.

In Alexandria, with one or two honourable exceptions, the civilian population had written off the British, and were taking what steps they could to remove, sell or otherwise dispose of their property in anticipation of the Axis take-over which was almost hourly expected. Rommel had even broadcast the name of the house he intended to use as his headquarters in Alexandria. (One of the honourable exceptions to this general panic mounted a machine-gun on the reception desk of his Alexandria hotel so as to give the Germans a proper welcome.) Altogether it was touch and go.

On the evening following Churchill's arrival, a meeting was held, attended by all the luminaries past and present of the British High Command.

Wavell had come from India, Smuts from South Africa, General Brooke, the Chief of the Imperial General Staff (C.I.G.S.), had come with Churchill, and the 'locals' General Auchinleck, Admiral Harwood for the Royal Navy and Air Marshal Tedder for the Royal Air Force, were all present. 'We did a lot of business with a very great measure of agreement,' Churchill wrote, 'but all the time my mind kept turning to the prime question of command.'

Naturally, in a matter of this importance, the Prime Minister would rely on the advice, in the first place, of the C.I.G.S. It was his duty to appraise the quality of the generals appointed to high command. 'I first offered the Middle East Command to him,' Churchill went on.

General Brooke would, of course, have greatly liked this high operational appointment, and I knew that no man would fill it better. He thought it over, and had a long talk the next morning with General Smuts. Finally he replied that he had been C.I.G.S. for only eight months, he believed he had my full confidence, and the Staff machine was working very smoothly. Another change at this moment might cause a temporary dislocation at this critical time. It may be also that out of motives of delicacy he did not wish to be responsible for advising General Auchinleck's

American-made Sherman tanks, used by the British in North Africa from the latter part of 1942. Churchill, claiming that he had 'gone on his knees' to persuade Roosevelt to send some of these tanks to Africa, protested vigorously when he was told in Cairo that they could not be used in battle for some weeks after their arrival

supersession and then taking the post himself. His reputation stood too high for such imputations; but I had now to look elsewhere.[20]

It was no easy matter to decide. Although they were naturally not consulted, the loyalty and feelings of the battle-hardened Eighth Army had also to be considered. There had been murmurs of distress when Wavell, who had been very popular in the field, had been replaced by Auchinleck. Who now was to re-establish their confidence?

One name stood out from all the others and that was someone already there in the desert, to whom the troops were devoted and whose appointment would avoid the necessity of a replacement being sent out from England. This was 'Strafer' Gott. The only snag, however, was that he had been reported as 'worn down with his hard service' and much in need of a break. On 5 August Churchill visited the Alamein positions and took the opportunity of seeing General Gott himself.

> As we rumbled and jolted over the rough tracks, I looked into his clear blue eyes and questioned him about himself. Was he tired and had he any views to give? Gott said that no doubt he was tired, and that he would like nothing better than three months' leave in England, which he had

not seen for several years, but he declared himself quite capable of further immediate efforts and of taking any responsibilities confided to him. We parted at the airfield at two o'clock on this afternoon of 5 August. By the same hour two days later he had been killed by the enemy in almost the very air spaces through which I now flew.[21]

There was thus no alternative to the two names originally suggested by the C.I.G.S. – General Alexander as Commander-in-Chief and General Montgomery as Commander of the Eighth Army. Both had worked together at Dunkirk and there was no doubt that they would make an excellent team, the only inhibiting factor being that both would have to come out from England without previous experience of the desert and that this, therefore, might be taken as a reproach to the Eighth Army. In fact some of the Desert Rats did take it in this way but this 'bloody-mindedness' did not last for long, and in any case the matter had become so pressing that no further delay could be brooked. Accordingly on 7 August, after deeply regretting that Gott had just been shot down in the air and killed, Churchill cabled to the Deputy Prime Minister at home:

> C.I.G.S. decisively recommends Montgomery for Eighth Army. Smuts and I feel this post must be filled at once.

Pray send him by special plane at earliest moment. Advise me when he will arrive.

Unfortunately, a day previously Montgomery had been appointed to command the British First Army which had been allocated to the 'Torch' operation. Now he had to be replaced after twenty-four hours in the job and after he had in turn replaced Alexander. Faced with a third British commander in two days, it is small wonder that Eisenhower asked rather plaintively 'whether the British were taking ''Torch'' seriously'. In Cairo, however, there was no doubt about this at all. The great shake-up had begun. Perhaps the most suitable launching motto for this is the quotation from Job which Montgomery afterwards used for his memoirs: 'Yet man is born into trouble, as the sparks fly upward.'

And so Auchinleck left the scene. Almost alone of the generals concerned he never wrote his own account of these great campaigns, and it was thus perhaps inevitable, if unfair, that subsequent accounts of the Desert War have largely been based on the partisan outlook of Churchill, Montgomery and Rommel as their prime source. Such accounts may often undervalue Auchinleck's

role. However much Alexander and Montgomery changed the overall atmosphere at that point of the war, the long and gruelling preparatory work put in by previous commanders, of whom Auchinleck was the latest, formed the essential basis on which the new team worked; and although the actual plans for a possible retreat appear to have been stressed in the narratives of Churchill and Montgomery, there were also well-laid plans for an attack.

Today, most military historians and analysts would probably agree that an important turning-point, perhaps often overlooked, is that of the battle of 'First Alamein'. It was here that Rommel's advance was finally and definitely checked. It is human nature to throw the limelight on the man or men who achieved final victory but credit must be given, even belatedly, for the perseverance, guts and energy which Wavell and Auchinleck put into the very difficult tasks they were given. Yet it is an undeniable fact that the arrival of Alexander and Montgomery coincided with a marked upsurge of morale in the Allied forces. Policies may not have changed immediately, but the effect of new personalities was decisive.

From the end of June until well into October the Eighth Army resisted all attacks on the Alamein-Qattara positions but was unable to break out of it. A tank of the 22nd Armoured Brigade south of El Alamein, July 1942

5
'TORCH' PLANNING, LOGISTICS AND TRAINING

Back in London there were few signs as yet of the great American invasion soon to overwhelm the British Isles. Only in London in the environs of Grosvenor Square and the south-east corner of St James's Square in a modern office building were American uniforms to be seen in any quantity. Norfolk House now became the headquarters of the Supreme Commander of the Allied Expeditionary Force.

Undoubtedly Eisenhower had taken on a 'king-size' job. 'In modern war,' he wrote, 'the personalities of senior commanders and staff officers are of special importance.'[1] He might have added that the task of integrating two staffs with almost nothing in common except the English language (and a cynic would have added, not much of that) was perhaps the most difficult assignment any commander of either nation could have been given at that time. Initially denigrated behind his back, sneeringly called more of a chairman than a general, Ike soon confounded his critics with the power of his own bland personality. Ike generated a cohesive instead of a divisive power which he applied to all problems where a split might endanger the operation. New techniques

fired by a transatlantic energy began to replace the previous set rigidity. There were new ways of doing things, less barrack-square discipline and a more free-and-easy interchange of ideas.

Ike had first to master his own distaste for the North African operation, which he felt had been forced through against the better judgement of General Marshall and himself. Lieutenant-Commander Harry Butcher, U.S.N., his Aide and diarist, remarks that Ike privately thought that the decision made on 22 July 'could well go down as the blackest day in history particularly if Russia is defeated in the big Boche drive now so alarmingly under way'.[2]

However, the decision had been taken and he set about loyally putting it into effect. The invasion of North Africa 'necessitated a complete reversal in our thinking', Eisenhower wrote,

> and drastic revision in our planning and preparation. Where we had been counting on many months of orderly build-up, we now had only weeks. Instead of a massed attack across narrow waters, the proposed expedition would require movement across open ocean areas where enemy submarines would constitute a real menace. Our target was no longer a restricted front where we knew accurately terrain, facilities and people as they affected

military operations, but the rim of a continent where no major military campaign had been conducted for centuries. We were not to have the air power we had planned to use against Europe and what we did have would be largely concentrated at a single, highly vulnerable base – Gibraltar – and immediate substantial success would have to be achieved in the first engagements. A beachhead could be held in Normandy and expanded, however slowly; a beachhead on the African coast might be impossible even to maintain.[3]

The Combined Chiefs of Staff had decreed that 'Torch' was to be – or appear to be – an American expedition in order, if possible, to woo over the French. Eisenhower was therefore given an American deputy, Major-General Mark Clark, nicknamed the 'American Eagle' by Churchill, perhaps because of his aquiline nose. This appointment was an insurance in case any accident should happen to Eisenhower, and Clark also acted as Chief of Staff until Brigadier-General Bedell Smith could arrive. The 'Beetle' was to be a corrective to any idea that the Supreme Commander would be pushed around. A hard-driving somewhat Prussian-minded officer, Bedell Smith is on record as saying, 'Someone at the top has to be an absolute S.O.B. and Ike's not in a position to do it all the time. So that's my job.'[4]

Just as Rommel and Montgomery quickly imposed their strong personalities on the armies they commanded, so now Eisenhower faced the most daunting task of setting his own somewhat milder stamp on the amorphous, conglomerate forces which were thrown together under his command. This must be counted as no small achievement in itself, and Eisenhower began, as did Rommel and Montgomery, with his own personal staff. This comprised Lieutenant-Commander Butcher, U.S.N., a charming and genial man who had formerly been a vice-president of the Columbia Broadcasting Service and whose only failing was, perhaps, an over-zealous enthusiasm for public relations. The other principal Aide was Captain Ernest (Tex) Lee, described variously as an administrative titan, a red-tape artist, office chieftain and official worrier, and it was through Tex, for instance, that Eisenhower 'bucked up' the 'Snowballs', as the U.S. Military Police were called when they first began to appear in London with their white helmet liners, white belts, white gloves and white leggings.

Ike's orderly, who did everything from shining shoes to shopping, was a black-haired, blue-eyed Irish sergeant called Micky McKeogh, and the team was completed by Ike's personal driver – an innovation which caused eyebrows to be raised, since this was the only woman in the team and she was English. Kay Summersby, whose somewhat saucy independence did so much for women's lib before the term was invented, typified the new spirit Ike infused into the 'Torch' command. He followed this up by at once asking Colonel Oveta Culp Hobby, the Director of the U.S. Women's Army Corps in Washington, to send over 5,000 WACs, which was then just a third of all the WACs there were. Ike said firmly that he'd seen what British women in their various services could do in wartime and 'if you don't send me WACs over here I'm just going to hire a regular army of civilians'. He got an advance cadre of five WAC officers.

'Eisenhowerplatz', as Grosvenor Square was nicknamed, and British hospitality, soon threatened the quiet personal life which is an absolute essential to anyone at the top. So Telegraph Cottage in Richmond Park was put at the Supreme Commander's disposal and, having lost

a whole afternoon's work as the result of a lunch with King Haakon of Norway, 'from July onward I did not, during the war, accept any invitations except from the Prime Minister or from members of the American or British armed services. These always had business as their primary object.'[5]

Eisenhower was a good 'picker of men', and one of the methods he used was always to play poker or bridge with anyone destined for high command, since he reckoned that the qualities needed to play either game well were similar to those needed for success in war. One of Ike's favourite poker players was Major-General Carl Spaatz, who was Chief of the U.S. Eighth Air Force and who was also known as 'the Thinker'. This rather unspectacular balding man was given to moods of grim silence, matched by a cold impatience. Spaatz was not the man for a cosy chat at U.S. Air Headquarters at Bushey Park, but Eisenhower took full advantage of his 'thinking bouts' and, since Spaatz also had a taste for poker which he played for astronomical stakes, they got on very well together.

The other great character who first made his mark in the 'Torch' operation was Ike's oldest and closest friend, General George C. Patton. 'Old Blood and Guts' had been given command of the Western Task Force which would be landed at Casablanca. With his highly polished cavalry boots and tailored jodhpurs, Patton exuded a superb self-confidence and turned out to be one of the most glamorous, dramatic and successful generals of the Second World War. Patton could scarcely have differed more from his British stable-mates and perhaps it was lucky, for the sake of Anglo-American co-operation, that it was the U.S. Navy and not the Royal Navy which had to convey him to Casablanca. 'Never in history' Patton declaimed, 'has the Navy landed an army at the planned time and place. But don't worry! If you land us anywhere within fifty miles of Fedala and within one week of D-Day, I'll go ahead and win.'[6] Whether this was true or not, it could not be taken as either understanding or appreciative of the naval role in conveying and delivering the largest landing force there had yet been in the history of the world – and this across thousands of miles of hostile sea.

Indeed, the jealousy and cleavage between the U.S. Army and Navy quickly came out at the early staff meetings. 'No one was in authority,' Eisenhower wrote, 'so no decisive action could be planned. Dozens of different ideas affecting strategy, tactics, organization and supply were discussed interminably. These discussions were complicated by service and personal prejudices, and by varying convictions regarding the usefulness of the air in ground operations.'[7]

The British, on the other hand, managed to present a more or less solid front, possibly because the same jealousies and divisions had been partially neutralized by three years of war. 'We had an important meeting', Admiral Ramsay wrote in July, 'of Paget, Sholto Douglas, Mountbatten, Eisenhower and myself, at which I took a leading part and managed to get things agreed to as I wanted. Eisenhower is a sensible chap, I think, and anxious to get on with things'[8] – a somewhat British under-statement which sounds patronizing in cold print, but was in fact the very opposite.

Ramsay stands out as the key planner in the whole 'Torch' operation. Two years previously he had masterminded the successful evacuation of over 300,000 men from Dunkirk, and his cool, Lowland Scot personality proved to be ideal for the present job. He was quiet but tough. Ramsay's long suit was moral courage. His career had been abruptly ended just before the war because of a disagreement he had had with his commander-in-chief whilst Chief of Staff in the Home Fleet. Thus he was serving now as a retired officer which, in those days, implied a lower status than that of an active service officer. Indeed, Ramsay was not reinstated on the active list until the spring of 1944 just before the Normandy invasion.

History is apt to paper over the differences between personalities – especially when that history is written by the admirals, generals and politicians who took part. It is also liable to adjust with hindsight certain opinions and values which were different at the time. It may seem extraordinary now but as things were in 1942, the American Chiefs of Staff would not agree to a retired British Admiral being appointed as the naval leader of the expedition. Ramsay was good enough to plan it, but not to be given responsibility for actually carrying out his own ideas. An active service admiral was considered essential, and this was why Admiral Sir Andrew Cunning-

ham, then the British First Sea Lord's representative on the Combined Chiefs of Staff in Washington, was appointed to the job.

The U.S. Chiefs of Staff continued to be unenthusiastic about the North African operation, and this fact of life had somehow or other to be altered or at any rate bypassed. On 12 August Cunningham wrote from Washington to the First Sea Lord that this lack of keenness 'would not matter a row of pins but it reacts on "Torch", for which there are few signs of enthusiasm and they do not seem to be getting down to it though they pay lip service to the usefulness of the operation . . . I am quite sure that King is dead against it, and that he has given it as his opinion that it is of no value to the war effort of the United Nations and this opinion of his is reflected all through the Navy Department.'[9]

Descending more into detail, the question of British naval command became further complicated because, in fact, three separate commands were involved – that of the naval part of the expedition, the command of the battle fleet and other ships covering the landings, and the command at Gibraltar, which was inevitably to play a key part in the launching and subsequent build-up of any expedition to occupy North Africa. Gibraltar also had continuing commitments for both Atlantic and Mediterranean convoys.

So what kind of naval officer was Eisenhower to be given for 'Torch'? A Naval Commander-in-Chief, under the Supreme Commander to direct operations alongside the latter in close consultation? A naval officer of comparatively junior rank on the staff of the Commanding General? A naval officer of high standing as his naval adviser or Naval Chief of Staff?

The First Sea Lord's initial idea had been not to have a Naval Commander-in-Chief at all, but it soon became apparent that if the Supreme Commander had to deal with three separate British naval authorities in addition to a somewhat uncooperative U.S. Naval Staff, unnecessary difficulties would be loaded on to his back. A high-powered British Admiral was therefore considered essential, and although 'A.B.C.' (as Cunningham was known throughout the service) did not put himself forward, he was given the job. However, this had to be kept a close secret.

Cunningham did not join Eisenhower in London but remained at his desk in Washington. This he found irksome after his brilliant command of the Mediterranean Fleet, but in the event it proved to be just as well, since Admiral King had no intention of yielding an easy victory to the British.

King wanted command of the Casablanca landing to be independent of the main expedition and given to the American Naval Commander-in-Chief, Atlantic. King is alleged to have said: 'I fought under the goddam British in the First World War and if I can help it no ship of mine will fight under them again.'[10] Whether he actually said this or not, it was certainly his attitude – although he had no objection to British ships being put under his own command – and this chauvinism did not make the Anglo-American partnership any the easier. Eventually Cunningham got him to compromise. The Casablanca force was to be under the Commander-in-Chief, Atlantic, until it had passed a certain longitude, after which it would come under the orders of the Supreme Commander. The U.S. Naval Force itself was put under the command of Vice-Admiral H.

Kent Hewitt, U.S.N., with, of course, General Patton in command of the troops.

There were also command problems on the British side. Up to now Ramsay had been working under the aegis of the Chief of Combined Operations. Now Mountbatten, in addition to responsibility for the development of landing craft and for the training of their specialized personnel, was a member of the British Chiefs of Staff committee. He had been entrusted with preparing the Dieppe raid, an operation Ramsay thought highly questionable. Ramsay, in turn, and until the switch to 'Torch', was the Naval Commander-in-Chief of the Expeditionary Force. As such, he was responsible not only for planning the invasion of Europe, in conjunction with the Allied Commanders-in-Chief and the Chief of Combined Operations, but also for training the whole British Army and part of the Royal Navy in amphibious operations.

This was no bed of roses. However, moral courage, goodwill and plain speaking on both sides cleared the air and disposed of the friction which unfortunately continued to mar the relationship between the U.S. Army and the U.S. Naval

Far left: Lieutenant-General Carl A. Spaatz, Commanding General, United States Eighth Army Force and 'one of Ike's favourite poker-players' with Major-General James H. Doolittle commanding the air forces in the western sector of French North Africa

Left: Brigadier-General Walter Bedell Smith (wearing the uniform of a Lieutenant-General in this photograph taken in 1944 or later) was Eisenhower's Chief of Staff for Operation Torch and afterwards for Operation Overlord

Below: High-level conference. Seated, right to left: General Eisenhower; General Marshall; Winston Churchill; General Sir Alan Brooke, Chief of the Imperial General Staff; and Anthony Eden, Foreign Secretary and formerly Secretary of State for War in Churchill's wartime government. Admiral Cunningham stands immediately behind Churchill with Alexander and Tedder on either side of him

Following page: Major-General George S. Patton, Jr (photographed after his promotion to Lieutenant-General) commanded the troops assigned to the landings in French Morocco. He was one of Eisenhower's oldest and closest friends

authorities. On 18 June Ramsay had been promoted to Acting Admiral and re-appointed as the Naval Commander-in-Chief, Expeditionary Force. He and Mountbatten had a candid talk as a result of which he wrote to Mountbatten saying:

I think our meeting last week served an excellent purpose in promoting goodwill between our respective staffs, taking it for granted that such has always existed between our two selves personally. I should like to feel equally assured that it will also result in satisfactory concerted planning between our staffs.

I know the difficulties in the way but I am firmly convinced that they have got to be overcome in order that we may derive the full benefit from your specialized knowledge and experience.

The outstanding problem at the moment, as I see it, is the ambiguity of your position . . . as long as you are tied by the heels to the Chiefs of Staff meetings, I fail to see how you can at the same time properly carry out your functions as Head of the Combined Operations Organization with all its ramifications.

I freely admit that I am not happy about the state of training and discipline among personnel of special surface ships, landing craft and special beach parties. It is not anything like up to standard and, with the great expansion which is upon us, it is likely to deteriorate rather than improve unless it is taken in hand now and given close personal attention and supervision.

I do not think you can do this with your other commitments, and if you are to retain the latter I think you should co-opt the services of a Flag Officer on the active list of outstanding ability, and turn the whole task over to him under your general direction.

The state of training and discipline affects me very closely . . . I must, therefore, in some way have a say in it, with access to establishments to inspect and report etc. It is a most important subject and I recommend it to your early and close attention. Time won't admit of delay.[11]

On 23 July Ramsay wrote:

Things have been in a proper mess in higher direction circles, owing to the American desire to do something quickly, yet not knowing what it is possible to do. Consequently their perspective is all wrong and they have had to be shown it.[12]

Ramsay's influence grew all the time. His dry Scottish humour, backed by his undoubted knowledge and experience, made his forceful views acceptable and he commented:

No doubt after years of war we look more closely at things before we say what we will or will not do, whereas the Yanks are new at the game and have the enthusiasm of beginners . . . however they are as good for us as we are for them.[13]

Once the 'Torch had been lit' and passed to Ramsay to get on with it, he called his staff together and in his concise, quiet, conversational way put them in the picture in fifteen minutes. He said it had been left to him to pass on as much or as little of the plan as he thought fit, but that in his view the best form of security was to tell them the whole story. The task was immense.

In three months full naval plans had to be made and the necessary operation orders issued. In this short time objectives had to be selected and beaches reconnoitred. Forces had to be allocated and trained in entirely new techniques. Supplies and military equipment had to be built up and a system of 'combat loading' devised. Briefly this was to ensure that ships were loaded on the basis of first in last out, so that the right vehicles and weapons would be immediately available to troops landing on a hostile shore (as a footnote to this and something which A.B.C. never let his staff forget, one of the first items to be landed in Algiers after the assault turned out to be a couple of dentist's chairs). Landing craft with trained crews had to be made available for the transfer of supplies from ship to shore.

Above all, this vast process had to be developed under a cloak of complete secrecy, each stage being planned in conjunction with Americans 3,000 miles away, using different equipment and separate techniques. In addition, a deception plan had to be devised and put into operation to bemuse not only the enemy but also the British and American peoples. Thus, for example, Canadian troops were issued with Arctic clothing for a supposed operation in Norway: American troops were told that their tropical clothing was intended for use in the Persian Gulf.

Moreover, there was still disagreement at the top, even by the end of August when Dill returned to London to give the British Chiefs of Staff a progress report. Preparations in the United States, he said, were still hanging fire because there was as yet no firm decision as to where the forces should land, and delay was being caused by the still unreconcilable differences between the U.S. Army and Navy.

The American Chiefs of Staff were highly worried about possible Spanish reactions to the invasion. Gibraltar, they thought, might well be besieged and the whole of the Spanish coast, in addition to Spanish Morocco, turned into hostile territory. Cunningham argued, correctly as it transpired, that Franco would calculate that he had already lost his chance of entering the war on favourable terms. However, if he did decide to move against an Anglo-American occupation of North Africa, there could be no doubt that Spanish coastal towns were very vulnerable to sea and air attack. Franco might well get more than he had bargained for. Cunningham went further and said that if only they were bold enough to go as far east as Tunisia and to land in Bizerta, the hammer blow would have a far more immediate effect. But this the U.S. Navy resolutely refused to consider. In their opinion the Mediterranean was a highly dangerous and suspicious area. The risks of going even as far east as Algiers were hardly worth taking.

However, at the beginning of September – possibly aided by a visit to Washington by Ambassador Murphy and certainly after some very plain speaking by Churchill – the situation brightened. Definite decisions were at last taken. The British would land at Algiers and Oran. The Americans would stay out of the Mediterranean and make themselves responsible for Casablanca. In the British view the Casablanca invasion might prove to be the riskiest of all, for the simple reason that the Atlantic rollers made a landing possible on only one day out of five.

Both Roosevelt and Churchill had hoped for a mid-October invasion date but, because the forces assembling in the United States could not be ready earlier, the expedition could now not be mounted before the end of that month. 'What is the use of putting up an Allied Commander-in-Chief or Supreme Commander', Churchill complained in a letter to Harry Hopkins: 'if he cannot have the slightest freedom in making his plan or deciding how, when and where to apply his forces? Eisenhower's position has been a very painful one . . . frankly I do not understand what is at the back of all this . . . I thought there was agreement with Marshall and that King had been paid off with what he needed for his Pacific war . . . now I have a deep and growing fear that the whole of the President's enterprise may be wrecked bit by bit . . . with every day's delay the Germans have a better chance of forestalling us. . . .'[14]

It was a long, angry, well-argued letter which, perhaps luckily for future Anglo-American accord, was never sent. It was about to go when Roosevelt put his foot down and called his Chiefs of Staff to order. On 4 September he cabled Churchill agreeing to reduce the combat loaders which the American Chiefs of Staff had required for Casablanca and to release them for the Oran and Algiers side of the operation. He added: 'We are getting very close together', and it was evident that the President had been making his power felt. Churchill quickly agreed with the latest proposals and sent Ramsay to Washington with the naval requirements which Cunningham would need in order to argue his case in detail. The torch might be said to have been properly lit by the exchange of two short telegrams on the 5 and 6 September, the first from the President which simply said, 'Hurrah!' and the reply from Churchill, 'O.K. Full blast.'

At last the vast, intricate planning could now proceed for firm and agreed objectives and round-the-clock staff work at Norfolk House, in Grosvenor Square and in Washington began. No operation comparable in size had ever before been undertaken in the history of the world. At one

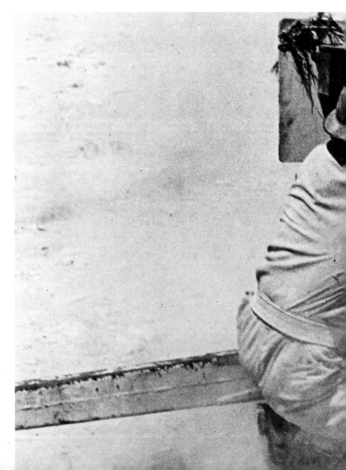

stage the staggering total of 879 ships were to be at sea directly concerned with the operation and converging on the target from the United Kingdom and the eastern seaboard of the United States. These would include 229 British and 105 U.S. warships, 12 British convoys of 334 ships and 3 American convoys of 211 ships. The thought of what a couple of U-boat packs could do to this conglomeration of shipping became almost too appalling to be considered for long. In the event and because of a combination of very nearly faultless planning, a workable deception plan and the incalculable factor of luck, complete tactical surprise was to be achieved. But in September and October 1942 such a result, although planned for, could only be thought most unlikely to occur. That it happened as it did was an extraordinary feat – overshadowed two years later by the Normandy landings, yet in the autumn of 1942 all but incredible.

For practical purposes Eisenhower and his staff had only six weeks in which to plan and mount the operation. Then before the end of September an incident occurred which jeopardized the entire operation and caused it to be further postponed.

Because of the strain thrown on the resources and organization at Gibraltar, an additional British Commodore had been sent out to the Rock to help with the berthing and general administration of the considerable number of auxiliary craft, tugs, tankers, colliers and ammunition vessels which would be using the harbour. On 26 September Commodore Parry's Secretary, Paymaster Lieutenant J. H. Turner, R.N., flew out from England in a Catalina which never reached its destination. A little later this officer's body was washed ashore near Cadiz. On it was found a letter to the Governor of Gibraltar written by General Mark Clark, giving the target date of the operation (which was then 4 November), and saying that General Eisenhower would reach Gibraltar on D − 2 or 3. The letter reached the Governor, via the Spanish authorities, apparently unopened, but another letter addressed to Commodore Parry had been opened by the

action of sea-water and as other articles from the ill-fated aircraft were still drifting ashore, it had to be assumed that any of them might have passed through enemy hands and therefore that the whole 'Torch' plan would be compromised.

The Governor's warning arrived in London on 28 September and with some considerable misgiving the operation was put back to 8 November, the last practicable date from the weather point of view. After the war it was discovered that the key letter had not, in fact, been opened by 'the gentlemanly Spaniards' and therefore the vital information it contained never reached German Intelligence and the O.K.W. However, the fact that it might have done so generated the macabre idea in British Intelligence that such an incident should be put to a more deliberate use in the future to pass decoy information to the enemy.

During the planning of 'Torch' the security factor became more and more crucial. As the date approached, the whole operation turned more and more into a real life 'cliff-hanger' which would put to shame any Hollywood film of the time. Two years later, when the Normandy assaults were being planned, there could be no

question of strategic surprise since it was then patently obvious that a vast invasion was being actively prepared. The most that could then be hoped for would be tactical surprise which, astonishingly, was also to be achieved. When 'Torch' got under way, however, the Germans could only guess at the scale of any operation which the Allies might mount.

The strategic picture, in which German-occupied Europe had long been the dominating feature, led Axis intelligence to concentrate on a possible cross-Channel strike as being the likeliest use of Allied resources at that time. They were aware, of course, of the value which an island race must always set on control of the seas, and also of the impossibility of defending thousands of miles of European coastline against a determined invasion. But they thought, correctly, that the British had their hands more than full trying to regain the initiative in the Battle of the Atlantic.

The possibility of a landing in French North Africa was certainly considered, but it did not carry much weight and in any case, with Laval manipulating the aged Marshal Pétain at Vichy, there must be, they thought, at least a reasonable

chance of French resistance in defence of their colonial empire. All things considered, the O.K.W. felt that any unusually large concentration of ships entering the Mediterranean through the Straits of Gibraltar would be for the relief of Malta. They therefore concentrated their Luftwaffe and U-boat power in the Sicilian narrows. In the event they were to be taken completely unawares.

Seen from the Allied side the attitude of the French became a major hazard to the 'Torch' planners. Once again – as in 1940 – the moment you said 'the French' the next question was always '*Which* French?' On 3 September, when cabling the President about Ramsay's visit to Washington, Churchill had said, 'Delay due to change already extends three weeks. Free French have got inkling and are leaky. . . .' After the fiasco of Dakar when the Free French were fired on instead of being welcomed two years previously and because of de Gaulle's porcupine personality, both British and Americans were unanimous that he must be kept out of it and told nothing until the last possible moment. The lifting of an eyebrow might give the whole operation away.

De Gaulle might see himself as a latter-day Jeanne d'Arc, but very few other Frenchmen did and, taking it on from there, who of the Vichy lot could possibly be trusted? Darlan? He had had to yield political power to Laval and therefore could no longer bluff all and sundry into thinking he had Pétain's authority to impose his will – except, and it was a big exception, so far as the French Navy was concerned.

But the French Navy was still smarting from the deadly stroke the British had dealt it at Oran a few days after the Armistice in 1940, when the greater part of the French Atlantic Fleet had been sunk after refusing either to join the British or immobilize themselves. Feelings were bitter. They would certainly resist with force any British naval action and there was no guarantee that the Americans would fare any better. The bulk of the civilian population both in metropolitan France and in French North Africa remained apathetic and had no wish to be dragged into the war again on any excuse.

Such was the general situation in which Robert Murphy – with Roosevelt's full backing – got down to work.

Men of Vichy. Front row, left to right: Pétain, Darlan, Pierre Laval. Second row, flanked by generals: Darquier de Pellepoix, Commissioner-General for Jewish Affairs. On the right, in civilian clothes, is General Auguste-Paul Noguès, the Vichy government's representative in French Morocco

6
BEHIND THE SCENES

Eisenhower planned the invasion of North Africa in the hope that it would be bloodless, but that if it were not then overwhelming force must be available to crush any and all resistance without the slightest delay. However, it was thought just possible that force would not be necessary. It was further calculated that this non-violent result could perhaps be achieved through some careful intricate manoeuvring by the Allied diplomatic and intelligence services. Such, of course, was not the task of an afternoon.

The arena in which the British Ambassador in Madrid and the American Ambassador in Vichy worked and had their being differed from the military scene in North Africa to such an extent that they might have been operating in separate kinds of world. War has been defined as the extension of politics by force: diplomacy and the intelligence on which it depends can normally do a better job and do it with far greater economy but, for success, those who operate the scene must clearly understand what diplomacy can and cannot achieve. Conditions and working facilities differed so much in Portugal, Spain, occupied and unoccupied France and the kaleidoscope of

Tangier, Morocco and Algeria, that a short consideration of each area must be made if the whole is to have any meaning at all.

In Spain, the British worked under comparatively hostile but weak conditions. In Portugal, which was England's oldest ally, there was a balance. In France, no British presence was evident except that connected with the underground which was just beginning to burgeon. The Americans, however, were in a very different situation. Until the North African assault, United States neutrality continued to be a powerful and stabilizing factor in France, Spain, Portugal and North Africa.

America was strong and America had the wheat without which the whole area would have starved. That a sufficient dribble of wheat got through was the result of a carefully calculated arrangement with the Royal Navy, a process watched and understood by the Germans. This also entailed a certain amount of bartering behind the scenes since vital raw materials might indirectly and unofficially be set against the unhindered passage of escaped prisoners of war in a fluid, almost volatile, situation dictated in the end by who was

going to win the war or who was thought to be winning the war at any given moment.

Contrasts of personalities and their points of view were vivid. Marshal Pétain had been his country's ambassador in Spain until the fall of France. When, before the war, he had been asked to go back to Paris to arrest the deterioration of the Daladier government, he had replied: 'What would I do in Paris? I have no mistress'[1] – a remark which revealed the reality of the French political situation. Sir Samuel Hoare, on taking up his appointment as British Ambassador in Madrid in June 1940, was informed that the British Embassy in that capital existed only on German sufferance. His reaction was to rent a house right next door to the German Embassy and tour the city with a Union Jack on the bonnet of his Rolls-Royce. This, too, had its effect.

There were other factors such as the role of the Roman Catholic Church, whose activities in every area were closely watched by all parties and not least by President Roosevelt from across the Atlantic. The President had established informal diplomatic relations with the Holy See in 1939 with the appointment of Myron C. Taylor, a prominent Protestant, as his envoy, and as Robert Murphy, himself a Catholic, wrote: 'I cannot imagine any Roman Catholic President ever so fascinated as was Roosevelt with the thought of the Church in world politics.'[2]

In Spain, where German influence was as strong as in any of the occupied countries of Europe, and where a German Jew called Lazar controlled the Press, the main fact of life was that a small, corpulent, bourgeois dictator, who himself had Jewish blood in his veins, was contriving to steer an uneasy course between neutrality and non-belligerence. 'Franco', the British Ambassador reported, 'has the voice of a doctor with a good bedside manner, a big family practice and an assured income. He could almost never be drawn into a discussion that involved Question and Answer and it was even more difficult to penetrate the cotton wool entanglements of his amazing complacency.'[3]

At lower levels the various naval and military attachés went about their business of licensed spying, of garnering essential intelligence and of playing each other off whenever opportunity offered, and, in the case of the British Naval Attaché, Commander Alan Hillgarth, together with his colleague, Geoffrey Birley, in Gibraltar, of virtually conducting a private war.

Lisbon and Tangier were the principal foyers for international espionage, with Madrid and Gibraltar ranking close behind, but it was the various personalities in the field who really made the running, such as the American Naval Attaché to France, Commander Roscoe Hillenkoeffer; the German Ernst Achenbach who, with his Californian wife, ran the German Embassy in Paris until the arrival of Otto Abetz; Pierre Dupuy, the Canadian Minister at Vichy who took care of British interests after diplomatic relations had been severed; Felix Cole, the U.S. Consul-General in Algiers; and the colourful Colonel William Eddy, a United States Marine officer who had been wounded in the First World War and whose knowledge of Arabic had secured him the post of U.S. Naval Attaché in Tangier.

The French personalities in Vichy and in French North Africa exhibited an even greater range of opinion and talent, and it was Murphy's assessment of each which more than anything else affected the planning and the outcome of 'Torch'.

'Mr Murphy,' as Eisenhower put it somewhat formally,

who had long been stationed in Africa, was early taken into the confidence of the President of the United States and informed of the possibility of military action in that region. With his staff of assistants, he not only conducted a continuing survey of public opinion, but he did his best to discover among the military and political leaders those individuals who were definitely hostile to the Axis and occupying their posts merely out of a sense of duty to France. Affable, friendly, exceedingly shrewd, and speaking French capably, he was admirably suited for his task.

When the decision for 'Torch' had definitely been taken, Murphy was recalled to Washington for a conference with the President and, arising out of this, was dispatched to London to brief Eisenhower. Since his presence in London and a meeting with the Supreme Commander might well have given the game away, Murphy was provided with a fictional commission as a Lieutenant-Colonel McGowan ('no one pays any attention to a mere Lieutenant-Colonel') and flew to London in uniform and under conditions of the greatest secrecy. As luck would have it he bumped into Don Coster, one of his Vice-Consuls in Africa, soon after landing at Prestwick. 'Why, Bobby, what are you doing here?' Coster asked and forthwith found himself arrested and held incommunicado until after the landings had taken place.

'From Mr Murphy', Eisenhower went on,

we learned the names of those officers who had pro-Allied sympathies and those who were ready to aid us actively . . . he told us very accurately that our greatest resistance would be met in French Morocco, where General Auguste Paul Noguès was Foreign Minister to the Sultan. He gave us a number of details of French military strength in Africa, including equipment and training in their ground, air and sea forces. From his calculations it was plain that if we were bitterly opposed by the French a bloody fight would ensue; if the French should promptly decide to join us we could expect to get along quickly with our main business of seizing Tunisia and attacking Rommel from the rear. It was Mr Murphy's belief that we would actually encounter a mean between these two extremes. Events proved him to be correct.[4]

How did Murphy arrive at this not too startling conclusion? And how was it that his advice, which affected not only the operation itself but also what happened afterwards, could fairly be described as invaluable, if not unique? The short answer in the vernacular is that Murphy knew the form better than anyone of any nationality available at that time. This, too, had not come about in an afternoon. Murphy was an outstanding career diplomat at a time in American history when such men were thin on the ground. The greater part of his working life had been spent in Europe. More importantly, he understood Europe and Europeans in a way that few of his compatriots in positions of power did at that time.

Murphy had lived and worked in Germany and France through the twenties and the thirties when Hindenburg had yielded to Hitler and when there had been thirty-seven French Governments in the ten years between 1930 and 1940. When he had been the U.S. Consul at Munich he had met and talked with Hitler. He had served under Ambassador Bullitt in France just before and during the early part of the war. This brilliant and intelligent ambassador had been very critical of British policy as conducted by Baldwin and Chamberlain, but also held to the opinion that the United States would never repeal its Neutrality Act.

In 1940 Murphy had 'enjoyed a half-hour with Ambassador Kennedy, who told me of his bad health, his discontent over returning to London, his belief that everything he could do there could just as well be done by a $50 a month clerk, that he wanted to quit but didn't see how he gracefully could before the elections.'[5] On 9 May 1940, the day Hitler began his *Blitzkrieg* which resulted in the fall of France, Murphy had been told by Raoul Dautry, the French Minister of Armaments, that 'the entire French Armament programme had been based on the assumption that attack would not come for another year'. Murphy had been in Paris as the Germans approached and the French Government – especially the Foreign Office – was burning its records in a rare old panic, and the city had been covered with a pall of black smoke like Dante's *Inferno*. Since he knew and understood the French, Murphy remained in Paris and in Vichy during and after the time the Germans had taken over. Inevitably he came to meet and thus to assess every Frenchman in any position of power.

Then, recalling him to Washington for consultations in the autumn of 1940, Roosevelt made him one of his 'personal representatives' and told him henceforth to communicate direct with the President. He had already become invaluable.

After he returned to Vichy in November 1940, it had been agreed that Murphy's talents could best be employed on a roving commission. After all, he was one of the few people who could still legitimately move around. So whilst Admiral Leahy minded the shop in Vichy, Murphy began the first of many visits to French North Africa, where he reached an accord with Weygand.

A number of American Vice-Consulates were opened, and Murphy was surprised to be able to confirm what Commander Hillenkoeffer had earlier reported, namely that the Nazis were leaving French North Africa very much to its own devices, few Germans and Italians were in evidence, and the French were continuing to administer the province much as they had done before the war. This attitude opened the door to intrigue. By 1942 it was estimated that some 200,000 Europeans, mostly French, had filtered across to French North Africa as refugees in the broadest sense. These comprised people of all classes, trades and aptitudes, and naturally their presence generated a thriving black market in everything from food to military information. Murphy, trusted by all, moved easily and with good humour through this morass of official and unofficial personages, all paying careful lip service to the régime whilst developing private and sometimes dangerous resistance to Vichy.

This resistance, covering as it did every shade of opinion and interest, threw up a loosely linked and wary leadership which, for working purposes, became known as the Committee of Five. This was headed by Jacques Lemaigre-Dubreuil who had been the president of one of the largest oil concerns in France. After Dunkirk he had made himself *persona grata* with the Germans by re-opening his factories to supply their needs, a fact which at that time would certainly have been misunderstood in London. Described by another French collaborator as 'sure of himself, speaking loudly, his angora hat at a tilt and displaying an innate taste for being observed', Lemaigre-Dubreuil moved about freely 'disguising his conspiracy, like Ali Baba, in so many barrels of oil'.[6]

Man Friday to Lemaigre-Dubreuil was a thin little man in his forties with pale grey, staring eyes. This was Jean Rigault, who had managed a pre-war right-wing paper, *Le Jour Echo*. Next came a dashing figure, Henri d'Astier de la Vigerie, a forty-year-old nephew of Cardinal d'Astier, with black feline eyes and the delicate bronzed features

Top left: General Charles de Gaulle. In Allied eyes a symbol of
French resistance to Nazi oppression, but widely regarded in France
as a British puppet. He was not told before the landings that the
Allies were about to invade French North Africa

Top centre: Marshal Philippe Pétain. A successful commander of
troops and a sincere patriot according to his light, but doomed to
become a focus of controversy in two world wars. In 1917 some
Frenchmen praised him, but others branded him as a defeatist,
because he approved offensives he thought were bound to fail

Top right: General Noguès (left) with General Alphonse Juin,
Commander-in-Chief of the French land forces in Algeria

Far left: General Gentilhomme, commander of the Free French
contingent in Syria

Left: General Henri-Honoré Giraud. Chosen by the Allies to
organize local support, but he proved to have little following in
French North Africa

Right: Pierre Laval, eminence grise of the Vichy government,
gives evidence at Pétain's post-war trial

of a Spanish aristocrat who radiated charm. Fourth came Colonel A. S. von Ecke, a great brusque redheaded Dutchman of fifty with a barrel chest and rugged voice, known as 'Robin Hood', who had spent twenty years in the Foreign Legion and who had currently been put in charge in North Africa of Pétain's youth movement 'Les Chantiers de la Jeunesse'. Van Ecke thus had a large reservoir of ardent and willing talent to call on. Finally, there was a small man with a paunchy figure, long pointed nose and bald head. Jacques Tarbé de Saint-Hardouin was a career diplomat and had been Chef de Cabinet to a right-wing Premier of France, Pierre Étienne Flandin. Because of his position Hardouin could and did spend much time with Murphy without exciting suspicion. In addition he had the asset of an elegant young Turkish wife who ran a salon to entertain *le grand monde* of North Africa.

These then were the Five. Lemaigre-Dubreuil travelled to and from France. Saint-Hardouin stuck closely to Murphy. Van Ecke issued false passes. D'Astier set about spreading the plot and recruiting new members and Rigault kept the archives which, for safety's sake, he consigned to an ascetic young Jesuit who hid them in the Convent of the Sisters of Notre Dame d'Afrique. Earlier in the year Murphy had written to Sumner Welles, his Under-Secretary of State, saying that, 'In essence their purpose is the establishment in French North Africa of a provisional Government operating independently of Metropolitan France. They are searching for and hope to find shortly a military leader.'[7] This was, of course, long before the 'Torch' idea took shape.

The answer to this last problem turned out to be General Giraud. This six-foot-three General – who had escaped from a German prisoner-of-war camp in the First World War disguised as a woman and then as a circus performer, being aided by none other than Nurse Edith Cavell – had been held since 1940 in the 'escape-proof' hilltop fortress of Koenigstein on the German-Czech frontier. In May 1942 he made a dramatic escape with the help of a wire-filled rope smuggled to him in cans of ham and partly woven from tattered linen. During the summer of 1942 Giraud had taken charge of the North African conspiracy, appointing General Mast as his deputy on the spot. Giraud's role in 'Torch' was to be full of excitement, hope and distress.

But why was Giraud necessary when the Allies had de Gaulle in London? The prime reason was that, broadly speaking, no one in any position of power in metropolitan France or in French North Africa wanted to have anything whatever to do with de Gaulle. This was not entirely de Gaulle's fault (even allowing for Dakar). Instead, it highlights a deep distrust of the British. As Lemaigre-Dubreuil put it: 'The African Army on the whole disliked the British. Too much French blood had been shed fighting them at Mers-el-Kebir (Oran), in Syria and at Dakar. All this may have been necessary for the British, but it was humiliating and costly to France.'[8] The implication behind this was that de Gaulle could only be a British puppet. How untrue this was, history has now made abundantly clear. It was not known, however, in the Algeria of 1942.

So much for the pro-American, if not pro-Allied, consensus in French North Africa. How did the situation look from the Axis point of view? Hitler's attention remained firmly on the Eastern Front, and only reluctantly could he be lobbied into handing down decisions about the Mediterranean, especially since Rommel continued to give him the glamorous victories he required.

Among the lower echelons of the German High Command there had been a creeping and growing

exasperation with the French and, to a lesser degree, with the Spaniards after the map of Europe had been so drastically changed in the summer of 1940. Hitler's one meeting with Franco had been totally disastrous, the Fuehrer commenting that, rather than go through that again, he would prefer to have all his teeth drawn out.

Interminably at Wiesbaden the French members of the Armistice Commission argued, prevaricated and generally secured concession after concession – or when the screw was turned, contrived to delay its effect and generally to emasculate the German control of France. However, there were casualties along the line.

In November 1941 Weygand had been abruptly retired from his command of French North Africa following a threat by the Germans to occupy the whole of France, and in April 1942 Laval replaced Darlan in political control at Vichy. Now, at any rate, the Germans felt they had the right man in the right place. To a certain extent they were right but Laval, whose ignorance of the *Herrenvolk* was matched only by a supreme confidence in his own ability to outsmart them, continued to play the rule book in such a way that German tolerance, never the strongest Teuton feature, became stretched almost to breaking point. It could scarcely be described as a satisfactory state of affairs.

If the French led their German masters up the garden path, Admiral Canaris, the head of Abwehr or German Intelligence, assisted the process by supplying Hitler and the O.K.W. with pretentious and nugatory information from the Iberian peninsula. At times this became something of a farce, climaxing in the fact that the vast Allied invasion of North Africa was to reach its destination undetected. How did over 350 secret agents in the field plus the huge Abwehr headquarters in Lisbon and Madrid contrive such a fiasco?

Nazi spies had established themselves strongly in Spain by the summer of 1939 when Franco had won the bitter civil war. A year later, after the fall of France, Hitler decided to 'drive the English out of the Western Mediterranean by taking Gibraltar and closing the Straits'.[9] This was easier said than done. However, relying on Franco's support, an ambitious operation (code-named 'Felix') was planned, the groundwork for which was entrusted to Admiral Canaris and his organization. This entailed two requirements – the coaxing of Spain into supporting the venture and the reconnoitring of the Rock and its environs. This became, in the words of Ladislas Farago, 'reminiscent of a Mack Sennett comedy'. Led personally by Canaris, an intelligence team made its way to the outskirts of Gibraltar 'to study the

The chances of enlisting support for the Allies in the French overseas empire were not enhanced by the British invasion of Syria in 1941. The use of Free French troops, in particular, was much resented. Left: A British anti-aircraft gun on the road to Damascus

Following page: An 88-mm gun in action

95

terrain, the possible difficulties of the assault and to develop a basic attack plan'.[10]

Watched with somewhat schoolboyish delight by Commander Hillgarth and his team, whose own agents in that area had been longer established and were in general more reliable, 'Canaris's reconnaissance venture developed into a farcical tour. Never in the history of espionage', Farago writes,

was a mission like this mounted by such distinguished spies – the Chief of Intelligence in person, flanked by his top-ranking aides, Colonel Pieckenbrock and Commander Wilhelm Leissner (alias 'Gustav Lenz') the Abwehr chief in Spain. In a manner typical of his way of doing such things, he also sent another team of snoopers to the Rock, practically behind his own back.

Assembled in the greatest secrecy, it was headed by a dour, no-nonsense sabotage expert, Captain Hans-Jochen Rudloff, who had conducted highly irregular operations during the French campaign.

This double mission was soon to be followed by a veritable avalanche of reconnaissance ventures, until Spain became the number one tourist spot for the Abwehr.

All one had to do to get himself a vacation was to think up an idea that had some bearing on 'Felix' and he was assured of a holiday in Andalusia. One intelligence unit after another was dispatched to the area around the coveted Pillars of Hercules, one ignorant of the other and working at cross purposes, during a brief period of manly hilarity in the Abwehr which was not otherwise noted for its sense of humour.[11]

But however much the Spaniards wanted Gibraltar, they were not prepared to have the Germans march through Spain to take it for them, and by January 1941 'Felix' had been shelved. The Abwehr was left with the aftermath of a huge and wasted effort except for one vital asset – two villas at Algeciras equipped with the best instruments of surveillance which the German optical and electronic industries could produce.

From here a watch was kept on traffic through the Straits of Gibraltar and also upon the Rock itself. Such became the intensity of this watch that Berlin claimed to know what the Vice-Admiral Gibraltar was having for breakfast even before the tray was put in front of him on the terrace of the Mount. This 'mechanical' surveillance was backed up by reports, for which the Germans paid well, from Spanish fishermen and, of course, from certain members of the many thousands of Spanish workers who crossed each day for work in the dockyard.

With all this going for them, it may well be

continued on page 129

Left and below: Rommel. A master of desert tactics, but much inclined, according to his critics, to risk outrunning his supplies. Among his treasured possessions was a well-thumbed copy of Wavell's book on the art of generalship

Left and below left: Monty. Cautious, thorough and painstaking. Second Alamein made him famous; good judges regard Alam el Halfa and Medenine as his most successful desert battles

Right and above right: The Western Desert, 1942 *Top:* A soldier of the Afrika Korps scans the desert through a twin-lens periscope. *Bottom:* A German machine-gun post

Left and right: German
troops in front of the
Alamein-Clattarn position,
September 1942

Previous pages: German and
Italian troops mount guard
at Bardia after its recapture
in 1941

Left: The Axis Powers responded to 'Torch' by rushing troops to Tunisia in transport aircraft. German grenadiers disembark at a Tunisian airfield from a Ju 52

Right: North Africa – unloading vehicles for the Afrika Corps

A mobile column of the Long Range Penetration Group

Tunisia, March 1943. A Lockheed P 38 (Lightning)
aircraft down in flames

Above: More work for the regimental cobbler after a desert battle. *Right:* Bir Hacheim – two of the attackers pause for a smoke

Above: Dust, Sollum, 1941. *Left:* Rommel and entourage.
Right: Heat of the desert – two German officers sit down
for a meal under camouflage netting.

The Central Mediterranean
Left: Italian cruisers on convoy duty. *Right:* A choppy sea off the Libyan coast. *Below right:* Operation Torch – an American tanker on fire off the Moroccan coast

Over page: Douglas Boston (DB7) medium bombers over the Western Desert. One of the first American aircraft ordered by the British Government after the outbreak of war, the Boston was extensively used both by the R.A.F. and by American Army Air Forces

Left: Air lift – a German air transport base in Cyrenaica;
the aircraft are Ju 52 transports and Bf (Me) 110 twin-
engine fighters. *Above:* Tunisia, 1943 – Hurricane bombers
attack German tanks

Above: A failure in the Battle of Britain but valuable in the desert – the Bf (Me) 110 twin-engine fighter and ground-attack aircraft. *Left:* A successful American naval fighter – the Grumman Wildcat

Below: The Bristol Beaufighter – introduced in Britain as a night fighter but used in Africa in a variety of roles

Left: According to the magazine *Signal*, a German fighter group in North Africa adopted the custom of paying ceremonial honours to its standard before each combat mission. This can scarcely have been done when aircraft had to take off in a hurry. *Right:* German Bf (Me) 109 single-seater fighters over the Western Desert. *Below right:* The wreckage of a Ju 52 transport aircraft brought down in North Africa

Over page: PZKW Mark IV tanks in the Western Desert pass a knocked-out British tank. A PZKW Mark IV tank could do 10 m.p.h. across the desert or up to 26 m.p.h. on a hard road. Its 30-mm armour was reinforced in models introduced in 1941–42 by 30-mm face-hardened steel plates

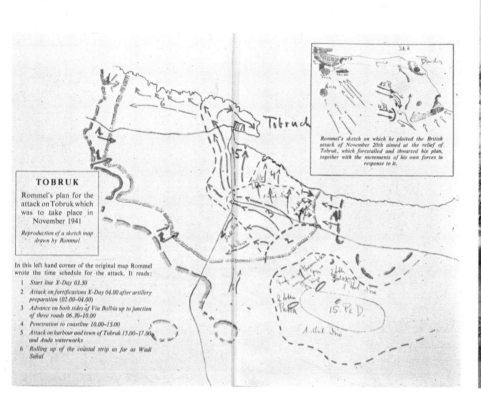

TOBRUK

Rommel's plan for the attack on Tobruk which was to take place in November 1941

Reproduction of a sketch map drawn by Rommel

Rommel's sketch on which he plotted the British attack of November 20th aimed at the relief of Tobruk, which forestalled and thwarted his plan, together with the movements of his own forces in response to it.

In this left hand corner of the original map Rommel wrote the time schedule for the attack. It reads:

1 Start line X-Day 03.30
2 Attack on fortifications X-Day 04.00 after artillery preparation (02.00–04.00)
3 Advance on both sides of Via Balbia up to junction of three roads 06.30–10.00
4 Penetration to coastline 10.00–15.00
5 Attack on harbour and town of Tobruk 15.00–17.00 and Auda waterworks
6 Rolling up of the coastal strip as far as Wadi Sahal

Above left: The Axis assault on Tobruk – map of Tobruk with annotations by Rommel. *Left:* The desert in flower. *Above:* A British 4·5-inch gun in action, probably in Tunisia

Left: A German motor-cyclist and lorry plough through the desert, bound for Tobruk

Tunisia. *Above top:* Italian troops dig in. *Above:* German paratroops go into action. *Right:* 1941 – a German armoured car scatters the desert sand

Over page: In January 1943 – the month in which the Eighth Army effectively turned the Italians out of Libya – the magazine *Signal* printed this photograph of British troops allegedly captured somewhere in North Africa

continued from page 96

asked how complete tactical surprise was, in fact, achieved by the greatest armada in history ever to put to sea up to that time. The short answer is that the British with far fewer agents, but perhaps better chosen ones, had penetrated the Abwehr network. Skilfully and economically, certain key pieces of misleading information were fed to the Germans as part of the deception plan emanating from Norfolk House.

Since reports from Spain were only a part of the overall intelligence picture which Canaris presented to the High Command, and since in the end the German war effort was directed by Hitler, who relied on instinct as much as he did on fact, it was not an insuperable task to put in front of the Fuehrer what it was thought he would like to know. This is the fatal flaw of dictatorship.

The effects of the above flaw were compounded by Admiral Canaris. He had long believed that Hitler was bound to lead Germany to defeat if he remained at the head of affairs. He had a private contempt for Hitler and for the Nazi party which he did not always completely disguise and which led to the theory – never openly proved – that he was secretly working for the British. Canaris relied upon a network of spies in the United Kingdom who daily radioed reports which somehow got through despite all the sophisticated electronic measures used to suppress them. In fact every one of these agents had been 'turned round' by the British and all were thus carefully feeding information to the Abwehr and to the German High Command which the Allies wished them to have.

When the 'Torch' convoys set off from Loch Ewe in Scotland and from the eastern seaboard of the United States, Admiral Canaris and Colonel Pieckenbrock were on a visit to Copenhagen, and although after the event they confused their critics with carefully manufactured evidence to the effect that they had warned the High Command (even succeeding in befuddling so shrewd a man as Dr Goebbels in this matter), 'Torch' proved to be a fatal blow to the Abwehr in general and to Canaris in particular. Thereafter, the Admiral's position deteriorated to such an extent that his enemies, principal of whom was Walter Schellenburg, were soon daring to criticize him to the Fuehrer personally and to recommend his dismissal.

Second Alamein. A member of the crew of a knocked-out German tank surrenders to British infantry

7
THE WESTERN DESERT OPENS UP

August 1942. Across in Egypt Alexander and Montgomery had begun to make themselves felt. 'A leader', Harry Truman once said, 'is a man who has the ability to get other people to do what they don't want to do – and like it.' To begin with, though, nobody in Cairo headquarters liked it very much. A comfortable way of life was being thoroughly upset – it was worse than annoying, it was inconvenient. Now Alexander was to take care of Cairo, Montgomery the Desert.

'My whole working creed', Montgomery himself declared, 'is based on the fact that in war it is "the man" that matters. . . . I hold the view that the leader must know what he himself wants. He must see his objective clearly and then strive to attain it; he must let everyone else know what he wants and what are the basic fundamentals of his policy . . . it is necessary for him to create what I would call "atmosphere" and in that atmosphere his subordinate commanders will live and work.'[1]

There was little doubt in the Eighth Army about the atmosphere Monty created as soon as he gained command. He began by getting everyone – literally – on the run. Monty believed first in physical fitness. Back in England his entire

headquarters staff had had to turn out on one afternoon each week and do a seven-mile run. 'There were many protests,' he wrote, 'but they all did it, even those over forty, and they enjoyed it in the end – some of them.'[2] Back in Cairo the 'Groppi Grenadiers' and the rest of the staff of Middle East Headquarters in Cairo were about to undergo the biggest shake-up of their lives. The new broom was to sweep very, very clean indeed.

It began at the top. Monty had previously served under Auchinleck in Southern Command in England and said, 'I cannot recall that we ever agreed on anything.' Now he was to take over the battle-hardened Eighth Army from 'the Auk'. No sooner had Monty reached Cairo than

> Auchinleck took me into his map-room and shut the door; we were alone. He asked me if I knew he was to go. I said that I did. He then explained to me his plan of operations; this was based on the fact that at all costs the Eighth Army was to be preserved 'in being' and must not be destroyed in battle. If Rommel attacked in strength, as was expected soon, the Eighth Army would fall back on the Delta; if Cairo and the Delta could not be held, the Army would retreat southwards up the Nile, and another possibility was a withdrawal to Palestine. Plans were being made to move the Eighth Army H.Q. back up the Nile. I listened in amazement to this exposition of his plans. I

asked one or two questions, but I quickly saw that he resented any question directed to immediate changes of policy about which he had already made up his mind. So I remained silent.[3]

With hindsight this stark account by Montgomery of what happened is, perhaps, unfair to Auchinleck. The retiring Commander-in-Chief had planned to defeat Rommel's armour in the neighbourhood of the Alam el Halfa ridge. Contingent plans for a withdrawal to the Nile Delta, if the worst came to the worst, had been made about the time of First Alaméin: but that battle had been won.

The new Commander-in-Chief, Alexander – 'calm, confident and charming' – had ordered Monty 'very simply to destroy Rommel and his Army'. The meeting with Auchinleck had taken place on 12 August and Monty had been told not to take over command until the 15th, after spending two days in the desert 'getting into the picture and learning the game'. So Monty set off for the desert the next day at 0500 hours.

On arrival he found the situation to be

> quite unreal and, in fact, dangerous. I decided at once to take action . . . I told General Ramsden he was to return at once to his Corps; he seemed surprised as he had been

placed in acting command of the Army, but he went. I then had lunch, with the flies and in the hot sun. During lunch I did some savage thinking. After lunch I wrote a telegram to G.H.Q. saying that I had assumed command of Eighth Army as from 2 p.m. that day, 13 August; this was disobedience but there was no comeback. I then cancelled all previous orders about withdrawal.[4]

During that morning he had acquired a Chief of Staff and an A.D.C. The latter, John Poston, was a young officer in the 11th Hussars who had been with Gott and who knew the desert well. The Chief of Staff was Brigadier 'Freddie' de Guingand, a man almost completely the opposite of Montgomery. 'He lived on his nerves and was highly strung; in ordinary life he liked wine, gambling and good food. Did these differences matter? I quickly decided they did not; indeed differences were assets.'[5]

Even before he took over command, Montgomery had realized the magnitude of the task he faced. He knew he could not tackle it alone. He needed someone to help him, a man with a quick and clear brain, who would accept responsibility, who would work out the details and leave the commander free to concentrate on the major issues. 'I knew that if I once got immersed in the details of the "dog's breakfast" that was being set in front of me, I would fail as others had failed before me.'[6] De Guingand proved to be exactly the man Montgomery was looking for and they stayed together for the rest of the war.

No sooner had he assumed command than he issued orders that in the event of enemy attack there would be *no* withdrawal; we would fight on the ground we now held and if we couldn't stay there alive we would stay there dead. I remembered an inscription I had seen in Greece when touring that country with my wife in 1933. It was carved by the Greeks at Thermopylae to commemorate those who died defending the pass 2,000 years ago and its English version is well known:

> 'Go tell the Spartans, thou that passest by,
> That here, obedient to their laws, we lie'

We would do the same if need be.[7]

Again to be fair to Auchinleck, Montgomery has acknowledged that the plan for the battle of Alam el Halfa was based on one prepared in Auchinleck's time.

On the evening of the day he took over, Monty addressed his headquarters staff. They listened to him in stunned silence. As he commented himself – one could have heard a pin drop if such a thing was possible in the sand of the desert.

I introduced myself to them and said I wanted to explain things. Certain orders had already been issued which they knew about, and more would follow. The order 'no withdrawal' involved a complete change of policy and they must understand what that policy was, because they would have to do the detailed staff work involved. If we were to fight where we stood the defences must have depth; all transport must be sent back to rear areas; ammunition, water, rations etc. must be stored in the forward areas. We needed more troops in the Eighth Army in order to make the 'no withdrawal' order a possibility. There were plenty of troops back in the Delta, preparing the defence of that area; but the defence of the cities of Egypt must be fought out *here* at Alamein. . . .[8]

Spartan though he was, Monty had more wisdom than that of a mere martinet. He disliked the atmosphere he found at this hot, fly-ridden, uncomfortable desert headquarters and this, he considered, destroyed morale. He gave orders that the headquarters would move as soon as possible to a site on the sea shore near Air Force Headquarters, where they could work hard, bathe and be happy (one of the first things which had struck him – and which Tedder amply confirmed – was that the Army and the R.A.F. were fighting separate wars). There the Air Force and the Army would work out a plan together to go over to the offensive. He had only been a few hours in command; the old hands might think his knees were still very white, but already the atmosphere had changed. Now the Eighth Army had a full-time commander. There was no more uncertainty in the air.

However, there still remained a great deal of leeway to make up and the 'old hands' might well be forgiven for their scepticism. They had seen it all happen before. At this early stage Montgomery was simply another general taking over with great ideas which the conditions of the Desert War would no doubt soon modify. He had yet to come up against Rommel. A measure of disbelief was fully justified. They would wait and see.

When researching this book I asked Laurence Cotterell, himself an ex-Desert Rat, to set down a few notes about the Libyan campaign to counterpoint the official papers and the generals' and politicians' memoirs which tend to dominate the record. Some of the notes he gave me illuminate other parts of the picture:

(1) Bear in mind the extreme popularity of Wavell so far as any true Desert Rat was concerned.

(2) Remember the extraordinary camaraderie which existed between men of the Eighth Army and men of the Afrika Korps, creating a bond much firmer than any which existed between desert soldiers and their own countrymen in other theatres of war.

(3) There is also the cult of Rommel to be considered. The adulation among British troops was such that an Order of the Day had to be issued to try to counteract it. This naturally led to an intensification of the cult.

(4) Remember the widespread unpopularity among the desert troops, particularly the old hands, of Montgomery who was very much a politicians' general and a civilians' general, and whose military support came only from the 'new boys' he brought out with him from England.

(5) The distrust of politicians was more marked in this theatre than in others and not even Churchill was a popular figure with desert troops, despite his visits – mainly after they had left the desert. This was on account of his con trick when he told the veterans in Tripoli that they would henceforth be doing their soldiering in green fields. His listeners took this to mean a spell in Britain and further service no further away than Western Europe. In fact he was talking about Sicily and Southern Italy. [This, of course, refers to a later period in the war.]

(6) This was an ideal war and the ideal theatre, since it was nothing but an arena made of sand, and men brought together to fight and survive, or fight and die, with no buildings or homes to be damaged and no women, children or other civilians to get in the way. Consider also the extraordinary ignorance among desert soldiers of the battle situation. With a fluid situation and no landmarks, one could just see what was happening as far as the eye could reach and if one wanted to know what the general desert situation was it was better to tune in to the B.B.C. to find out.

(7) Water is a factor you will doubtless bring into perspective, because it was the rarest and most precious commodity for both sides and one which cemented a fellow feeling. I have never yet heard of a case of a well being poisoned.

(8) Finally the other natural element which controlled the whole situation was sand, sand – and sand again.

Throughout August both sides were hard at work reorganizing, regrouping, extending their minefields, probing for information and collecting reinforcements. 'Both sides sought to use the

breathing space', Rommel wrote, 'to refit their forces and bring up fresh troops . . . but shipping from Britain or America required two to three months for the journey round the Cape to North Africa and we therefore had a few weeks' grace before the immense reinforcements (other than normal routine replacements) no doubt planned for the Eighth Army after the fall of Tobruk could reach African soil. We reckoned on mid-September. . .'[9]

Generally speaking (and with the exception of the cover plan preceding the Battle of Alamein), the intelligence services of both sides in the Desert War provided their respective commanders with reasonably accurate estimates of the forces available on the other side. Rommel calculated that by 20 August, a week after Montgomery had taken command, the British would have 70 infantry battalions, 900 tanks and armoured vehicles, 550 light and heavy guns and 850 anti-tank guns available for action. This estimate was approximately correct if the forces refitting behind the front and those disposed for defence of the Nile Delta were included.

Rommel had four German and eight Italian divisions (two of each being armoured) but, as Liddell Hart observes, 'a comparative reckoning of the two sides in number of divisions is, of course, no true comparison. Rommel's were being made up to strength much more slowly than the British, and his Italian divisions were too poorly equipped to be reckoned on the same terms as the British or German – apart from the question of fighting spirit.' The 300 American Sherman tanks which were going to make such a welcome addition to British strength were still on their way up the east coast of Africa.

Churchill had gone on to Moscow for his first meeting with the Russian dictator before Montgomery's arrival, but on 17 August the Prime Minister returned to Cairo *en route* to London. The new team of Alexander and Montgomery had only been operating for a few days, but already results were visible. These helped to offset news of the Dieppe raid which had just taken place and which, in spite of the grim casualty figures, had to be classified as 'a costly but not unfruitful reconnaissance in force'. It may have provided essential experience for a future cross-Channel invasion: in August 1942 it did nothing for the

British war image at that time.

However, the six days which Churchill spent in Cairo undoubtedly did help enormously to build up morale, in spite of the slightly cynical opinions of the 'old hands'. Churchill, privately enjoying himself like a schoolboy on a treat, got out and about and up to the front line as often as he could. A contemporary eye-witness account of one of these visits conveys very clearly what it was like:

The desert stands where the desert stood. Nothing much is changed. The flies are bad about here, and netting is essential if one is to get any peace at all – or any food. Lizards sit tightly on the sunny sides of rocks contemplating heaven alone knows what in such desolation. Scavenger beetles go about their eternal tasks, performing impossible feats of strength and cunning in hiding bits of refuse and rubbish. Dogs of all shapes, sizes and colours amble furtively round the camp, instantly ready to yowl and run with their tails between their legs at any sign of displeasure. There are a lot of Bedouins about, and they stalk majestically around, clasping a few eggs in lean brown hands and seeking to trade them for tea or sugar. A few donkeys crop non-existent grass and appear to like it – one of the *real* mysteries of the East.

The road runs along the top of a ridge parallel to the sea and separated from it by low sand hills that are of purest white. The sea is always incredibly blue. Something must have happened to it since the ancient Greeks called it 'wine coloured'. There are no clouds in the sky. The sun burns more and more brassily as it climbs and the desert stretches away south, east and west, to lose itself in dancing heat-waves.

In this setting Mr Churchill came to see the men of the Eighth Army. We all thought he had rather the air of a pleasant headmaster who had come along to see how his pupils were getting on; only one wasn't too sure that he hadn't a birch concealed somewhere. Perhaps it was the fly-whisk he carried which fostered this idea.

The little procession of cars churned up great clouds of dust as they bumped over the road. Troops already at work scarcely bothered to raise their heads. A few did, and saw the P.M. smiling at them and prodding two fingers in the air in the 'V' sign. They stared and scratched their heads and peered questioningly at the following cars. We nodded vigorously in answer to their unspoken question.

On again until near to the forward positions held by the Australians, the scene changed. Word of his coming had in some way outpaced the cars. So everywhere troops were running to the road, lorries were stopping and men were tumbling out of them.

Away to the west the guns banged away sullenly and grumbled in the heat. Up north, tiny planes glinted in the sun as they dived and twisted, and the rattle of their fire came to us briskly but softly on the breeze. It was a normal sort of morning on the Western Desert Front.

For hours in the evening we sat discussing this visit and discovering hundreds of hidden and contradictory mean-ings. Churchill – Wavell – Smuts! What does it all mean? There are great days ahead.[10]

Whatever feelings of loyalty men on the spot might have towards officers who had been suddenly replaced, there was one meaning which all could gather from these sudden and extraordinary visits. 'The Eighth Army', another observer wrote at the time, 'has occasionally felt that it was battling on alone, and that its trials and tribulations, its successes and failures, were not sufficiently appreciated at home. Now we feel someone is really taking an interest in us.'[11]

It is intriguing to speculate on what might have happened had Hitler seen fit to visit his African front. Rommel and the lean, taut troops he commanded also felt forgotten and neglected, and if it were true to say, as General von Raven-stein did, that 'the desert is a tactician's paradise but the Quartermaster's hell'[12], then the long, continuing and largely unsuccessful struggle which Rommel was forced to wage against the Com-mando Supremo in order to obtain anything like adequate supplies must be placed high on the balance sheet of results.

But Churchill did not only spend his time in

Egypt in joy-rides to the front.

> In the fullest accord with General Alexander and the C.I.G.S. I set on foot a series of extreme measures for the defence of Cairo and the water-lines running northward to the sea. Rifle-pits and machine-gun posts were constructed, bridges mined and their approaches wired, and inundations loosed over the whole wide front.
>
> All the office population of Cairo, numbering thousands of staff officers and uniformed clerks, were armed with rifles and ordered to take their stations, if need be, along the fortified water-line.
>
> The 51st Highland Division was not yet regarded as 'desert-worthy' but these magnificent troops were now ordered to man the new Nile front. The position was one of great strength because of the comparatively few causeways which cross the canalized flooded or floodable area of the Delta. . . .[13]

By this time, too, another vital convoy – or rather five ships out of fourteen (including the famous American tanker *Ohio*) had got through to Malta. The loss in men and ships was grievous but, revictualled and replenished with ammunition and vital stores, Malta revived. British submarines returned to the island and, together with striking forces of the R.A.F., managed to regain a dominating position in the central Mediterranean. By not invading the George Cross island when it was literally at its last gasp, Hitler had lost the initiative on the eve of what was soon to prove the most decisive battle of the war to date.

> The safe arrival of the convoy enabled me to invite Lord Gort to Cairo. I greatly desired to hear all about Malta from him. Gort and his aide-de-camp, Lord Munster (who was a Minister when the war began, but insisted on going to the front) arrived safely. They were both very thin and looked rather haggard. The General and his staff had made a point of sharing rigorously the starvation rations of the garrison and civil population. They were cautiously renourished at the Embassy. We had long talks and when we parted I had the Malta picture clearly in my mind.[14]

So the Churchill visit came to an end. Before leaving Montgomery to get on with it, Churchill had written in his personal diary: 'May the anniversary of Blenheim, which marks the opening of the new Command, bring to the Commander-in-Chief of the Eighth Army and his troops the fame and fortune they will surely deserve.'[15] Churchill also sent a report to the War Cabinet in London which aptly summed up the fruits of his visit. It was dated 21 August, two days before Churchill set off home and ten days before Rommel was to attack for the last time at Alam Halfa.

Previous pages
Top left: General Sir Alan Cunningham. Chosen to command the Eighth Army (formerly the Western Desert Force) although he had no experience of desert warfare and had never commanded an armoured force, he was relieved of his command during Operation Crusader on the grounds that he had done extremely well but was beginning to think defensively
Top centre: General the Hon. Sir Harold Alexander, Auchinleck's successor as Commander-in-Chief, Middle East. How far Churchill was right in thinking that the Eighth Army lost confidence in its leaders after its retreat to the Alamein-Gattarn position is still a controversial question. Top right: Churchill with Smuts, during his famous visit to Cairo, August 1942
Bottom right: Monty, earmarked for command of the First Army in Operation Torch, but appointed to command the Eighth Army when commander designate, Lieutenant-General W. H. E. Gott, was killed on 7 August 1942
Following pages
Top left: Prelude to Second Alamein. Lieutenant-General H. Lumsden, commanding the 10th Corps, confers with his divisional commanders. Left to right: Major-General Raymond Briggs (1st Armoured Division), Lieutenant-General Sir Bernard Freyberg, V.C. (2nd New Zealand Division), Major-General Alec Gatehouse (10th Armoured Division), Lumsden, Major-General Charles Gardiner (8th Armoured Division)
Bottom left: Photograph taken by official war photographer on the last day of First Alamein
Top right: Between battles. A near miss on a gun position south of Alamein
Bottom right: PzKw Mark IV tank, used by the Germans in the Western Desert from 1941.

Have just spent two days in the Western Desert visiting H.Q. 8th Army. Brooke, Alexander, Montgomery and I went round together seeing 44th Division, 7th Armoured Division and 22nd Armoured Brigade, and representatives of the New Zealand Division. I saw a great number of men and all the principal commanders in the XIIIth Corps area, also again Air Marshal Coningham, who shares headquarters with General Montgomery.

I am sure we were heading for disaster under the former régime. The Army was reduced to bits and pieces and oppressed by a sense of bafflement and uncertainty. Apparently it was intended in face of heavy attack to retire eastwards to the Delta. Many were looking over their shoulders to make sure of their seat in the lorry, and no plain plan of battle or dominating will-power had reached the units.

Since then . . . a complete change of atmosphere has taken place . . . the highest alacrity and activity prevails . . . however it seems probable that Rommel will attack during the moon period before the end of August . . . if not he will be attacked himself at greater relative disadvantage in September. This would fit in well with 'Torch'. . . .[16]

The war had been in progress for three years and yet now these changes and the events with which they were involved were on a time scale of days – the vast 'Torch' operation being only weeks away. A tremendous, almost tangible tension had begun to build up.

'I had now to go home on the eve of battle,' Churchill wrote,

and return to far wider but by no means less decisive affairs. I had already obtained the Cabinet's approval of the directive to be given to General Alexander. He was the supreme authority with whom I now dealt in the Middle East. Montgomery and the Eighth Army were under him. So, also, if it became necessary, was Maitland-Wilson and the defence of Cairo. 'Alex', as I had long called him, had already moved himself and his personal headquarters into the desert by the Pyramids. Cool, gay, comprehending all, he inspired quiet, deep confidence in every quarter.[17]

Rommel, whose inspirational powers were certainly the equal of Alex and Monty combined, watched the August days go by with mounting exasperation. Where was the logistic support he so badly needed to push on to the Nile? 'It is always a bad thing when political matters are allowed to affect supply or the planning of operations,' he wrote, and in view of this opinion, the following supply figures for August 1942 speak for themselves:

For the German element of the Panzer Army:
   8,200 tons (32% of requirements)
For the Italian element of the Panzer Army, the Italian troops in Libya and the civilian population:

25,700 tons (800 tons of which were for civilian needs)
For the German Luftwaffe:
   8,500 tons

'Cavallero,' Rommel went on, 'who from time to time visited the front, often promised to have all manner of things put right. But it just as frequently happened that on his next visit he would say with a laugh that he had made many a promise in his time and not all of them could be kept.'[18]

The cause of the trouble, very apparent to those at the business end, lay in the over-organization and muddle which bedevilled the Italian supply staffs. Rommel therefore proposed to the O.K.W. that control of Mediterranean shipping should be vested in Field-Marshal Kesselring with special powers. 'Kesselring', as Rommel wrote, 'had a personal interest in helping us at Alamein; he had considerable strength of will, a first-class talent for diplomacy and organization and a considerable knowledge of technical matters.'[19] Kesselring also had the Luftwaffe and Goering behind him. Thus he could tap support at the highest level whenever there might be differences of opinion with the Commando Supremo in Italy. Rommel's proposal, however, was not adopted. This 'Quartermaster's hell', more than any other factor, determined the outcome of the Desert War.

But by the end of August another matter cropped up which caused the gravest anxiety, and that was the health of Rommel and of some of his commanding generals. Rommel himself was simply exhausted. He had been nineteen months in Africa and according to his doctors had stood the climate, the heavy colds and the digestive troubles from which he suffered longer than any other officer over forty, 'an astonishing physical feat . . . true there is no immediate danger but unless he can get a thorough rest some time, he might easily suffer an overstrain which could leave organic damage in its train.'[20]

In fact Rommel had been suffering frequent attacks of faintness but was trying with all his strength to remain on his feet. After one medical examination the doctor and the Chief of Staff, General Gause, signalled to O.K.W. that Rommel was not in a fit condition to command the forthcoming offensive, but as Rommel felt that the only man who could replace him was Guderian and as Guderian was 'unacceptable' to the Fuehrer, Rommel carried on, his health luckily improving just before his last offensive. But as he wrote to his 'Dearest Lu' on 24 August, 'at the rate we've been using up generals in Africa – five per division in eighteen months, it's no wonder that I also need an overhaul some time or other.'[21]

So the end of August came, and with it the waning of the full moon indispensable to a Panzer offensive. The petrol and ammunition which Rommel had been promised by the Commando Supremo had still not arrived, but any further delay would mean giving up all idea of resuming the offensive. 'However, Marshal Cavallero informed me that the tankers would arrive under heavy escort in a matter of hours, or at the latest next day and in the hope that this promise would be fulfilled and trusting in Field-Marshal Kesselring's assurance that he would fly across up to 500 tons of petrol a day in an emergency, I gave the order for the attack to open on the night of 30–31 August.'[22]

'If our blow succeeds,' Rommel wrote to his wife, 'it might go some way towards deciding the whole course of the war. If it fails, at least I hope to give the enemy a pretty thorough beating. Neurath has seen the Fuehrer, who sent me his best wishes. He is fully aware of my anxieties.'[23]

Professor Horster (Rommel's doctor) commented that 'Rommel left his sleeping truck on the morning of the attack with a very troubled face. "Professor," he said, "the decision to attack today is the hardest I have ever taken. Either the Army in Russia succeeds in getting through to Grozny and we in Africa manage to reach the Suez Canal or. . ." He made a gesture of defeat.'[24]

Montgomery, too, required an early and decisive victory but for different reasons.

What I now needed was a battle which would be fought in accordance with my ideas and not those of former desert commanders . . . I had taken command of truly magnificent material but officers and men were bewildered at what had happened and this had led to a loss of confidence . . . this loss of confidence, combined with the bellyaching which went on and which was partly the cause of it, were becoming dangerous and could only be eradicated by a successful battle: a battle in which Rommel was defeated easily, and must be seen to have been beaten, and with few casualties to the Eighth Army . . . I could not myself attack: Rommel must provide that opportunity for me. But in order to reap the full benefit, I must correctly forecast the design of his expected attack and determine in advance how we would defeat it. This was not difficult to do. My intelligence staff were certain the 'break-in' to

our positions would be on the southern flank: this would be followed by a left wheel, his armoured forces being directed on the Alam Halfa and Ruweisat ridges. I agreed and my plans were based on this forecast.[25]

It was obvious to Montgomery that Rommel could not simply bypass the Eighth Army and carry on eastwards to Cairo. Had he done this, Montgomery would have descended on his rear with 400 tanks and that would have been the end of the Afrika Korps. But Montgomery did make his southern flank mobile, at the same time deciding to hold the Alam Halfa ridge in strength with the 44th Division and locating his tanks just south of its western end.

Once I was sure that the enemy main thrust was being directed against the Alam Halfa ridge, I planned to move the armour to the area between the west of the ridge and the New Zealand positions in the main Alamein line. I was so sure that this movement of my own armour would take place that I ordered it to be actually rehearsed; and when it *did* take place on the morning of 1st September I had some 400 tanks in position, dug in and deployed behind a screen of 6 pounder anti-tank guns. The strictest orders were issued that the armour was not to be loosed against Rommel's forces. It was not to move. The enemy was to be allowed to beat up against it and to suffer heavy casualties.[26]

Put very simply, Montgomery turned the 44th Division, 22nd Armoured Brigade and 10th Armoured Division into a solid fortress which he invited Rommel to attack. As General von Mellenthin wrote:

Montgomery is undoubtedly a great tactician – circumspect and thorough in making his plans, utterly ruthless in carrying them out. He brought a new spirit to the Eighth Army and illustrated once again the vital importance of personal leadership in war.

Since we could not pierce the Eighth Army front, we had to seek a way round the flank, and Rommel adopted a plan broadly similar to that of Gazala. The Italian infantry, stiffened by 164 Infantry Division and other German units were to hold the front from the sea to a point ten miles south of Ruweisat Ridge; the striking force consisting of 90 Light Division (on the inner arc of the circle), the Italian Armoured Corps and the Afrika Korps was to swing round the British left flank and advance on the Alam Halfa Ridge. This was a key position well in rear of Eighth Army, and its capture would decide the fate of the battle. In case of success 21 Panzer was to advance on Alexandria and 15 Panzer and 90 Light towards Cairo.[27]

The attack began on the night of 30–31 August and to turn the British front south of Alam Nayil, it was necessary to pierce a thick minebelt stretching almost to the Qattara Depression. It soon became clear that things were not going at

all in the way Rommel intended. The British minefields proved to be deeper and more elaborate than Rommel had imagined. By dawn the leading units had not reached their objectives and were only eight to ten miles east of their own minefields. This threw the whole timetable out of gear, giving Montgomery time to regroup his forces as planned and allowing the R.A.F. to plaster the minefield gaps. General Nehring, Commander of the Afrika Korps, was wounded and had to be replaced by Colonel Bayerlein. General von Bismarck, the Commander of 21st Panzer, was killed by a mortar bomb.

At this point Rommel very nearly called off the attack. However, Bayerlein's resolute leadership got the Afrika Korps through the minefields and this decided Rommel to press on again. He was now to be hindered by two other events – one was the discovery of a false 'going-map' which crafty British intelligence had planted in no-man's-land. This the Germans took to be authentic and it led the Panzers into soft sand causing them to waste even more precious petrol in getting out. The second event was a heavy sandstorm which greatly added to the hardship of the march, but did give some welcome protection from British air attacks.

Because of refuelling problems and the somewhat laggardly progress of the Ariete and Trieste Divisions as they cleared lanes and threaded their way through the British defence system, no attack on Alam Halfa could be launched until the evening of 31 August. However, when the Afrika Korps did attack, supported by Stukas, they exhibited their usual determination and their new Mark IV Special tanks with their high velocity 75-mm guns inflicted considerable damage on the dug-in 'fortress' Grants. However, as Montgomery had calculated, the defence held and the attack failed.

'After nightfall,' Rommel wrote,

our forces became the target for heavy R.A.F. attacks, mainly on the reconnaissance group . . . with one aircraft flying circles and dropping a continuous succession of flares, bombs from the other machines, some of which dived low for the attack, crashed down among the flare-lit vehicles of the reconnaissance unit. All movement was instantly pinned down by low-flying attacks. Soon many of our vehicles were alight and burning furiously. The reconnaissance group suffered heavy casualties.

Needless to say the promised petrol had not arrived, and German and Italian supply traffic

through the British minefields found itself seriously harassed by 7th Armoured Division south of Rommel's salient. Since a frontal attack on the Alam Halfa position was not going to work, Rommel would normally have swung east and tried to manoeuvre the British out of their positions. Lack of petrol made this impossible.

'The next morning,' Rommel went on,

> after disposing of a few command matters, I drove through the area occupied by the Afrika Korps. Between ten and twelve o'clock, we were bombed no less than six times by British aircraft. On one occasion I only just had time to throw myself into a slit trench before the bombs fell. A spade lying on the soil beside the trench was pierced clean through by an 8-inch splinter and the red-hot metal fragment fell beside me in the trench . . . in the afternoon I shifted my Command Post and in view of the bad supply situation, again considered whether to break off the battle.[28]

In one sense the decision was immaterial. A shortage of fuel prevented even a large-scale withdrawal. The Afrika Korps had to remain where it was, being ceaselessly eroded by bombing and shellfire.

On 3 September Rommel's striking force was nevertheless in full retreat, leaving behind 50 tanks, 50 field and anti-tank guns and about 400 derelict vehicles. By 6 September the battle was over. However, a redeeming feature, from the German point of view, was that Rommel retained a hold on important British minefields on the southern flank.

'I have sometimes been criticized for not following up Rommel's withdrawal,' Montgomery wrote;

> there were two reasons . . . first I was not too happy about the standard of training of the Army and also the equipment situation was unsatisfactory . . . secondly I was not anxious to force Rommel to pull out and withdraw 'in being' back to the Agheila position. If we were to carry out the mandate, it was essential to get Rommel to stand and fight and then to defeat him decisively. This had never happened to him before; he had often retreated but it was always for administrative reasons. It was obvious that we would prefer to bring him to battle, when we were ready, at the end of a long and vulnerable line of communications – with ours short. Such would be his situation if he stood to fight at Alamein.[29]

Von Mellenthin comments: 'No doubt these are cogent arguments but one feels that Rommel's reputation and his well-known brilliance in counter-attack had much to do with Montgomery's caution.'[30]

8
THE 'TORCH' IS LIT

September 1942 saw the most intense planning activity in London and Washington for the 'Torch' operation, and this planning had to be combined with training and other preparatory work elsewhere in the United Kingdom and in the United States. Moreover, everything needed to be done in the profoundest secrecy in the sense that although, obviously, an expedition of some kind and on some scale was being prepared, only a handful of staff officers in Norfolk House knew the when and the where.

This period culminated in the issue of the Naval Orders for Operation Torch which were in eight parts and which were issued in sealed envelopes, conveyed 'By Hand of Officer' and in Top Secret bags between 3 and 20 October. The physical production of these detailed orders became something of a saga in itself. In fact the task merits the word 'colossal' when scaled against the facilities available at that time both in personnel and material. The orders were given the short title TON (Torch Orders Naval) and had seven enclosures, the titles of which convey some idea of the parameters of the operation. They were:

Over 200 warships, 1,000 aircraft, 70,000 troops and 350 merchant ships, including transports and landing ships, were required for the assault, the object of the operation being simply stated as 'the occupation of Algeria and French Morocco by combined British and American forces with a view to the early occupation of Tunisia'. The force had also to be strong enough to move into Spanish Morocco if Spain turned hostile.

Then, of course, once the assault had gone through, more troops, aircraft and stores would be required to complete the occupation of Tunisia as soon as the necessary ports had been captured. The composition and deployment of the forces which eventually took part in 'Torch' were as follows:

Air Forces

There were two areas of Allied Air Command, namely the Eastern Air Command (British) comprising the area east of Cape Tenez (36° 35′ N. 1° 20′ E. – 330 miles east of Gibraltar) under Air Marshal Sir William Welsh. This area included the whole of the Western Mediterranean 'to seaward'. The Western Air Command (U.S.) – the area west of Cape Tenez under Major-General James Doolittle – comprised the 12th U.S. Air Force. The Eastern Air Command was serviced by the R.A.F. Both commands were under the orders of the Allied C.-in-C., General Eisenhower.

The muster of aircraft was as follows:

| | Air Marshal Welsh | | General Doolittle | | |
	Gibraltar	Algiers	Oran	Casabalanca	Total
Catalinas	24	–	–	–	24
Hudsons	20	20	–		40
Bombers	–	72	57	114	243
Fighters	–	162	320	240	722
P.R.U.	6	6	–	–	12
					1,041[1]

Though the initial assaults were to be supported by seaborne aircraft, it was essential that the maximum possible strength of fighter aircraft should be available as soon as airfields were captured. It was therefore planned to fly from Gibraltar 160 fighters to each of the Oran and

Casablanca areas, and ninety to the Algiers area within three days of the attack. Thereafter the build-up was to reach, at the end of seven weeks, a total in all types of aircraft of 1,244 in the Western Command and 454 in the Eastern Command.

The Axis forces opposing them were estimated at about 600 aircraft to which might be added nearly 500 Vichy, as follows:

	Luftwaffe Sicily	Italy Sicily, Sardinia, Tripoli	Total	Vichy North Africa
Bombers	106	134	240	185
Fighters	36	195	231	218
Reconnaissance	27	102	129	83
			600	486

Allied Military Forces

The assault forces to be landed to capture the three ports numbered approximately 70,000:

Eastern

(Algiers) Task Assault Force under Major-General Ryder, U.S. Army.

Two U.S. Combat Teams, 39th and 168th	9,000
Two British Brigade Groups, 11th and 36th	9,000
Two Allied Commandos, I and VI	2,000
	20,000

The landing at Algiers was to be followed up by the British First Army under Lieutenant-General K. A. N. Anderson.

Centre

(Oran) Task Assault Force under Major-General Lloyd R. Fredendall, U.S. Army.

Three U.S. Regimental Combat Teams, 16th, 18th and 26th	13,500
One Armoured Combat Command (plus 180 tanks)	4,500
First Ranger Battalion	500
	18,500

This landing was to be followed up by an American Force.

Western

(Casablanca) Task Assault Force under Major-General George S. Patton, U.S. Army. This was to sail direct from the United States and planning had necessarily to be carried out in Washington.

Five U.S. Regimental Combat Teams 7th, 15th, 30th, 47th and 60th	22,500
One Armoured Combat Command	4,500
One Regiment	2,000
One Armoured Combat Team (2 Battalions)	2,000
	31,000

These were to be transported with 250 tanks in 12

Combat Loaders, 10 Auxiliary combat loaders, 6 Cargo ships and 1 sea train.

The follow-up forces in this area were to be entirely American. Except at Algiers where the landing and assault were to be carried out by British and U.S. Forces, the assaults were to be made by U.S. Forces. At Oran and Algiers the naval forces for escorting, disembarking and supporting were British. At Casablanca they were American.[2]

Early in October two new details of considerable importance were woven into the general plan. The first was a decision to employ a battalion of parachute infantry to be flown all the way from England, to seize the airfields of Tafaroui and La Senia, south of Oran. The second was a decision in favour of direct frontal attacks against the ports of Algiers and Oran. In both cases the nearest main landings had to be a full day's march distant, and it was feared that the delay might afford time for the blocking of these vital ports, and the sabotaging of shipping and harbour installations.

For the plans as finally approved, there were not available in the United Kingdom sufficient forces, British or United States, with the necessary amphibious training. A programme was therefore arranged to afford the best training possible in the short time available. This training took place at the Combined Training Centre near Inveraray in western Scotland. A new United States naval base was rushed to completion in the same area, and several regimental combat teams were put through a short course there. Those crews which arrived last from the United States had to be hurriedly trained, though the training was pressed forward with energy by the ground-force commanders.

Naval Forces

The great assembly of British naval forces was under the command of Admiral Sir Andrew Cunningham, Bart. as N.C.E.F. (Naval Commander Expeditionary Force) with Commodore R. M. Dick as his Chief of Staff. It was rendered possible only by reducing convoy forces in the Atlantic to the narrowest possible limits.

The naval forces were constituted as follows:

Eastern Naval Task Force (Algiers)   – E.N.T.F.
Centre Naval Task Force (Oran)   – C.N.T.F.
Western Naval Task Force (Casablanca) – W.N.T.F.
Force H
Force R
Force Q

Force H (Vice-Admiral Sir Neville Syfret) consisted of 3 capital ships (1 detached to C.N.T.F.), 2 aircraft carriers (1 detached to C.N.T.F.), 3 cruisers and 17 destroyers. Force H was to act as a covering force to the landings at Algiers and Oran guarding them against any excursion of the Italian Fleet. Attached to it was Force R – 1 corvette, 2 tankers and 4 trawlers for fuelling purposes.

Force Q – 2 cruisers and 3 destroyers – was to cruise off the Azores to cover the U.S. Casablanca landing against a possible attack by surface craft in the Atlantic.

The Eastern Naval Task Force under the command of Rear-Admiral H. M. Burrough in the H.Q. ship *Bulolo* consisted of 67 warships and 25 merchant vessels.

The Centre Naval Task Force under Commodore T. Troubridge in the H.Q. ship *Largs* consisted of 70 warships and 34 merchant vessels.

The Western Naval Task Force under Rear-Admiral H. K. Hewitt, U.S.N. consisted of Flag Group (Force W), 1 cruiser (flag of Commander W.N.T.F.) and 4 submarines acting independently; a Fire Support Group of 2 capital ships, 3 cruisers and 20 destroyers. Aircraft-carrier group of 4 aircraft-carriers, 1 A/A cruiser and 9 destroyers; Minesweeping Group of 5 Fast and 3 Slow minesweepers. The Assault Convoy consisted of 12 combat loaders, 10 auxiliary combat loaders, 6 cargo ships, 1 sea train and 2 oilers.[3]

The task of translating the agreed plans into firm operation orders was entrusted to Commodore Dick (Cunningham's Chief of Staff), Captain C. Douglas-Pennant (Ramsay's Chief of Staff) and Commanders Barnard, Brownrigg, Durlacher and Power (who had been on Cunningham's staff in the Mediterranean Fleet). These officers naturally worked in the closest co-operation with specialist British and American officers from all three services. Orders were dictated continuously for several days to a team of eight Wren stenographers working in spells of four on duty and four standing by. The orders were printed under the closest security by the Oxford University Press and were only just available before some of the slower convoys were ordered to sail. The printers themselves were held incommunicado until the expedition had taken place.

This staff work was a very considerable achievement and of it Eisenhower wrote: 'The tremendous pressure under which we worked is hard to appreciate for any who have not shared in the experience of planning a great allied operation in modern war.'[4]

It was equally difficult to classify the various time-absorbing problems which, apart from operation orders, ranged from Red Cross affairs to the need for shipping white cloth to the Arabs who insist on it for burial shrouds and would kill to get

it. 'Press conferences were almost obligatory since the problem of morale, both in the United States and in England was never far from our minds.'[5]

'A constant menace throughout', one staff officer wrote, 'were the Chequers dinner-parties whence our headmen would return full of bright new ideas which had to be resisted strongly because they were far too late to be incorporated in the orders.'[6] Moreover all plans had to be co-ordinated with the U.S. Navy. 'This was by no means simple,' Eisenhower wrote,

> and it required a great many conferences. Two of the [U.S.] Navy's capable officers had been assigned by Admiral King to assist in planning and they were welcomed by Brigadier-General Alfred M. Gruenther, chief American planner, with the statement that there were a thousand questions the Navy could help to answer. 'We are here only to listen' was their answer. I knew that if I could talk personally to Admiral King there would be no difficulty, but under the circumstances these snarls had to be worked out with care and patience.[7]

Time pressed down inexorably on them all. Moreover, inspections of training had to be threaded in with the planning, and these inspection trips became, perhaps, the most depressing feature of the entire preparatory period.

> There was an evident lack of skill, particularly among ship companies and boat crews. However, since these had been assembled at the last minute, to minimize interference in Allied shipping programmes, we hoped and believed that major errors revealed by the exercises would not be repeated in actual operations. This proved to be the case.[8]

One incident reveals how dangerous these last-minute preparations could be. Eisenhower was told by a troop commander whose unit was embarking the very next day that they had just received their final consignment of 'bazookas', the infantryman's best weapon of defence against tanks. This commander was completely at a loss as to how to teach his men in the use of this vital weapon. 'I don't know anything about it myself', he told Eisenhower, 'except from hearsay.' This did not augur well for the day. . . .

It was not only in London that personality problems became at times as important as logistics. Just as the British Middle East Command had had its crisis of generalship which was resolved in August so, too, did the Americans in the preparation of their own first great operation of the war. General Patton is the supreme example of this.

Early on, Eisenhower had asked for Patton to command the Casablanca expedition and General Marshall had assigned this colourful but undeniably talented officer to the command. Patton had then come over to London where he had been thoroughly briefed on his role in the overall plan. However, as Eisenhower wrote:

Hardly had he returned to Washington, before I received a message stating that he had become embroiled in such a distressing argument with the Navy Department that serious thought was being given to his relief from command. Feeling certain that the difficulty, whatever its nature, was nothing more than the result of a bit of George's flair for the dramatic, I protested at once, suggesting that if his personality was causing any difficulty in conferences, the issue could be met by sending him out with his troops and allowing some staff member to represent him in the completion of planning details. In the event the matter was passed over.[9]

So the great expedition approached its point departure. The main hazards had all been considered or 'appreciated', in military parlance. These comprised among others the sufficiency of carrier-borne air support during the initial stages, the efficiency of Gibraltar as an erection point for fighter aircraft to be used after landing fields had been secured, the weather, the recent experiences of Malta convoys, the character of resistance of the French Army, the attitude of the Spanish Army and the possibility that German air forces might rapidly enter Spain and operate against Allied lines of communication. One paramount question remained – what would the French in Morocco and Algeria really do in the event of an Anglo-American assault? Would they acquiesce or would they fight?

This problem hinged on General Giraud, and and was to be the only one in which Robert Murphy's considered assessment proved to be wrong. Murphy, aided by the Committee of Five, knew the scene better than anyone else, and he had been convinced that General Mast in Algeria and General Béthouart in Morocco, who were risking their lives to assist the Allies, were correct in assuming that if General Giraud could be taken into North Africa – ostensibly to aid in an uprising against the Vichy Government – there would be an immediate response. All North Africa would flame into revolt under a leader universally respected and popular.

To clinch this matter, Murphy insisted that a high-ranking officer from the Supreme

Commander's staff should go to North Africa for a definitive conference. This had to be organized with the same secrecy as the operation itself. It was a mission of extreme danger. Any Allied officer caught in the act would be interned. Any French officer would be tried by Vichy as a traitor. Obviously Eisenhower could not go himself. Instead he decided to send his Deputy, General Mark Clark.

Lieutenant N. L. A. Jewell, R.N., in command of H.M. Submarine *Seraph*, was detailed to carry out one of the riskiest and at times funniest minor operations of the war. It took place late in October. The meeting had been arranged at a lonely house on four kilometres of private beach between two rocky headlands some fifty miles west of Algiers. The house stood near the mouth of a small stream called the Oued Messelman and was known as a smugglers' haven. A copse of pine trees hid both the house and the beach from the road between Cherchel and Gouraya but the whole coastline was patrolled by coastguards.

Major-General Clark, Brigadier-General Lemnitzer, Colonels Holmes and Hamblen, together with Captain Gerauld Wright, U.S.N., left Lon-

don by air for Gibraltar on 19 October, duly embarked in the submarine and set off for the rendezvous as planned. Compulsory boat drills, however, delayed them and they did not arrive at the rendezvous until 0400 hours on the 21st, by which time the captain of the submarine decided it would be too dangerous to get the party ashore before daylight.

In the meantime Murphy and one of his Vice-Consuls called Knight, plus Rigault and d'Astier de la Vigerie (of the Committee of Five) had left Algiers without being observed. But the whole night no one came ashore. So at about six in the morning the 'French party', realizing that something had gone wrong, returned to Algiers only to discover shortly afterwards by a coded radio message from Gibraltar that the operation had been postponed for twenty-four hours. It was difficult for them to find plausible excuses to make another long journey from Algiers in a matter of hours. Even getting the necessary petrol was difficult.

But after various excitements, all of them – including General Mast – again reached the villa. By this time the various arrivals and departures

had aroused the curiosity of the local villagers, and an Arab night-watchman had decided to take a look at this lonely, usually deserted villa. A fifty-franc note and the explanation that a party of girls was expected, managed to dispose of this (backed up by the unloading of hampers of food and wine from the cars), and just after midnight the submarine surfaced and four folboats or kayaks made their way ashore.

General Clark was in the last boat, which overturned, and he had to swim for it. The French who had arrived in plain clothes but who had then changed into uniform remarked on General Clark's carbine which he carried . . . 'A General with a rifle? What sort of army is this?' Murphy was more friendly. 'Welcome to North Africa!' he said, to which Clark replied, 'I'm damned glad we made it'.[10] They hid the rubber boats away in the olive groves, and took some four hours' sleep in the 'unkempt and much used Victorian canopied beds' and then, after a breakfast of bread, jam and sardines, got down to one of the most bizarre conferences of the war.

Although no co-operation could be expected from the French Navy – a fact which had already been appreciated – General Mast said that, given four days' notice, he could guarantee that there would be little or no resistance from French military and air forces. He also guaranteed free entry into Bône, the most easterly port in Algeria. An arrangement would also be made with General Giraud in France to ensure his co-operation.

The mission ended as dangerously as it had begun, the Deputy Supreme Commander being very nearly drowned on his return to the submarine. The outcome, however, was considered as extremely encouraging. No changes in the plans for 'Torch' were made, and although after the event the French contingent felt that the Americans might have taken them more into their confidence as to the timing of the operation, the mission was unquestionably a success and must, on reflection, have saved a large number of lives. That same night, as General Clark and his party were struggling with their small canoes in a choppy sea off the coast of Algeria, the first of the slow 'Torch' assault convoys sailed from the United Kingdom.

A couple of days later, on 24 October 1942, the

Left: The first prisoners of war. French troops captured by the Americans soon after the initial landings

Following pages
Left: The U.S.S. Augusta *fires her 8-inch guns*
Right: The submarine H.M.S. Seraph *(Lieutenant N. L. A. Jewell, R.N.). On the eve of 'Torch' she carried Major-General Mark Clark, with four companions, to a secret rendezvous with representative Frenchmen near Algiers. She also embarked General Giraud from a beach near Toulon and transferred him to a Catalina which took him to Gibraltar*

American Western Task Force under the overall command of the fiery, unpredictable General Patton and the naval command of the quiet, far less 'combustible' Rear-Admiral Hewitt set sail from Hampton Roads, Virginia, on an operation described by Patton in his will as 'about as desperate a venture as had ever been undertaken by any force in the world's history'.

Never a man for under-statement, Patton with his colourful personality, bad language and power of instant rage had twice come within sight of dismissal during the six or seven weeks which he had had to plan his side of 'Torch'. Patton was a deeply religious man powered by a strong sense of his own destiny. When he had first been summoned to Washington from the Indio Desert in California, where since March he had been running the Desert Training Centre, Patton had taken one look at the initial plans for 'Torch' and had told General Joseph McNarney, Marshall's Deputy, that such plans were for the birds. 'I need a great many more men and a lot more ships to do the job.' The American Chief of Staff's immediate reaction had been to order Patton back to Indio. Badly shaken, Patton then

spent two days in sober reflection, after which he came to the conclusion that, 'Maybe I could do the job after all with the forces your stupid staff is willing to give me.'[11] So Marshall allowed him back to Washington where, on the third floor of the old Munitions Building on Constitution Avenue, he got down to detailed planning.

But command of the Western Task Force, the only entirely 'unblended' part of the operation, entailed a very close co-operation with the U.S. Navy. The task of safely transporting Patton's forces across 3,000 miles of U-boat infested Atlantic was intimidating enough without the Navy's being subjected to Patton's Rabelaisian invective. After one of the early explosive conferences, Admiral Hewitt went straight back to Admiral King saying, in effect, that either Patton be sacked or the U.S. Navy would not co-operate. King, lukewarm as he was to the 'Torch' idea, formally passed on the request to Marshall and for a time it seemed likely that Patton would be sacrificed for the general good of the whole.

However, wiser counsels prevailed. Marshall persuaded King and King, in turn, urged Hewitt to take Patton 'for better or for worse, accepting

his outbursts of rage as an occupational hazard'. Not only was Patton's ebullient personality unlikely to endanger the enterprise, it would more probably ensure its success. 'Anyway,' Marshall declared, 'Patton is indispensable to "Torch".'[12]

Patton sustained his own confidence by prayer (any moment of destiny would be likely to find him down on his knees) and by reminding himself of the motto which dominated his thinking – 'Do not take counsel of your fears.' It was excellent advice, but it in no way helped to sophisticate a man who saw the problem he had been given in basic military terms and who became bewildered when Colonel 'Wild Bill' Donovan of the newly formed Office of Strategic Services (father to the C.I.A.) got into the act. Donovan, with the best intentions in the world, confused the planners with North African intelligence which had about as much value as a travel brochure.

One dire result of this was that Patton, suddenly convinced that he must not offend Moslem opinion, decided to bypass Rabat on religious grounds. In the event such decisions were to have very nearly fatal results.

However much private gloom these political interferences engendered (the State Department did not even point out to the invading U.S. Commander that Algeria was a province of France under direct rule by Vichy, whereas Morocco was a Protectorate ruled by the Sultan and only 'guided' by General Noguès, the French Resident General), Patton had continued to assemble and train his 34,000 men in the Solomon Island training area of Chesapeake Bay, and on 3 October signalled to Eisenhower: 'You can rest assured that when we start for the beach we shall stay there, whether dead or alive, and if alive we will not surrender. When I have made everyone else share this opinion, as I shall certainly do before we start, I shall have complete confidence in the success of the operation.'[13] Some might say that this was whistling in the dark, but the fighting spirit behind these brave words could also be seen as similar to that which Montgomery was instilling into his command 6,000 miles away and which, in the end, was to result in the strategic pincers being firmly and successfully closed on the Axis forces in North Africa.

There was nothing pastel about Patton, and no one lasted with him who did not measure up to

Patton (two stars on helmet) about to disembark at Fedhala the day after the initial landings

the high standards he set. Of the eight officers closest to him in the planning of 'Torch' – all of whom took passage with him in the U.S.S. *Augusta* – five were to survive and continue with 'Old Blood and Guts' till the ending of the European War in May 1945. These were General Geoffrey Keyes, Colonels Gay, Mullar and Hammond and his Deputy Chief of Staff, Lieutenant-Colonel Paul D. Harkins.

A couple of days before he set sail, Patton called on the aged General Pershing, who had given him his start in Mexico in 1916 and who was then dying in the Walter Reed Hospital in Washington. He also called on General Marshall in the Pentagon and, by special invitation, on the President in the White House. To all of them he declared: 'I will leave the beaches either as a conqueror or a corpse.'[14] Then on 23 October he boarded a C.47 for Norfolk, Virginia, and from there drove to Hampton Roads where the U.S.S. *Augusta* was waiting. The vast 'Torch' convoy was an impressive sight and to Patton it was privately reassuring. The fourteen-day passage across the Atlantic of the American component had begun.

The Command Headquarters for the entire British and American assault was to be Gibraltar, and on 28 October when over 650 ships were at sea, headed for the 'Torch' areas, Admiral Cunningham, whose connection with the operation was still being kept a dead secret, set off for Plymouth in plain clothes, accompanied by those of his staff who had not flown on ahead. Ramsay was to stay in London as the rear link and Cunningham sailed in *Scylla*. Later he wrote:

I remember being greatly shocked by the wholesale destruction of Plymouth which had been wrought by the German bombers. The devastation was frightful, and it occurred to me that a glimpse of it might have been of service to some of my American friends in peaceful Washington. The *Scylla* sailed at once for Gibraltar. Even the ship's company had no knowledge of where they were bound or what I was doing on board. The better to keep it dark we had arranged for a dummy signal to lie casually on the captain's table intimating that I was bound for the Far East after calling at Gibraltar.[15]

Cunningham and his staff, of which I was one, arrived at Gibraltar on 1 November and immediately occupied the bare, somewhat eerie offices deep under the Rock which had been prepared for the Supreme Commander. There was no other place to use which would have been safe from air

attack, but the anxious time which now began in the cold, damp, stagnant air of the tunnels where the feeble lighting and the constant drip, drip, drip of water through the rock only added to the tension was – even when I remember it after thirty years – more difficult to endure than the subsequent invasions of Sicily and Normandy. This was because of the vast sea distances which the armada had to traverse.

Nearly three weeks elapsed between the sailing of the first of the convoys and the assault itself. During such a time a whole range of disasters could so easily happen affecting all or part of the operation. You cannot hold your breath for three weeks but it felt like that, and we read every signal which came through with apprehension tinged at times with alarm.

We had no means of knowing the German Staff appreciation, made as late as the 4 November, which said: 'The relatively small number of landing-craft and the fact that only two passenger ships are in this assembly at Gibraltar, do not indicate any immediate landing in the Mediterranean area or on the North-West African coast.'[16] Nor could the experts rely on German agents in Algeciras and La Linea taking the large collection of aircraft on the North Front at Gibraltar as merely preparations for yet another reinforcement of Malta. So there we all sat waiting, keeping the rats from eating our soap, and almost literally holding our breath.

The Supreme Commander flew out in one of a flight of five Fortresses on 5 November. The cover story for this was that Eisenhower was paying a visit to Washington at the President's request. Even Eisenhower's arrival added to the tension, since by some accident the plane in which he was flying was unreported in London hours after it had landed at Gibraltar. This gave the rear link in Norfolk House a nasty time and the superstitious, amongst whom were most of those in the know, thought the auguries were bad.

However, in spite of it all, there was an exhilaration very apparent among the soldiers, sailors and airmen who had been thrown together on and underneath the Rock similar to that before a big prize fight. All of us were part of a huge, calculated gamble. We had done – or we thought we had done – everything in our power to ensure success. Now it really was in the lap of the gods.

9
ALAMEIN

In the Western Desert the six weeks following the battle of Alam Halfa were spent by the Allied and Axis armies in somewhat different ways. The Allies were, so to speak, breathing in deeply in preparation for the great attack; the Axis were regrouping and resting their forces in order to hold on to their positions, whilst a last desperate attempt could be made by a sick Rommel to secure the food, petrol, ammunition and spares which were essential not only to survival but for any further advance into Egypt.

Except for an unsuccessful Allied attempt to raid Tobruk on 14 September and some daring raids by the Special Air Service Regiment, the Long-Range Desert Group and other guerrilla-type forces, plus the normal probing and skirmishing along the front line which both sides maintained, almost no heavy fighting took place. Germans and British watched each other intently, picking up and laying down minefields, recovering, repairing and replacing tanks and armour and, in the case of the Allies, developing a vast, secret and in the event successful deception plan. Allied Intelligence considered it impossible to hide from the enemy the fact that an attack of

some kind was about to be launched. So Montgomery decided to plan for tactical surprise and to conceal from the enemy the exact places where the blows would fall and the exact times.

The Alexander–Montgomery team was working well. Montgomery wrote that Alexander backed him up in every detail and that he was 'the perfect Commander-in-Chief to have in the Middle East, so far as I was concerned – he trusted me'.[1] Both considered that, for any attack to be successful, a full moon period would be necessary. Moreover, as about a week's 'dog-fighting' would be likely to occur before a break-through, then ideally the moon should be waxing and not waning. This limited the timing to the last week in September or four weeks later, when the full moon would be on 24 October.

Back in London and with the Russians and the 'Torch' landings in mind, Churchill demanded a September attack. Montgomery flatly refused. He would not move before he was fully prepared and that, he said, would be on the night of 23 October. Since the word 'must' had been used by Churchill for the September offensive, Montgomery bluntly retorted that in that case someone

else would have to be found to do it. Not many people stood up to Churchill in so direct a way, but perhaps because Montgomery's stock stood high after Alam Halfa 'we heard no more about a September attack'.[2]

On 22 September Rommel turned over the command of his Panzer Army to General Stumme, recently recalled from the Russian front. 'In spite of the excellent care of the good Professor Horster,' Rommel wrote, 'my health had grown so bad . . . that it had become essential for me to embark on a long course of treatment in Europe without further delay.'[3]

The day Stumme arrived, yet another abortive conference took place between Marshal Cavallero, Lieutenant-Colonel Otto (Rommel's Quartermaster) and Rommel himself. 'I complained of the frightful state of our supplies and . . . as usual Cavallero promised to look after our interests.'[4] As usual, of course, nothing happened.

Stumme, who was to die in the front line a month later, exhibited displeasure when Rommel told him that 'I proposed to cut short my cure and return to North Africa if the British opened a major offensive. He supposed that I had no confidence in him. But that was by no means the case; it was merely that I was convinced that even the most skilful Panzer General would be unable to take the right decisions in an emergency on the Alamein front unless he were familiar with the British. Words alone cannot impart one's experience to a deputy. On the Alamein front there was a great difference between quiet and critical days.'[5]

Those last two sentences contain much wisdom about the Desert War, but no amount of front-line expertise could be effective if the Panzer Army had no petrol to keep the tanks moving and, even worse, if there were 'growing sick parades caused by bad rations'.

The day after Rommel left Africa he was in Rome. 'I discussed the situation with the Duce. I left him in no doubt that unless supplies were sent to us at least on the scale I had demanded, we should have to get out of North Africa.' But, in a sense, Rommel found himself a prisoner of his own success. 'The Duce still did not realize the full gravity of the situation. All through the past two years . . . in spite of this lack of response, things had never actually gone wrong . . . we were always told, "You'll pull if off all right. . . ."'[6]

A few days later, Rommel faced up to the Fuehrer himself, demanding that the ratio of the German to Italian supply quota should be raised and stating categorically and in detail: 'It is only by the fulfilment of the conditions I have stated that the German troops, who are bearing the main brunt of the fighting in Africa, will be able to maintain their hold on this theatre against the finest troops of the British Empire.'[7]

During this conference Rommel realized that the Fuehrer and his headquarters staff were deluding themselves into a false optimism.

Goering in particular was inclined to minimize our difficulties. When I said that British fighter-bombers had shot up my tanks with 40-mm (American) shells, the Reichsmarschall, who felt himself touched by this, said: 'That's completely impossible. The Americans only know how to make razor blades.'

I replied: 'We could do with some of those razor blades, Herr Reichsmarschall.' Fortunately we had brought with us a solid armour-piercing shell which had been fired at one of our tanks by a low-flying British aircraft. It had killed almost the entire crew.[8]

Hitler, like Mussolini, disposed of his awkward customer by promising the impossible. The *Nebelwerfer* (multiple rocket projectors) and the *Siebelfaehren* (shallow draught barges to carry

A.A. guns) which he said would arrive were simply not being produced – as the result of incorrect production figures – in sufficient quantities to make such a supply possible.

So, after a press conference had been forced on Rommel at which 'I could not, of course, give a true picture of the situation', the Field-Marshal departed to a mountain resort near Vienna to try to patch up his health. Here he brooded on the tremendous and discouraging war potential of the U.S.A. and on the news from Africa that the British now had a 2-to-1 superiority in tanks, and might be expected to launch a major attack at any time. It was not the best cure for a very sick man.

Meanwhile, at Alamein, the British were perfecting their plans, not least of which was a large-scale 'visual deception' designed to mislead the enemy as to both the date and the sector in which the main British thrust would be made. This would be done by the concealment of real strength and intention in the north whilst advertising false signs of activity in the south. To carry out this huge piece of bluff, there had to be the most careful attention to detail, the whole plan being carried out on an 'Army' scale. Luckily the base facilities in Egypt were sufficiently large and well established to provide the considerable quantities of labour, transport and materials necessary for the mass-production of deception devices and their emplacement by means of the co-ordinated movement of hundreds of vehicles into the areas selected.

The idea behind it was simple enough. It was that enemy air photographs should continue to reveal the same story every day. In the event they did and 'Bertram' (the code name for the camouflage plan) was an unqualified success, for which Lieutenant-Colonel Richardson, whose 'baby' it was, received the highest praise.

Montgomery had decided that the main thrust in the coming offensive would be made in the north. This required a large dump, for example, near the station of Alamein containing 600 tons of supplies, 2,000 tons of petrol, oil and lubricants (POL) and 420 tons of engineer stores. The site was open and featureless and it was of paramount importance that the existence of this and similar dumps should not become known to the enemy.

A complete dummy pipeline was therefore laid down to the south. It ran for about twenty miles from a point just south of the real water point at Bir Sadi to a point four miles east of Samaket Gaballa. The pipe trench was excavated in the normal way. Five miles of dummy railway track, made from petrol cans, were used for piping, which were strung out alongside the open trench and moved on as the trench was filled in. Dummy pump houses were erected at three points, and overhead storage reservoirs at two of these points.

Concurrently with this southern development, the positions in which infantry divisions were to spend the day of the attack were dug and camouflaged a month before and whilst X Corps, for instance, was training round Wadi Natrun, the bulk of its transport together with that of the Highland and New Zealand Divisions was collected in its final assembly area, plus dummy vehicles to the number of those still training. When these divisions actually moved into these areas, dummies were erected in the training areas. Thus no change was apparent.

The dumps themselves were concealed by the gradual extension of existing ones under camouflage and also by setting up groups of stores to resemble trucks and tents which were already in place. A new water point near El Alamein station was concealed and not brought into use until the battle had begun. In the last few days before the offensive opened, fighter cover was intensified over the northern sector so as to discourage any fresh reconnaissance in detail.

Wireless traffic, the monitoring of which provides a valuable source of intelligence, continued to be routed via the training areas long after the Corps itself had moved. Then again, early in October, the whole Army was put on hard rations for a few days, the fresh ration contract in the Delta being abruptly stopped. This was a false alarm designed so that a repetition of it later in the month would cause no comment. Finally, only Commanding Officers themselves knew of the plan of battle, other regimental officers not being told until 21 October and the men not until the 22nd or the 23rd. From 6 October no visitors could enter the area of the Eighth Army without General Montgomery's personal authority.

These varied preparations behind a stabilized front were made possible by containing air supremacy. Marshal Tedder, who was no slouch at putting the R.A.F. first and who firmly believed that 'the air was the architect of victory', as Smuts had suggested earlier in the year, declared himself to be 'much heartened to discover that cooperation with the Army had further improved, thanks, at least in part, to the lead given by Montgomery on this subject. It was most refreshing to find in Eighth Army Advanced Headquarters the embryo of a real Operations Room copied directly from our own mobile operations room.' But he could not help adding somewhat waspishly: 'I took it upon myself to tell the soldiers that it was the first sign I had seen of their being able to collect and sift information about their battle, and consequently the first sign I had seen of their being able to control it'[9] – a remark not overloaded with tact but which, no doubt, had justification. Tedder's policy was for the R.A.F. first to gain and then to keep air supremacy, thus being able, once the battle had started, to direct its main effort into close support. By late September the British had such an ascendancy in the air that they were able to keep Axis reconnaissance aircraft away by flying continuous patrols in daylight. Axis landing grounds at Daba and Fuka were attacked early in October when the Luftwaffe lost thirty aircraft.

The real Alamein air offensive, however, did not begin until the night of 18 October with an intensified attack on Tobruk and a night-strafing of the railway running along the coast. The following day, increasing attacks were made on the landing-grounds at Daba, on troop concentrations on all sectors of the front and, of course, on road and rail traffic between Mersa Matruh and Sidi Barrani.

A fortnight before the battle began, paths were being cleared through enemy minefields by the sappers and the military police whose job it was to clear and to mark the mines. No set of men more fully gained or more properly deserved the admiration of their comrades than those engaged in this tricky and dangerous business of 'lifting mines'. Rommel had managed to place – not always in the best positions from his point of view – some 500,000 mines of every kind.

Vast numbers of captured British bombs and shells were built into the defence, arranged in some cases for electrical detonation . . . our outposts were provided with dogs to give warning of any British approach. We wanted to ensure that the work of clearing the minefields proceeded at the slowest possible speed and not until after our outposts

had been eliminated. Most of the mines available in Africa were unfortunately of the anti-tank type, which infantry could walk over without danger. They were, therefore, comparatively easy to clear.[10]

Again unfortunately for the Afrika Korps, large sections of the minefields were not continuously observed by German artillery and could therefore be lifted with fewer casualties and less delay than might have been expected.

That phrase so frequently heard on the communiqués of the time – 'A path was cleared through the enemy's minefields' – sounds deceptively simple but this, in a contemporary description, is what it entailed:

The men in front are a reconnaissance section, rather like the bayonet men in the old grenade fighting in trenches. The two men on their flanks are tommy-gunners. Their job is to make any enemy encountered by the reconnaissance section keep their heads down. The party behind them, carrying what look like sections of gaspipe, are the torpedo party; and their gaspipes are Bangalor torpedoes to blast a path through barbed wire.

The dusty tramp just behind them, carrying a revolver, is the section officer, and the men on either side of him are carrying rolls of tape to mark the cleared channel.

The next party, looking like housemaids with Hoovers, are the men working the mine detectors – not the least contribution to the victory was the timely arrival of

enough of these instruments, which were turned out by British factories as a rush job. These Hoover men actually locate the mines. The party behind mark the mines with little flags. The next party render them innocuous – 'delousing' is the Army name for their job. Behind them comes the section N.C.O. and, last of all, the men to mark the entrances to the gaps with notice boards and special lamps, visible only to oncoming troops.

The job is difficult as well as elaborate. For example, during the battle, one section officer had three trucks blown from beneath him in eight minutes. The parties were nearly always exposed both to close-range and long-range fire, and often had to improvise methods other than those of the drill-book.

Here is a veteran Australian mine-lifter demonstrating his methods to a visitor: 'I walk along like this and I give a kick here and a kick there. Now if you look, you'll see I've got one.' And indeed with his second gentle kick, he had uncovered a French-made mine. He proceeded to 'delouse' it. Meanwhile he talked. 'Yes, I've been doing this since Tobruk – the time when we held it. No my lot have never had any casualties from mines or booby-traps. You get a sense for them, I suppose. I've pulled up thousands.

'Now the other night when we began this attack, we had a fair job to do. They were as thick as thieves, these mines, and booby-traps in between them. Then there was that barrage going on; but best of all there was a bright moon. We had a bit of shelling, of course, but that's not the trouble you think it is. No, it's machine guns on fixed lines.

They're unhealthy.'

The Australian and his section had cleared a wide path through the minefield and the casual way they moved about and the lack of respect they showed for mines and booby-traps alike were a little worrying to the observer. As they worked some enemy 75's began shelling, and some of the bursts were only ten or twenty yards away.[11]

So the great Battle of Alamein began on 23 October 1942, 'turning the tide of war in Africa against us', Rommel wrote, 'and, in fact, probably representing the turning-point of the whole vast struggle. The conditions under which my gallant troops entered the battle were so disheartening that there was practically no hope of our coming out of it victorious.'[12] In fairness to Wavell and Auchinleck, it should be borne in mind that Montgomery went into the attack with a superiority of roughly 2 to 1 in combatant strength and some 1,100 tanks to Rommel's 500 to 550 (of which 300 to 350 were of inferior quality). In addition Montgomery had nearly 1,000 medium or field guns, about 800 6-pounder anti-tank guns and some 500 2-pounder anti-tank guns. The 6-pounder had been used for the first time in substantial numbers at Alam el Halfa.

Experience had taught the British that in the early stages of an attack it was useless to throw armour against prepared positions. Montgomery, therefore, intended to use his infantry to exploit two good passages through the minefields supported by a very powerful barrage from the ground and air. The main attack, then, was to be delivered by General Oliver Leese's XXX Corps composed of the 9th Australian, the 51st Highland, 2nd New Zealand and the 1st South African Divisions. Further south near the centre of the line the 4th Indian Division would be used to create a local diversion. In the far south near the Qattara Depression the 7th Armoured Division would make a diversionary attack with the object of distracting attention and pinning down enemy reserves, especially the 21st Panzer Division.

Then in the north when the two corridors through the minefields had been properly secured, General Lumsden's X Corps comprising the 1st and 10th Armoured Divisions would sweep through and establish themselves near Tel el Aqqaqir for the expected counter-attack of the Panzer Army. Numerically on the ground and in the air, the odds were heavily against the Germans.

At 2140 hours the British opened a barrage of

Previous pages: British and Australian infantry advance to the assault

Right: Second Alamein. The Eighth Army opens its preliminary bombardment on the night of 23 October 1942
Far right: Among the distinguished prisoners taken at Second Alamein was General Ritter von Thoma, here seen climbing out of the armoured scout car which brought him in. Veteran of the Spanish Civil War and the Polish campaign, he regarded Rommel as a master of the tactical but not the technical aspects of armoured warfare. In September 1942 he obtained a long-coveted appointment in North Africa, but was captured after holding it for a mere six weeks

immense weight over the whole line, eventually concentrating on the northern sector. The Germans had never before experienced such drumfire and this was to continue throughout the entire Alamein battle.

In addition to the artillery of the attacking and holding divisions, Montgomery concentrated a total of 540 guns of a calibre greater than 105 mm between Hill 35 and Deir el Shein. In all, 1,200 guns were employed in the opening bombardment, which from the receiving end appeared to be done with extraordinary accuracy, resulting in heavy casualties.

The Italian 62nd Infantry Regiment was the first to crack under this. They left their line and streamed back to the rear. By 0100 on 24 October the British had penetrated the main defences to a depth of six miles. Two battalions of the German 164th Infantry Division were also obliterated.

However, the density of the minefields now being encountered in depth slowed down the British advance. Daylight had come before even one corridor had been sufficiently cleared for armour to pass through. Indeed the entire day was spent hung up in the minefields and, whereas

Montgomery had expected the armoured divisions to fight their way through, he gained the impression that there was a fear of tank casualties and a lack of eagerness on the part of senior commanders to push on. 'It was clear to me that I must take instant action to galvanize the armoured divisions into action . . . I therefore sent for Lumsden and told him he must "drive" his divisional commanders, and if there was any more hanging back, I would remove them from their commands and put in more energetic personalities. This produced immediate results in one of the armoured divisions. By six that evening the armoured brigade of 1st Armoured Division in the northern corridor was out in the open; it was then attacked by 15 Panzer which was exactly what I wanted.'[13] However, it was clear that the battle was not going according to plan.

The full deployment was completed the following morning, by which time the four armoured brigades of X Corps, comprising 700 tanks, were through and were covering the mouth of the six-mile breach, ready for the expected counterattack.

A few miles to the west at his headquarters on

the coast, General Stumme (Rommel still being in Austria) heard the 'tornado of fire' begin but, as few reports seemed to be getting through from the front, he decided to go there and see for himself. This is what Rommel would have done, but Rommel would also have taken an escort vehicle and a signals truck. Stumme took a staff officer, Colonel Buechting, and no one else.

Intending only to go as far as the headquarters of 90th Light Division in the region of Hill 21, the car in which he was travelling unexpectedly came under fire. Colonel Buechting was killed. The driver immediately swung the car round and drove at top speed out of range. Stumme had leapt out but remained clinging to the outside of the car. This the driver did not notice, intent as he was on getting away. When he did look round, the Commander-in-Chief had vanished, his body not being found till the following morning. It was presumed he had had a heart attack and had simply fallen off. This, however, was not known for twenty-four hours. What *was* known was that General Stumme had disappeared and Colonel Buechting was dead.

'On the afternoon of the 24th,' Rommel wrote,

I was rung up on the Semmering [Austria] by Field-Marshal Keitel, who told me that the British had been attacking at Alamein with powerful artillery and bomber support since the previous evening. General Stumme was missing. He asked whether I would be well enough to return to Africa and take over command again. I said I would . . . in the evening I received a telephone call from Hitler himself . . . in view of developments at Alamein he found himself obliged to ask me to fly back to Africa and resume my command . . . I took off next morning. I knew there were no more laurels to be earned in Africa . . . but just how bad the supply situation really was I had yet to learn.[14]

This he did when he arrived back in Africa at dusk on the 25th.

All was not well, however, on the British side. Fatigue and depression plus the heavy casualties added up to a widespread feeling that the offensive might have to be broken off. Montgomery continued to have opposition from his subordinate commanders who had to be pressurized to advance against their better judgement. One divisional commander was discovered to be nearly ten miles behind his leading armoured brigades and received a curt telephone call from Montgomery himself: 'I spoke to him in no uncertain voice and ordered him to go forward at once and take

charge of his battle; he was to fight his way out and lead his division from in front and not from behind.'[15]

At a conference at his Tactical Headquarters at 0330 hours on the 26th, Montgomery made it abundantly clear to his Corps commanders that there would be no departure from his plan. The armoured divisions were to fight their way forward from the minefield area into the open where they could manoeuvre. Any wavering or lack of firmness now would be fatal and if the two generals were not for it 'then I would appoint others who were'.[16]

By 0800 on the 26th all the armour was out in the open and in the position Montgomery had hoped to achieve twenty-four hours previously. There then followed three whole days of almost static fighting in which the cost of what Liddell Hart calls 'the direct approach – the offensive spirit unguided by subtlety of mind' started to weigh down even Montgomery himself and 'I began to realize from the casualty figures that I must be careful. I knew that the final blow must be put in on 30 Corps' front, but at the moment I was not clear exactly where. But I had to be ready for it.'[17]

What it was like at the front itself comes out vividly in the official account of how Lieutenant-Colonel V. B. Turner commanding the 2nd Battalion of the Rifle Brigade won the Victoria Cross at Tel el Eisa and Kidney Ridge:

Lieutenant-Colonel Turner led his men in a night attack over 4,000 yards of difficult country, and captured his objective, together with forty prisoners and two 88 mm guns. He then reorganized the position for all-round defence against the counter-attack. This position was so isolated that replenishment of ammunition was impossible and no support could reach the battalion owing to the heavy concentration and accuracy of the enemy's fire.

From early morning until late in the evening the battalion was subjected to repeated attacks by nearly 100 German tanks, which advanced in successive waves, all of which were repulsed with heavy losses to the enemy, 35 tanks being burned out and another 20 immobilized.

Throughout the action Lieutenant-Colonel Turner never ceased to move in turn to each part of the front as it was threatened. Wherever the fire was hottest and the fighting fiercest, he was to be found, bringing up ammunition, encouraging his men and directing the fire of his guns. Finding a six-pounder in action alone of its platoon, the others having been knocked out, he himself acted as loader and destroyed five enemy tanks at point-blank range. While manning his gun he was wounded in the head by a machine-gun bullet; but he refused all aid until the last remaining tanks had been destroyed, when only one shell for his gun was left.

His superb bravery and complete disregard for danger resulted in the infliction of a severe defeat on the enemy's armour in one of the finest actions of the war, and set an example of courageous leadership which was an inspiration not only to the whole battalion, which fought magnificently but also to the entire Eighth Army in the critical opening days of the offensive.[18]

Montgomery decided to keep up frontal pressure with minor attacks whilst regrouping and resting the bulk of his troops, at that moment an almost inevitable decision. Rommel, too, was regrouping and this was to mark the end of what Montgomery's Head of Intelligence had called 'corsetting'. Up to now, because of their unreliability, Italian units had been flanked on either side by German ones, to stiffen their resolve and make up for their inferior equipment. British Intelligence had long ago worked out that if only this 'corsetting' could be unlaced and the Italians grouped together, then at once there would be the ideal weak point to attack. Now this had come about – and at a critical time.

The Germans had been pulled north to counter the main British attack, the Italians being left bunched together to the south. The dividing line between them appeared to be just north of the original northern corridor punched through by the British. As soon as Montgomery appreciated this, he at once changed his plan. He decided to attack the point of junction but overlapping well down on to the Italian front. Montgomery took this decision at 1100 hours on 29 October, and the question was then how soon a really hard blow could be delivered.

In the almost extrasensory, instinctive conditions of the Desert War, the British – the Allies – guessed correctly that Rommel was back. They did not then know that General Stumme had been killed, but whoever had taken over from Rommel (in fact command had devolved upon General Ritter von Thoma) had shown an unusual and welcome indecisiveness in his handling of the battle so far which told Allied Intelligence that – at any rate until the 29th – the Germans were not sure whether the main attack would be pressed in the north or in the south. However, once the old familiar grip on the situation seemed to be reasserting itself and German

forces started to concentrate in the north, Montgomery did everything possible to convince Rommel that previous German calculation had been right, i.e., the main attack was going to be in the north.

To make this plausible, 'Thompson's Post', as the thumb-shaped salient stretching up to the sea was known, had to be secured, and this fell to some of the toughest troops then fighting in the world – the 9th Australian Division. They advanced due north across the coast road, after heroic fighting, and having been told to stay there, did. Rommel was drawn. All through 30 and 31 October the Germans tried to hammer the Thumb. The Australians yielded not an inch and gradually the whole German reserve, which included the 21st Panzer and the 90th Light, were sucked into this northern trap. 'What, in fact, I proposed to do', Montgomery wrote, 'was to deliver a hard blow with the right and follow it the next night with a knock-out blow with the left. The operation was christened "Supercharge".'[19]

This period was the severest test of Montgomery's will-power and nerve which he had yet endured. Not only, earlier in the battle, had his subordinate commanders made it clear that they thought his use of armour wasteful and dangerous, he now had the Chiefs of Staff on his back.

> I was visited at my Tactical H.Q. by Alexander and by Casey [the Australian who was Minister of State in the Middle East]. It was fairly clear to me that there had been consternation in Whitehall when I began to draw divisions into reserve on 27 and 28 October, when I was getting ready for the final blow. Casey had been sent up to find out what was going on . . . I told him all about my plans and that I was certain of success and de Guingand spoke to him very bluntly and told him to tell Whitehall not to bellyache . . . I was certain the C.I.G.S. [Brooke] would know what I was up to.[20]

Montgomery certainly needed no urging from London to take aggressive action. He knew Operation Torch would take place in Morocco and Algeria in little over a week. Rommel must be got on the run before then if the Eighth Army was to be of real help to 'Torch', and in any case Montgomery was determined to reach Tripoli first. In addition and more locally, the Martuba airfields needed to be captured so as to give adequate air cover to another desperately needed convoy from Alexandria to Malta due to leave in the middle of November. So 'Supercharge' was

Left: Second Alamein from the Axis side. A German dual-purpose 88-mm anti-aircraft and anti-tank gun

Following page: In the bag. Some of the 30,000 prisoners captured during the battle and the subsequent round-up

ordered to take place on the night of 31 October – 1 November, and actually did begin in the early hours of 2 November.

This was the moment of decision. The Highlanders and the New Zealanders attacked at night, gaps were driven into the line further south and the whole weight of the Eighth Army's armour erupted like a lateral volcano out of the bulge. Still obsessed with Thompson's Post, Rommel had been caught off balance, and before he could regroup, the 1st and 10th Armoured Divisions were in and amongst the Panzer Army. A tremendously fierce tank battle took place in the open at El Aqqaqir – thus causing an even greater waste of petrol by the Germans – and by nightfall on 2 November Rommel had started to disengage.

By now the Italians were ready to give up. The 4th Indian Division smote into the Trieste and Trento Divisions which collapsed, and through this hole the 7th Armoured Division poured with tremendous pressure. The next objective was Rommel's main stocks, dumps and workshops twenty miles west on the coast at Daba. Now the 4th–6th South African Cars tore through the gaps in the inner minefields and headed for El Daba to effect a junction with the Royals who were engaged in the most spectacular raid of the campaign.

The following account for the Ministry of Information by an anonymous writer of this extraordinary part of the desert battle begins by attributing 'the luck which attended our initial break-through to the splendid work of the infantry and the artillery which paved the way'. He then goes on to say that they left their location, passing through the minefields in single file without a shot being fired at them, a somewhat eerie experience, making them wonder what lay ahead.

In the event, however, the only impediment to their progress occurred when the first car ran into an 88-mm gun pit filled with dead Germans. Other cars, including three petrol bowsers, got stuck in slit trenches, but most of them pulled out when dawn broke and fought their way through to the leading column.

The enemy was too astonished to do anything as we came through, or else the Italian section thought we were Germans and the German section thought we were Italians. They waved Swastika flags at us with vigour and we replied with '*Achtung!*' and anything else we could think of which with an answering wave would get us through their lines.

As it grew lighter they stared and blinked at us. Although a warning artillery barrage had been going on all night, they couldn't believe their eyes. They would goggle at us from short range, see our berets, bolt away a few yards, pause as if they didn't think it was true and come back to take another look.

We passed within ten yards of the muzzles of an entire battery of field artillery. Right down the column we went, with Germans standing by their guns and, fortunately, failing to let them off.

As dawn broke we passed a man in bed. From the mass of vehicles and equipment surrounding him he was obviously an Italian quartermaster. We woke him up by tossing a Verey light into his blankets. He broke the record for the sitting high jump.

Into one of his lorries we heaved a hand grenade. The results on the lorry were most satisfactory, but they scared our second-in-command who, following in his armoured car, had failed to see us toss the grenade.

Picking our way through trenches and gun positions we came upon what was evidently a 'permanent' headquarters. Lorries were dug in, men were asleep everywhere. They were surprised to wake up and see their lorries go up in smoke one by one.

In the first quarter of an hour the two squadrons destroyed forty lorries simply by putting a bullet through the petrol tanks and setting a match to the leak. The crews of lorries which had got bogged down in the break through transferred themselves to German vehicles holding petrol. Spare men climbed aboard Italian vehicles mounted with Breda guns and on we pushed.

Germans panicked from their lorries into slit trenches. We had no time to take prisoners. We just took their weapons and told them to commence walking east. Few refused. The majority were most anxious to oblige us in every way, and readily assisted in draining vehicles we thought fit to immobilize.

The Italians asked for far greater consideration. They wanted to come with us, clinging to the sides of our armoured cars as they fought each other to come aboard. To stop these poignant scenes a troop leader asked for one of their officers. Half a dozen men stepped forward.

We explained we couldn't take them all and, skimming off the cream, pushed on with a colonel and two majors clinging for dear life round the muzzles of our two-pounders.

The columns of smoke climbing up from the lorries we burned attracted the attention of tanks and aircraft. We managed to dodge the tanks but the aircraft pestered us throughout the next four days.

One German pilot adopted a novel form of bombing. He had probably grown tired of aiming at the small target offered by an armoured car and, attaching a bomb to a piece of rope suspended from his Me. 109, flew over us, hoping to bump the bomb into our turrets. After twenty-four unsuccessful attempts, the bomb hit the ground and exploded, causing irreparable damage to his piece of rope.

The armour of our cars was excellent and the only casualties inflicted from the air were on the German lorries we shanghaied to come along with us. We had one personal casualty – one of the Italian majors swinging round a turret was shot off by one of his own planes.

Then the two squadrons parted, one continuing due west, the other going south-west. In the south we cut the Axis telephone lines connecting the left and right flanks of their Alamein line, and added a little more to the general confusion.

For the remainder of the first day we sat astride their lines of supply, holding up and destroying lorries as they arrived to supply front line troops. This highway robbery continued for another three days without variation, except that instead of burning vehicles and attracting attention of aircraft we merely rendered them useless.

Ever since we raided the headquarters we had had reprisals sent out after us. Slow-flying reconnaissance Storches came after us. We shot one down. We also came across some aircraft, a marvellous target for our bombers, and sent back the information that they were waiting on the airfield to be destroyed. In an astonishingly short space of time our bombers were over – and so were their aircraft.

There was an amusing incident when we came across a South African pilot who had been ground strafing. He was shot down practically under the wheels of one of our armoured cars. Expecting to be manhandled so far behind the enemy lines, he couldn't believe his eyes when he realized we were British.

And so we stayed fifteen miles behind Rommel's lines. The only real battle we had was on 5 November when our break through took place. Having waylaid a number of vehicles containing retreating German troops, we met up with several 50 mm anti-tank guns. Things looked black for us when we met the Fighting French coming west.

Fortunately for us, mutual recognition came quickly and together we compelled the enemy to leave behind anti-tank guns and some field guns which he had on tow.

With this our job was over. There was no need to return. The Eighth Army had come out to meet us.

The results of this extraordinary raid were:

For:

200 vehicles destroyed. At least 30 guns captured or destroyed containing nothing of smaller bore than 30 mm. Prisoners – nil. Eastward walking Germans and Italians with astonished expressions still on their faces when picked up by other units, were far too many to be counted.

Against:

7 Armoured Cars and three lorries. 3 men killed, 12 wounded.[21]

So the great break-through turned quickly into the long drive west. Rommel tried to stand and tried to evacuate such material as he could, but he no longer had a line with two firm flanks. The southern desert flank was wide open and the 7th Armoured Division had gone round it before Rommel could call a halt. General von Thoma,

the Commander of the Afrika Korps, was in the bag and the retreat, for a time, became a rout.

Tanks, guns, vehicles, stores were abandoned, burnt out and scattered along the roadside, while Rommel tried to break right away. Past Daba where the tank workshops were left almost intact, and a train was still steaming in the station; past Fuka, the Axis remnants streamed, pounded ruthlessly by the R.A.F. Tanks were abandoned in panic when they ran out of fuel, aircraft abandoned intact on the Daba landing grounds.

Nose to tail, two deep, the Eighth Army poured west, back past the old familiar places, tanks, guns without number, without an enemy aircraft disturbing them. In the other direction marched long columns of tattered, tired, dejected Germans and Italians, to join the four columns Rommel had abandoned in the southern part of the line and to continue their dreary march into captivity in Egypt, the land they had so nearly conquered.

The Axis had suffered its first great defeat of war, and the tide had turned.[22]

As Montgomery commented: 'Rommel had never been beaten before though he had often had to "nip back to get more petrol". Now he had been decisively defeated.'[23]

Hitler was furious. He is alleged never to have forgiven Rommel for this defeat. On 3 November Rommel had sent his A.D.C., Lieutenant Berndt, to report direct to the Fuehrer. He was to leave the Fuehrer's Headquarters in no doubt about the situation and was to indicate that the African theatre of war was probably already lost. He was to demand the fullest freedom of action for the Panzer Army. This of course meant a speedy retreat. Hitler retorted with an order demanding the impossible:

To Field Marshal Rommel.

In the situation in which you find yourself, there can be no other thought but to stand fast and throw every gun and every man into the battle. The utmost efforts are being made to help you. Your enemy, despite his superiority, must also be at the end of his strength. It would not be the first time in history that a strong will has triumphed over the bigger battalions. As to your troops, you can show them no other road than to victory or death.

Adolf Hitler[24]

Rommel's bitter comment on this was: 'Arms, petrol and aircraft could have helped us, but not orders.'[25]

What Churchill described as 'the hinge of fate' had turned and there was now to be no going back. The victory at El Alamein also provided the Allies with the best possible curtain-raiser to the imminent invasion of Morocco and Algeria, which was further to take the Axis powers completely by surprise.

Despite the close watch kept on Gibraltar and the Straits by Axis secret agents, 'Torch' achieved complete tactical surprise. Part of the invasion fleet on passage

10
'TORCH'

President to Prime Minister. 5th November 1942

I am very apprehensive in regard to the adverse effect that any introduction of de Gaulle into the 'Torch' situation would have on our promising efforts to attach a large part of the French North African forces to our expedition.

Therefore I consider it inadvisable for you to give de Gaulle any information in regard to 'Torch' until subsequent to a successful landing. You would then inform him that the American Commander of an American expedition with my approval insisted on complete secrecy as a necessary safety precaution. . . . Admiral Leahy agrees wholly with the thoughts expressed above.[1]

It was an extremely tricky situation. In spite of representing the core of French resistance and 'the flame of French honour', as Churchill phrased it, de Gaulle was neither liked nor trusted. De Gaulle had his headquarters in London where, in a sense, he carried on a private war with the other Allies and especially with his host country, Great Britain. In Washington President Roosevelt was vehemently hostile to de Gaulle and his movement. Who then was to speak for the French?

Until the North African invasion had taken place it was not known to the Allies that Admiral Darlan was himself in Algiers (where he was to be murdered that Christmas) because his son, Alain,

had been taken ill and he had come across from metropolitan France to be with him. Perhaps this was lucky since, had Eisenhower been forced to plan on negotiating with Darlan, a confused situation might well have become dangerously chaotic. What actually happened was bad enough and in the event circumstances shaped themselves in such a way that Darlan could take full advantage of Allied ingenuousness and come out, as he usually did, on top.

In the meantime General Giraud entered the scene physically instead of operating, as he had done up to now, through his Deputy in Algeria, General Mast, and the self-appointed Committee of Five. Giraud was 'procured' from off shore in the south of France with his full co-operation and consent by the same British submarine, H.M.S. *Seraph*, commanded by the same Lieutenant Jewell (but technically wearing the American ensign) which had been used for General Clark's visit to Algeria. Then once at sea Giraud was transferred to a flying boat and arrived at Gibraltar on 7 November 1942, the night the invasion went through.

However, the stiff and abrupt General was labouring under a grave misapprehension. He thought he would be appointed Supreme Commander in North Africa and that the American and British armies, of whose strength he had no prior knowledge, would be placed under his authority. So when the gallant but somewhat bedraggled figure in civilian clothes was taken to Eisenhower's 'dungeon' under the Rock, it was a shock when the facts of life were quickly but tactfully explained to him.

'I wanted him to proceed to Africa', Eisenhower wrote,

as soon as we could guarantee his safety and there take over command of such French forces as would voluntarily rally to him. Above all things we were anxious to have him on our side because of the constant fear at the back of our minds of becoming engaged in a prolonged and serious battle against Frenchmen, not only to our own sorrow and loss, but to the detriment of our campaign against the German.[2]

But General Giraud was adamant. His honour and that of France was involved. He was gritty, shaken and disappointed. After many hours of attempted persuasion, he said: 'General Giraud cannot accept a subordinate position in this command; his countrymen would not understand and his honour as a soldier would be tarnished.'

A suggestion was made to Eisenhower by the American and British political advisers that Giraud be placed in nominal command, with Eisenhower directing the actual operation. To this subterfuge the Supreme Commander refused to agree and after further hours of talk, Eisenhower told the French General that 'we would proceed with our campaign as if we had never met or conferred with him'. Giraud's goodnight statement was: 'Giraud will be a spectator in this affair.' French honour and Giraud's habit, like de Gaulle's, of referring to himself in the third person showed every sign of playing their classic role in history.[3]

'The political faces in our headquarters that night were long,' Eisenhower wrote, but fortunately a night's sleep changed the General's mind and the next morning he decided to participate on the basis required. It might have been better if he had stuck to his guns. The moment he was 'in' he wanted to re-vamp the whole operation, ignoring North Africa completely and, instead, switching the landings to the south of France. This extraordinary and emotional demand revealed an almost total incomprehension of the intricate and detailed planning required for any invasion and the subsequent maintenance, air support and such like which would have to be provided if the invading troops were not to be thrown back into the sea. The more one thinks about it, the more incredible Giraud's attitude becomes. In any case, even as he spoke, the troops were landing.

Algiers
The landings began punctually at 0100 hours on Sunday 8 November under Rear-Admiral Sir Harold Burrough, K.B.E., D.S.O., with his flag in H.M.S. *Bulolo* and although not everyone made the correct beach, the landing parties met with little or no opposition except on the 'Beer Red' beach. Weather conditions were fair with a north-easterly breeze, force 3. The assault on Algiers harbour carried out by two British destroyers wearing the U.S. Ensign at the yardarm and carrying some 600 U.S. combat troops had a very different reception.

In the meantime the occupation of Blida airfield was a notable achievement on the part of the Fleet Air Arm. Never before had a military airfield been occupied by British naval aircraft. Early on 8 November four carrier-borne Martlets attacked two French aircraft on the airfield. At 0800 hours, four more Martlets renewed the patrol under the command of Lieutenant (A) B. H. C. Nation. After circling the airfield for half an hour, Lieutenant Nation observed its personnel waving white handkerchiefs. Having satisfied his carrier that he was over the right airfield – it was marked BLIDA in large white letters – Lieutenant Nation received permission to go in. Telling the others to keep watch, he landed and accepted a written statement from the Station Commandant to the effect that the base was at the disposal of the Allied armies for landing purposes. He then remained at the airfield until a party of Commandos and Rangers arrived.

Meanwhile, the destroyers *Broke* and *Malcolm* had made an ill-fated assault on Algiers harbour. The object of this was to prevent the sabotage of harbour installations and of the twenty-five ships then in port. The two destroyers were to crash through the booms protecting the northern and southern entrances to the harbour, place themselves alongside selected quays, land their American troops and remain there unless otherwise ordered. The whole operation, code-named 'Terminal', was under the command of Captain H. St. J. Fancourt, R.N., with Major Snellman, U.S. Army, in charge of the three companies of U.S. troops taking part.

H.M.S. *Broke* (Lieutenant-Commander A. F. C. Layard, D.S.O., R.N.) and H.M.S. *Malcolm* (Acting Commander A. B. Russell, R.N.) were two somewhat aged destroyers (the *Broke* had been built in 1924) which had been adapted for convoy duties. In the case of the *Broke* this had entailed the removal of one boiler-room and the addition of more fuel capacity for endurance. Both destroyers had left Belfast during the last week in October with one of the slow convoys to Gibraltar which they had delivered safely. They had then refuelled, slipping from the oiler in the Bay of

The landings at Oran. Left: The battleship H.M.S. Rodney *and the cruiser H.M.S.* Sirius *off the coast*

Following pages: The British landings at Algiers

Gibraltar at 0100 hours on Friday 6 November to rendezvous with the cruiser *Sheffield* en route to Algiers and take on the U.S. combat troops at sea.

The two ships were ordered to carry out the attack at 0140 hours on the 8th. There was no blackout in Algiers, but navigating into the right positions proved to be much more difficult than had been foreseen. By 0345 hours the final approach was made but *Broke*, passing the wrong side of the buoy, missed the southern entrance of the port and the *Malcolm* fared no better.

A 'troublesome' gunfire from the Forts began – allowance must be made for British understatement in the official account – and during the next two attempts *Malcolm* was heavily hit. With three boiler-rooms out of action she was forced to withdraw. By now it was dawn and *Broke* then made her fourth and successful attempt to ram the boom, cutting through it 'like a knife through butter' at full speed. 'The break through was smooth and effective. She swung to port and according to plan should have gone alongside the Quai de Dieppe.'[4] In the half-light, however, she mistook the layout of the harbour and berthed alongside the Quai de Falaise at the northern end of the Mole Louis Billiard instead, her coxswain being wounded by fire from a small French minesweeper as he steered alongside.

The American combat troops leapt ashore and captured the power station and oil installation as ordered, the next hour being comparatively quiet except for some desultory sniping.

> It was clear, however, that at any moment intensive crossfire might be opened on the ship from the Grand Mole but it was the Jetée du Nord battery which actually opened fire first. Some shells fell close and the *Broke* parted her lines, turned and reberthed alongside the Quai de Falaise, her bows pointing eastwards towards the harbour mouth ready to make a quick get-away if necessary.[5]

The general situation appeared to be satisfactory except for continued sniping, and Captain Fancourt recalled some of the boarding parties. During this period, Commander Layard recalls that he had some trouble in restraining the fighting spirit of his ship's company in the sense that they all wanted to go ashore to sort out the snipers. One Able Seaman actually did so without orders and, having located a particularly troublesome strongpoint, climbed up on the roof determined to clean it up. The roof collapsed and deposited him

right into the middle of a machine-gun nest, to the astonishment of himself and the incumbents. Seizing the advantage, Able Seaman Anderson shot the first man to come at him, whereupon the whole unit surrendered.

At about 0850, two French police officers and two civilians came aboard with a request that a United States officer should take over control of the town. Captain Fancourt at once sent an American army officer ashore with a British naval officer as interpreter, but this party failed to get through.

An atmosphere of Sunday calm prevailed, tempered only by an occasional 'Angelus' call to Mass, but Captain Fancourt asked that the Jetée du Nord Battery might be bombed at 1030 to cover a possible retirement.

About 0915 the *Broke* came under heavy attack from a new quarter. This fire, which appeared to be from a howitzer, was well controlled and three shells narrowly missed the ship.

Her position was no longer tenable and immediate action was clearly necessary. Reluctantly Captain Fancourt decided to abandon the harbour though the Jetée du Nord Battery had not yet been bombed. The general recall resulted in only a few United States troops being re-embarked before the ship got under way.

As she moved across the harbour she received numerous 3 and 4 inch hits. She repassed the boom more than four hours after entering harbour and at about 0940 steered towards Cape Matifu. Passing close under the Cape, which

was under bombardment from 'Hunt' class destroyers, she stood away to the westward with H.M.S. *Zetland* who had been bombarding Cape Matifu Fort. She had been forced to leave 250 men ashore and had suffered heavy damage. Eventually *Zetland* took her in tow but she sank the next day in deteriorating weather.[6]

Meanwhile, a state of confusion obtained in Algiers itself, due almost entirely to the presence of Admiral Darlan. Murphy had hoped he would have departed back to France before the Anglo-American descent but, absorbed with his son's attack of infantile paralysis, he had remained, staying in the villa of a French official, Admiral Fénard.

The main Allied hope in Algiers had been centred on General Juin, the French Military Commander, whose relationship with Murphy was intimate. A little past midnight on the 7th–8th, Murphy called on Juin to tell him that the hour had struck. As Churchill wrote:

General Juin, although deeply engaged and loyal to the enterprise, was staggered by the news. He had conceived himself to possess full command of the situation in Algiers. But he knew that Darlan's presence completely overrode his authority. At his disposal were a few hundred ardent young Frenchmen. He knew only too well that all control of the military and political government had passed from his hands into those of the Minister-Admiral. Now he would certainly not be obeyed.

Why, he asked, had he not been told earlier of zero hour? The reasons were obvious and the fact would have made no difference to his authority. Darlan was on the spot and Darlan was master of all Vichy-French loyalties.

Murphy and Juin decided to ask Darlan by telephone to come to them at once. Before two in the morning, Darlan, roused from slumber by the urgent message from General Juin, came. On being told of the imminent stroke he turned purple and said: 'I have known for a long time that the British were stupid, but I always believed that the Americans were more intelligent. I begin to believe that you make as many mistakes as they do.'[7]

Darlan, whose aversion to the British now had a fine point put to it, realized that he must change his views. But he was still bound to Pétain 'in form and in fact'. By going over to the Allies, he realized he would become personally responsible for the complete take-over of unoccupied France, which would be the inevitable and immediate German reaction.

The most he could be prevailed on to do, therefore, was to ask Pétain by telegram for liberty of action. In the hideous plight in which he had become involved by the remorseless chain of events this was his only course.[8]

Darlan also took the precaution of arresting Juin, Murphy and his assistant, Kenneth Pendar, the American Vice-Consul at Marrakesh, and removed himself to Fort l'Empereur. At 1130 hours he sent a further telegram to Pétain saying that Algiers would probably be taken by the evening, and at 1700 hours, 'American troops having entered the city, in spite of our delaying action, I have authorized General Juin, the Commander-in-Chief, to negotiate the surrender of the city of Algiers only.' Mr Pendar was released from arrest and was given a safe-conduct to the American Commander.

The surrender of Algiers took effect from 1900 hours on Sunday, 8 November. Admiral Darlan then came under American power and General Juin resumed control of his command under General Eisenhower.

Oran

Things were very much tougher at Oran. Here the same principles as at Algiers applied. The port and its installations had to be secured with the minimum of destruction – in spite of the known intentions of the French Navy to resist at all costs – and the best way of achieving this was considered to be a surprise attack directly into

the harbour itself to be made by two ex-U.S. cutters, now renamed H.M.S. *Walney* and H.M.S. *Hartland*, filled with U.S. combat troops, the whole Oran area being invested – again in a similar way to Algiers – by beach landings at two places west and one place east of the town itself. The eastern landing in the 'Z' sector on the Gulf of Arzeu was to be on a far greater scale.

The attack opened at 0116 hours on 8 November under the command of Commodore Thomas Hope Troubridge, a bluff and very capable officer who flew his broad pennant in the headquarters ship H.M.S. *Largs*. In addition to 34 transports, he had under his command 70 warships including the aircraft-carrier *Furious*, the auxiliary carriers *Biter* and *Dasher*, 3 cruisers *Jamaica*, *Aurora* and *Delhi*, an auxiliary A.A. ship, 16 destroyers, 8 sloops and corvettes and 2 submarines.

Although the weather was favourable – calm, dark and with good visibility – the unexpected westerly set in the tideless Mediterranean interfered seriously with the landings, as it had done in the Algiers sector. In addition, the X-ray sector assault was delayed by thirty-five minutes by the chance appearance inside the sector of a small

French convoy of four ships steaming north-east and escorted by a trawler. Apart from the time taken to deal with this convoy, the minesweepers had been overrun by the assault vessels for whom they had to clear a channel and in the event the assault went through without this vital clearance.

There is little doubt that disaster would have struck had the French not been taken so completely by surprise and had there been any real opposition. Over all that happened in the Oran sector lay the shadow of resentment and wounded pride occasioned by the Royal Navy's destruction of the French Atlantic Fleet at Mers-el-Kebir in July 1940. Unlike Algiers, the real fighting began after the initial landings had been effected and, indeed, Oran itself was not to be captured until 10 November.

Meanwhile, the ambitious plan to seize the airfields by means of the largest paratroop mission to date had gone badly astray. The 2nd Battalion, 503rd Parachute Infantry, had set out from England in thirty-nine C.47s with instructions presupposing an unopposed landing, and had failed to receive a later message warning them of probable French opposition.

In addition to this built-in hazard, so to speak, the formation became partially scattered over Spain by bad weather. The leading elements which reached Tafaroui encountered flak and landed at La Lourmel, where they were joined by later elements. They then flew back to Tafaroui, the mission being regarded as a failure. However, the paratroopers proved to be a valuable addition to the combat troops who captured the Tafaroui airfield.

The assault into the harbour of Oran by the *Walney* and the *Hartland* was carried out under the command of Captain Frederic Thornton Peters, D.S.O., D.S.C., R.N., a retired officer who had been mainly responsible for its planning. Posthumously he was awarded the Victoria Cross and the American Distinguished Service Cross. The attack opened at 0245 hours as both ships with MLs 480 and 483 in company approached the harbour entrance. Sirens were sounded by the French and all lights in the town extinguished. For a time the small force circled off the entrance while an announcement was made in French by loud hailer from the *Walney*. The reply was hostile.

Left: American troops push inland to capture Maison Blanche airfield

Following pages: American troops move inland from a beach outside the port. The garrison of Oran capitulated at noon on the second day

A searchlight was then turned on the *Walney* and she came under heavy though inaccurate machine-gun fire. Followed by *Hartland* she at once turned away northwards, coming round in a full circle to charge the booms. At the same time ML480 went on ahead at full speed, laying a smoke screen, but hit the outer boom and was stopped under heavy fire half-way across it. She got off again just as *Walney* at her maximum 15 knots crashed through the booms and entered the harbour. Three canoes, manned by special parties, were then launched, but one at least was immediately sunk by gunfire. The *Walney* then continued up harbour at slow speed, being hit by a pom-pom of the Ravin Blanc battery.

Half-way up the harbour she narrowly missed ramming a French destroyer, which returned the courtesy by raking her with two broadsides at point-blank range. These wrecked her main engines and she then came under heavy crossfire from the cruiser *Epervier* lying alongside to the south, and from destroyers and submarines moored to the northward.

At last, blazing forward and amidships, she drifted out of control bows on to the jetty ahead of *Epervier*. An attempt to get heaving lines ashore failed and she drifted once more

slowly out into the harbour. Her guns were out of action, their crews virtually wiped out. Sixteen officers and men were lying dead on her bridge where Captain Peters alone survived.

Below only five officers and men of the landing parties remained alive amid scenes of indescribable carnage. Nothing further could be done and the ship was abandoned, her few survivors, including Captain Peters himself, being taken prisoner. Her end was near and between 0900 and 1000 she blew up and sank.[9]

A similar fate awaited the *Hartland*. She had been ordered to delay five minutes before following the *Walney* and as she neared the smoke-screen laid down by the MLs she was picked up by a searchlight and came under a blanket of fire from the Ravin Blanc battery. This killed or wounded nearly all her guns' crews and her captain, Lieutenant-Commander G. P. Billiot, R.N.R., was temporarily blinded by a splinter. Before he could recover his sight, the ship struck the breakwater but, undaunted, contrived to go astern and thus enter the harbour through the boom.

The *Hartland*'s objective was the Quai de Dunkerque, but alongside it lay the French destroyer *Typhon*, which treated her to a withering fire at point-blank range. Shells burst inside her hull, turning her messdecks full of waiting troops

into a burning shambles.

Then, with fires raging fore and aft, she drifted alongside the mole. Lieutenant-Commander Dickey, U.S.N., calling on his men to follow, at once leapt ashore to seize a trawler alongside, but only one unwounded man was able to obey before the ship, caught by the wind, drifted once more out into the harbour where she anchored under heavy fire. Though her British and American ensigns were clearly visible in the light of the flames, the French humanely ceased firing.

Despite desperate efforts to subdue them, the flames spread and, expecting her to blow up at any moment, Commander Billiot ordered the ship to be abandoned. By 0410 all survivors had left and at 0525 there was an explosion on board, but the *Hartland* remained afloat for some time burning furiously till she blew up with a devastating explosion which damaged buildings in a large area around the mole and left only wreckage floating on the surface of the water to mark her end.[10]

Both Captain Peters and Commander Billiot, though wounded, miraculously survived. However, by some grim irony of fate, the Catalina aircraft in which Peters was returning to England a few days later crashed on landing at Plymouth and he was killed.

Military operations continued all through the following day, the 9th, and on the morning of the 10th the 1st Infantry Division and Combat Team 'B' closed in for a final assault on the city of Oran. In spite of stiff resistance, armoured units penetrated the city by 1000 hours, and at noon the French formally capitulated to General Fredendall. Thus fifty-nine hours after the first landing the city of Oran was safely in Allied hands.

Casablanca

If the going had been tough in Oran, disaster came within a few inches of the Western Task Force and the Moroccan landings, under the overall command of General Patton. Here in this purely American operation what Ladislas Farago calls 'the dilettantism of the Intelligence effort and the snap judgements of the planners came home to roost. Now the consequences of the decision to substitute Mehedia for Rabat became abundantly and painfully evident.'[11]

Task Force Thirty-Four under the command of Rear-Admiral H. K. Hewitt, U.S.N. – the greatest war fleet ever dispatched from the United States and comprised of some sixty warships and forty transports – had left American waters between 23 and 25 October and had proceeded across the Atlantic in secrecy and without incident until, on 4 November, it was steaming on a north-easterly course between latitudes 31° and 32° N.

The Task Force was divided into a Covering Group, an Air Group and three Attack Groups. The Northern Attack Group was to operate against the Medhedia-Port Lyautey area, sixty-five miles north-eastward of Casablanca. The Centre Attack Group was to take care of the Fedala–Casablanca area and the southern Attack Group was to land in the Safi area, 110 miles south-west of Casablanca. A glance at the map shows the distances involved and the essential part which communications would play in such a three-pronged and distended operation. In the event communications were to break down almost completely.

The strategic reasons for the above plan are obvious. All three landings, if successful, would secure the narrow coastal plain at the foot of the Middle Atlas mountains, through which ran all the principal roads and railways in French Morocco. Mehedia, the nearest landing-place to Port Lyautey, provided the best and most accessible airfield in Morocco on which to base naval aircraft. Possession of Port Lyautey would secure the railway that runs parallel to the border of Spanish Morocco through the Taza Gap to Algeria.

In the centre, the Fedala beaches were the nearest practicable landing-place to Casablanca, which in turn was the only large harbour on the Atlantic coast of Morocco and which was the headquarters of the French Navy. Casablanca also housed the uncompleted battleship *Jean Bart*. This great ship could not move but could – and did – fire her four 15-inch guns.

In the south, Safi covered the native metropolis of Marrakesh and its harbour provided the only opportunity of running Sherman tanks ashore for an assault northwards on Casablanca. The capture of Casablanca was to be the crux of the entire operation, and this meant that whilst the northern and southern attacks might fail without jeopardizing the success of the whole operation, the Fedala landings had to succeed, or disaster would almost be guaranteed.

Over all lay an unending anxiety about the weather. A landing on any Atlantic coast has perils on a different scale from those likely to be encountered in the Mediterranean. Atlantic rollers, the tide, and surf fifteen feet high, are

terrifying factors when a plan to land heavily armed men and equipment on a hostile shore is put into execution.

The American armada had been lucky in that a big pack of U-boats had been ordered to concentrate near Dakar and were therefore too far south to intercept the American troop convoys. The British, too, had been lucky in that another U-boat pack in the approaches to Gibraltar had been lured away by a mercantile convoy from Sierra Leone. This convoy became the sacrificial lamb which allowed the main 'Torch' convoys to get through unscathed. 'It looked impossible from the submarine chart', Admiral Ramsay wrote in London, 'that convoys could escape detection.'[12] To Eisenhower and Cunningham the strain was worse and, as Eisenhower was to write later on to Cunningham: 'I came to the conclusion that the hours that you and I spent together in the dripping tunnels of Gibraltar will probably remain as long in my memory as will any other. It was there I first understood the indescribable and inescapable strain that comes over one when his part is done – when the issue rests with fate and the fighting men he has committed to action.'[13]

To Admiral Hewitt out at sea and nearing his objective, the problem of the weather now became acute. The forecasts from Washington and London for D-Day were scarcely encouraging . . . 'Surf fifteen feet high and landings impossible.' Indeed Eisenhower had considered directing the Western Task Force to abandon the Moroccan Atlantic coast and instead switch to a Mediterranean landing, but on Cunningham's advice decided to leave it to the man on the spot. In the event this was a wise decision, since at the critical moment all communication between Gibraltar and Hewitt broke down.

Bad though the weather prognosis had been, Hewitt's meteorologist on board the U.S.S. *Augusta* considered that the storm was moving too rapidly to have any adverse effect on the beaches (in fact it had a delayed effect after the landings had taken place) and, taking one of the most courageous decisions of the war, Hewitt ordered the attack to be executed as planned. Fortune favours the brave and the meteorologist proved to be right. The weather abated sufficiently and at the right time for the landings to be made. The die was cast, the fleet dispersed before dark on

Previous pages: The landings in French Morocco
Left: Shells from the French battleship Jean Bart *fall near an American warship*
Right: Under pressure from the Americans, the French authorities in Algeria ordered a cease-fire on 10 November, two days after the initial landings. A French soldier outside a requisitioned building in Algiers talks to American G.I.s and a British sergeant

Right: Landing craft enter the harbour at Fedhala, some fifteen miles north of Casablanca

7 November, and the Western Task Force duly reached the Moroccan coast in fair weather before dawn on the 8th. What was the situation awaiting them?

The top Allied 'friend' in the Protectorate was General Marie-Émile Béthouart, the French Divisional Commander at Casablanca and in charge of the land defences of most of the Moroccan coast. Béthouart had been made privy to the plan and he was prepared to accept General Giraud as Supreme French Commander. Opposed to him were Admiral Michelier at Casablanca and the Resident-General Noguès, both of whom were in the dark as to the great Allied design, and both strong Vichy men. Béthouart's considered opinion was that when the moment came, both Noguès and Michelier would rally to the Anglo-American cause. To make sure of this, Murphy and the Five had urged Béthouart to arrest the Resident-General but this he was not prepared to do. He had no wish to be accused of supplanting his superior officer.

Instead, at 2300 hours on 7 November Béthouart assembled at his headquarters those of his officers whom he had taken into his confidence.

He told them: 'The Americans are landing tomorrow morning at five o'clock.' As Churchill wrote:

At midnight the party left Casablanca in three cars and two hours later took over the headquarters in Rabat, the capital, together with the telephone exchanges of the General Staff and the Post Office. Unluckily General Noguès's secret line was overlooked and during the next fateful hours the Resident-General was able to communicate freely with the Commanders of the main bases throughout Morocco.

On arrival at Rabat Béthouart sent his aide-de-camp to Noguès with written details of the discussions between Giraud and Murphy and of the imminent Allied landings.[14]

Noguès was an experienced and wily politician. Like most of the Vichy hierarchy, he had been indelibly impressed by the might of German power. He was also no fool. He knew what the Germans could do. With Gallic cunning he had so far managed to prevent any effective use of the facilities of Morocco by the German High Command. He was also aware that in Norway, Crete and lately Dieppe the Allies had not distinguished themselves. Therefore, when apprised of the forthcoming invasion in his own backyard by a nation which had not yet come up against German military skills, Noguès realized

that if it should turn out to be merely another Commando raid and if he failed to oppose it, the Germans would then have the excuse they wanted to take over the whole of French North Africa.

> But an American landing at Rabat, where he could judge for himself the magnitude of the effort and justify his surrender, to both the Germans and his own shifty conscience, would have decided the question . . . thus the decision to by-pass Rabat probably lost for Patton whatever chance there was of an unopposed landing.[15]

The decision to bypass Rabat, it will be remembered, was recommend by American Intelligence on the grounds that the city was a Mohammedan religious centre and that, in order not to offend Moslem opinion, it should be regarded, like Rome, as an open city.

In the event, the capture of Morocco took seventy-four hours, and the mistakes made by this 'green' American Expeditionary Force with its inadequate training justified Noguès in the calculations he made. At the point of decision, however, a high drama took place.

> On Béthouart's orders Noguès was surrounded in his residence by a company of colonial infantry. He was enraged. He arrested the aide-de-camp, who was his own nephew, and at once rang up Admiral Michelier at the naval base at Casablanca. He was told that there was no evidence of any Allied approach to the coast. This negative news determined Noguès's action.
>
> He ordered the 'Alert' and told Michelier to supersede Béthouart, now in Rabat. At that moment the American fleet of more than a hundred ships, carrying General Patton's landing force, was in fact but thirty miles away; but no word had yet reached Noguès even about the landings which were already in progress in Algeria.
>
> In this tense situation General Béthouart had every reason for anxiety. He alone had direct knowledge of the impending attack, but his coup in Rabat with his small band of supporters had merely placed all Morocco in a state of siege behind Noguès.
>
> At 5 a.m. Noguès received from the American Vice-Consul in Rabat a personal letter from President Roosevelt calling on him to aid the Allies. Two hours later, after the landings had begun, he informed Darlan in Algiers that he had rejected this United States ultimatum. Béthouart and his few adherents were surrounded.
>
> Noguès himself telephoned threatening to shoot the officers of the colonial regiment involved. All were arrested forthwith. Béthouart was tried by court-martial two days later and was not finally released till 17 November.[16]

Meanwhile the invasion began. In the north the sea was smooth, visibility was good and the lights of Port Lyautey were clearly visible. Only the heavy Atlantic swell was disturbing. After delays caused by unexpected difficulties in disembarking, the first attack waves landed a mile north of 'Blue' beach at 0505 hours (they should have landed on Blue and Yellow beaches at 0400 hours). The Red beach party clearly had no idea of its position and was starting up the river when hastily redirected. A landing on Green beach was made at 0540 hours through five to six feet of surf.

A French convoy had been passing as the invasion began. It was allowed to proceed and naturally alerted Port Lyautey. However, although surprise had been lost, the French offered no resistance while darkness lasted, but at first light a stiffening opposition began. Now the confusion and mistakes caused by insufficient training and a grave lack of supplies slowed up the advance. This was to continue all day.

> During the night conditions on the beaches, where heavy surf was preventing landing craft from withdrawing, presented a scene of the greatest confusion. Exits from the beaches could be used only by tracked vehicles; lorries, jeeps, light tanks and stores were piling up so fast that they could only be kept above high water mark with the greatest difficulty. Forces supposed to be landing on Green and Brown beaches were landing on Blue beach and searching vainly in the darkness for their proper units. Crews of stranded landing craft were wandering about aimlessly or tinkering ineffectively with their craft.[17]

All next day hard fighting took place. Medical supplies, water, tanks and ammunition were all urgently required and the troops were calling for them to be landed at all cost. In spite of mountainous surf thundering on to the beaches, landing craft were sent in a desperate attempt to answer this call. One by one they were swamped or stranded until by midnight only six remained afloat, seventy being reported as stranded on the beaches south of Mehedia the following day.

However, progress was made, and French tank infantry columns approaching from Rabat were driven off by aircraft from the battleship *Texas*. Early on the morning of 11 November, a message to General Truscott from the French Military Headquarters at Port Lyautey stated that on Marshal Pétain's authority all resistance would cease immediately. General Truscott at once ordered the cease-fire, and that day the Stars and Stripes floated triumphantly over Port Lyautey.

At Safi in the south similar difficulties beset the landing parties but by 0500 hours the harbour had been secured and the Battery Railleuse at Point de la Tour, which had been very troublesome, was silenced at 0715 hours, being captured

at 1206 hours. By 1430 hours success had crowned the operation and the town of Safi was in American hands. Only nine landing craft had been lost and Army casualties were estimated at ten killed and seventy-five wounded. Undoubtedly this was due to the early capture of the port before it could be sabotaged and it was attributed in the report to 'good fortune, good weather, surprise, retention of the initiative and accurate and overpowering gunfire. Certainly the defenders were fully alert with their defences manned, but in the darkness were unable to gauge the strength of the attack.'[18]

In the centre at the Fedala landings, it was touch and go. Nearly fifty per cent of the assault craft making the initial landings were wrecked by heavy surf in the opening stages of the attack. Moreover, although the first landing waves had encountered little opposition ashore, the landing of equipment and supplies was greatly hampered by heavy loss of landing craft through falling tide and heavy surf.

Then shortly after 0800 hours French aircraft and the Fedala batteries attacked both assault craft and beaches. This was followed by two naval battles between the U.S. Navy and the French, led by the cruiser *Primauget*. These actions delayed Patton's decision to land himself and dislocated the plans. In all, seven French ships were destroyed with 1,000 casualties. It was a sad irony that Captain Mercier of the *Primauget* longed for an Allied victory yet died on the bridge of his ship in the execution of his orders. As Churchill commented: 'We may all be thankful if our lives have not been rent by such dire problems and conflicting loyalties.'[19]

About noon, its morale badly shaken, the French Army asked for armistice negotiations. Rear-Admiral Hall, U.S.N., the expedition's Chief of Staff, went ashore with Major Rogers of the U.S. Marine Corps to discuss peace terms at Fedala. Eventually the Admiral proceeded to Casablanca to see the French Admiral Michelier. He arrived there coincidentally with the first 16-inch shells from the battleship *Massachusetts*. It was scarcely surprising, therefore, that his request for an interview met with a blank refusal and in such obnoxious circumstances negotiations were broken off.

At 1430 hours on 8 November Fedala fell. By nightfall 7,750 officers and men had been landed

Left: American troops disembark on beaches outside the town

Following pages: French coastal defence guns put out of action at Safi, on the southern flank of the assault

and the Americans controlled the town of Fedala, the harbour, the bridges over the river at both ends of the area, and the high ridges commanding the town and the beaches.

By now Patton was ashore, angrily discovering that there was little he could do to influence the course of the battle mainly because of a woeful lack of supporting weapons, vehicles and communications equipment held up by delays in unloading.

> Patton decided that this was the crux of the matter and began to intervene in this seemingly subordinate sphere of the operation. He summoned Lieutenant Stiller, his cowboy aide, and went down to the beach to see what they could do. 'The situation we found was very bad', he later wrote, 'boats were coming in and not being pushed off after unloading. There was shellfire and French aviators were strafing the beach. Although they missed it by a considerable distance whenever they strafed our men would take cover and delay unloading operations, and particularly the unloading of ammunition which was vitally necessary as we were fighting a major engagement not more than 1,500 yards to the south.'
>
> General Patton remained on the beach for about eighteen hours getting thoroughly wet all of that time, knocking himself out to speed the unloading at this one area, personally helping to push off the boats and trying to calm the nerves of his men, who kept faltering whenever a French plane flew over.[20]

Meanwhile, all contact with the Supreme Commander at Gibraltar had been lost. This brought the whole expedition into appalling danger. Radio communication failed and although Eisenhower tried every possible means of getting in touch, nothing got through except unintelligible signals. He tried sending light bomber aircraft to Casablanca to gain contact 'but after French fighters had shot down several of them we knew that this method was futile'.[21]

Eventually the minelayer H.M.S. *Welshman*, one of the fastest ships in the Royal Navy, which was preparing for a dash to Malta with vital supplies, was diverted to make contact with the Western Task Force. It was a clumsy and expensive way of finding out what was going on. This paralysis in communication was compounded on the spot by the U.S. Army Headquarters ashore having failed to take with them the joint code for high-grade messages, rendering impossible the retransmission by the *Augusta* of secret messages from Allied Force Headquarters to Western Task Force Headquarters ashore. On 10 November contact between the Army and Navy Head-

quarters virtually ceased.

Nevertheless the invading army had attained its immediate objectives and held an arc of 180° around the city of Casablanca, awaiting only the arrival of the Sherman tanks from Safi. Later on the 10th, Admiral Darlan broadcast an order calling on all French forces in North Africa to cease resistance and the following day an armistice conference took place between the French and the Americans at which it was agreed that naval and military hostilities should be suspended.

The United States had thus made its first big aggressive gesture of the war. The impact was shattering and the implications in depth sombre indeed for Hitler and Mussolini. The American giant, tethered by its uneasy neutrality before Pearl Harbor, had now snapped its bonds and was advancing upon its equally gigantic enemy. Those Germans and Italians in positions of high responsibility – and there were far more of them than cared or dared to open their mouths, except in private – were well able to read the writing on the wall. Rommel himself had long had a fascination and a respect for American strength, for American efficiency and for the immense resources which

could be tapped, manufactured and assembled 3,000 miles away from Luftwaffe attack. The conclusions to be drawn were not encouraging to the Axis powers.

American generalship had yet to be put to the test in battle but the 'stars to be' such as Patton, Mark Clark, Omar Bradley, Carl Spaatz and Eisenhower himself could already claim a resounding victory in their opening attack. The Americans had arrived on the scene with a loud, resonant bang. The first great gamble – of sending a huge armada across the Atlantic and of landing an expeditionary force in a semi-hostile and astonished North Africa – had been successfully achieved. This was but the start.

Thus ended the opening phase of Operation 'Torch'. By 11 November, only three days after D-Day, all the main French bases in North and North-West Africa from Bône to Safi were safely in Allied hands. After 20 November, the naval phases of the operation were limited to routine follow-up convoys, subject to no more than the normal hazards of sea passages in time of war. The political situation, however, was very far from being so simply arranged.

Aftermath of 'Torch'. Warships scuttled by the French at Toulon to prevent their falling into German hands when Hitler responded to the invasion of French North Africa by ordering his troops to occupy the whole of France

II
THE PINCERS CLOSE

The Germans reacted predictably and at once. They swept down through unoccupied France, taking over the whole country. They also made landings by air in Tunisia, the first German contingent arriving in the area on 9 November. There were two obvious reasons for this. One was to secure Rommel's rear by controlling Tunisia with its airfields and ports before the Allies could do so themselves. The other was to seize the French Fleet at Toulon and Bizerta or, at the very least, deny it to the Allies.

The Admiral commanding in Tunis was Jean Pierre Esteva. Very near to retirement and loyal to Darlan and Vichy, Esteva was nevertheless privately sympathetic to the Allies. Had the bold suggestion of taking 'Torch' as far east as Bizerta on the original assault been adopted, the next few months might well have turned out differently. On the night of 7–8 November when Esteva received from the hand of the American Vice-Consul in Tunis, Mr Doolittle, a personal message from President Roosevelt telling him of the invasion and seeking his support, he observed: 'The Allies had better hurry up as the Germans will be here in forty-eight hours.'[1] He was right.

On the morning of D plus one – 9 November – General Giraud, accompanied by Eisenhower's Chief of Staff, General Mark Clark, flew from Gibraltar to Algiers. Their mission was simple to state, almost impossibly intricate to achieve – namely to end the fighting and secure French co-operation against the Germans. Giraud was glacially received. It was already apparent that Darlan was the only man who mattered and that no one of any importance would accept Giraud as the Supreme Commander.

The local Resistance organization, so carefully fostered by Murphy and the Five, had already collapsed. By the next morning, the 10th, Clark was signalling Eisenhower that a deal with Darlan would be the only solution. The Supreme Commander, instead of being able to concentrate all his powers and attention on striking east with the minimum delay, was now compelled to waste invaluable time in the maze of local and Vichy politics.

'In Darlan we had the Commander-in-Chief of the French fighting forces!' Eisenhower wrote. 'A simple and easy answer would have been to jail him.' But Darlan still had control of the considerable French Fleet at Toulon and at Dakar. What a prize this would be! Eisenhower recalled that before leaving London, Churchill had said to him: 'If I could meet Darlan, much as I hate him, I would cheerfully crawl on my hands and knees for a mile if by so doing I could get him to bring that fleet of his into the circle of Allied forces.'

There was another pressing reason for a deal with Darlan, and it is not one properly understood even to this day by either British or Americans. The French character is deeply legalistic, and loyalty to the law and to the legal head of state was never stronger than in the Second World War. 'Without exception,' Eisenhower went on,

every French commander with whom General Clark held exhaustive conversation declined to make any move toward bringing his forces to the side of the Allies unless he could get a legal order to do so. Each of them had sworn an oath of personal fealty to Marshal Pétain, a name that at that moment was more profound in its influence on North African thinking and acting than any other factor. None of these men felt that he could be absolved from that oath or could give any order to cease firing unless the necessary instructions were given by Darlan as their legal commander, to whom they looked as the direct and personal representative of Marshal Pétain.[2]

Very few British and Americans understood the evidence of their eyes as they walked about Algiers. It was useless to talk to a Frenchman, civilian or soldier, unless one first recognized the Marshal's overriding influence. His picture was everywhere. Extracts from his statements were displayed on public buildings. No idea or proposal was acceptable 'unless the Marshal would wish it'.

In the house in Algiers in which I was billeted from November 1942 till April 1943, I faced a portrait of the Marshal at every meal I ate. My host was a retired Commandant d'Aviation called Deviterne, and a letter I had from him later on indicates what almost all Frenchmen in North Africa thought at the time:

> Answering to your opinion of the actual situation, I must tell you like General Giraud said recently to the American reporters: 'I cannot make policy!'
>
> Marshal Pétain was my chief to Verdun. Like the other soldiers who served under his command, I must look on him as the deliverer of my fatherland on the battlefield, like the protector of my invaded country. It is very possible that he may be, without seeming it, the harbinger of our efficient union with the Allies here . . . we don't know. History shall show us truth after! You can be sure that almost all Frenchmen will see *both* Generals Giraud and de Gaulle like the liberators of France.

But time, time, time was what mattered and the Germans, using Laval as their tool at Vichy, were quicker off the mark than London or Washington to whom reference would, in any case, have entailed a further delay. All the problems were now on Eisenhower's plate. Already four days had passed since the landings and nothing had been settled in the political sphere. It was all very well for the British and American Governments to order Eisenhower to co-operate with any French government he found in existence in French North Africa –

> I well knew that any dealing with a Vichyite would create a great revulsion among those in England and America who did not know the harsh realities of war.[3]

It did the same to those of us in the services on the spot. We could not – or we simply did not want to believe the evidence of our eyes. We felt at the time oddly let down. We did not understand. No more did Eisenhower.

> I determined to confine my judgement in the matter to local military aspects. Taking Admiral Cunningham with me I flew to Algiers on 13 November and upon reaching there went into conference with General Clark and Mr Murphy.[4]

Eisenhower was given an exhaustive review of the situation, being told by Murphy that the whole matter had now become a military one and that the Supreme Commander alone could give a proper decision.

It was now Friday. Much had happened since the Sunday *débarquements*. On the Tuesday Darlan had ordered a 'cease-fire' which Pétain had immediately cancelled (whilst telling Darlan by secret code that he still had his confidence and to play for time).

Darlan had tried to rescind the cease-fire but had been prevented from doing so by General Clark. In the meantime General Giraud, deeply shocked by his icy reception, had become convinced that Darlan was the only man able to bring French North Africa into the war on the Allied side, and when the Germans entered unoccupied France, he had offered to co-operate with Darlan. Those gallant French officers, Generals Béthouart and Mast, who had assisted the Allies, were helpless and in temporary disgrace.

Eisenhower, therefore, had to decide whether it was better to arrest Darlan, the local head of a neutral government with whom neither Britain nor America had gone to war, an action which would provoke continued fighting and cumulative bitterness – or do a deal. He chose the latter course. A final agreement with the French Army, Navy and Air Force officials was reached in the evening of Friday the 13th, and Eisenhower and Cunningham returned to Gibraltar that same night. The agreement gave the Allied Commander-in-Chief in a 'friendly, not an occupied territory' all the necessary legal rights and privileges for the conduct of military operations and the administration of his forces. The use of ports, railways and other facilities were likewise guaranteed.

In return, provided the French forces and the civil population continued to obey Darlan's directive to co-operate with the Allies, there would be no disturbance of the existing French administrative control of North Africa. No commitment to engage the British or American Governments in political recognition was made and as Eisenhower put it:

> Darlan was simply authorized, by the voluntary action of the local officials, and with our consent, to take charge of the French affairs of North Africa while we were clearing

the Germans out of that continent. He agreed also to place our friend, General Giraud, in command of all French military forces in north-west Africa.[5]

Five days had been lost and Eisenhower was to face instant and severe criticism from the British and American Press, but at least he could get back to trying to win his part of the war. It was not an hour too soon. Already Tunis and Bizerta had fallen under Axis control, Admiral Esteva's final telephone call to Algiers saying ominously, 'I now have a guardian', after which there was silence.

At no time in the fateful negotiations of 13 November did Darlan promise to bring the French Fleet over to the Allies. Admiral de Laborde at Toulon and Admiral Godfroy, under restraint at Alexandria, disliked the British (and especially the Royal Navy) and whilst in no way pro-German, preferred to continue their allegiance to Vichy. However, Darlan did state with conviction that the French Admiral at Toulon would never allow his ships to fall into German hands. This proved to be true, the French Fleet scuttling itself as the Germans were about to step on board.

Admiral Auphan, the Minister of Marine at Vichy who had wanted to stand by Darlan but who had been thwarted by Laval, resigned on 19 November, and on 27 November 1 battleship, 2 battle-cruisers, 7 cruisers, 29 destroyers and 16 submarines were among the 73 ships which sank in the port of Toulon. It is difficult to find any appropriate comment on this tragic monument to French pride, except to say that such a decision has never been forced upon the Royal Navy or the U.S. Navy.

In spite of the brilliant success of the 'Torch' assaults, Allied hopes of a speedy capture of Tunisia very soon began to fade. The French attitude was not at all what the invading forces had been led to expect, and this was a shock. Here was yet another instance of the failure by both British and Americans to understand French 'realism'. The voluminous, accurate and carefully reasoned intelligence reports furnished by Murphy had induced Roosevelt, Churchill, the Combined Chiefs of Staff and the Supreme Commander to expect a much more actively friendly reception. All of them, including the men on the spot, had got it wrong. Loyalty to the despised Vichy régime remained as inexplicable as ever. The Allies had believed that the French population in the region was bitterly resentful of the Vichy-Nazi domination. They had imagined they would be eagerly embraced as deliverers of France. If this was so, it was not apparent. Indeed, when the Germans started to bomb Algiers – and, once begun, air raids continued for some six months – an undercurrent of resentment started to flow. Perhaps the shock of the 1940 collapse – the fact that the French considered they had had their war – was still working its way out. There was a feeling of 'Why did you bring this war to us? We were satisfied before you came along to get us all killed.'

Not everyone felt like this, of course, just as there had been a few fair-minded people who saw the reason for the Royal Navy's destruction of the French Atlantic Fleet at Mers-el-Kebir in 1940 and accepted this disaster as a hazard of war, but General Anderson, the Commander of the British First Army, had this to say about the early attitude of the local population:

> Many mayors, station and post masters and other key officials with whom we had dealings as we advanced (for instance the civil telephone was, at first, my chief means of communicating with my forward units and with Allied Force Headquarters) were lukewarm in their sympathies and hesitant to commit themselves openly, while a few were hostile. I can safely generalize by saying that at first, in the Army, the senior officers were hesitant and afraid to commit themselves. The junior officers were mainly in favour of aiding the Allies. The men would obey orders.
>
> Amongst the people, the Arabs were indifferent or inclined to be hostile, the French were in our favour but apathetic. The civil authorities were antagonistic as a whole. The resulting impression on my mind was not one of much confidence as to the safety of my small isolated force should I suffer a severe setback.[6]

From another point of view this attitude was a sombre reminder to the invading forces that they had better succeed or else. . . .

Eisenhower decided to press on now without further delay. On 23 November he transferred Allied Force Headquarters to the Hotel St Georges, Algiers, despite cries of distress from his signals department, which said it could not be ready to move for another six weeks. He also made short shrift of an ill-timed suggestion from his rear Chief of Staff in London that the planned build-up for 'Torch' should be cut down and devoted to other strategic purposes 'in view of the initial successes and apparently certain outcome'. Eisenhower saw red:

Rather than talk of possible reduction we should be seeking ways and means of speeding up the build-up to clean out North Africa. We should plan ahead in orderly fashion on strategic matters but for God's sake let's get one job done at a time. We have lost a lot of shipping in the last few days and provision of air cover for convoys is most difficult. The danger of German intervention through Spain has not ceased. I am not growing fearful of shadows nor am I crying wolf. I merely insist that if our beginning looks hopeful, then this is the time to push rather than slacken our efforts. We have just started working on a great venture. A good beginning must not be destroyed by any unwarranted assumptions.[7]

A number of hard lessons had yet to be learnt.

The same urge to press on to a total victory animated Montgomery on the other side of the arena. In fact one of the mottoes he had pinned up in his caravan was Sir Francis Drake's prayer on the morning of the attack on Cadiz in 1587:

> Oh! Lord God, when Thou givest to Thy servants to endeavour any great matter, grant us also to know that it is not the beginning, but the continuing of the same, until it be thoroughly finished, which yieldeth the true glory.

With this in mind the pursuit proper began on 5 November and in twelve days advance elements of the Eighth Army – the 7th Armoured Division – had reached Msus, a distance of 560 miles. They had passed Sollum (270 miles) on the 11th, and the next day were at Tobruk (360 miles). Montgomery had been promoted a full General and made a Knight Commander of the Bath 'for distinguished services in the field'.

In a message of congratulation Monty issued to his troops on 12 November, he gave the tally of German and Italian fighting formations which at that time had ceased to exist. These were:

Panzer Army	*20th Italian Corps*
15th Panzer Div.	Ariete Armoured Div.
21st Panzer	Littorio Armoured
90th Light	Trieste
164th Light	
10th Italian Corps	*21st Italian Corps*
Brescia Div.	Trento Div.
Pavia	Bologna
Folgore	

The prisoners captured numbered 30,000, including nine generals. It was a more than promising start and a stiff challenge to Eisenhower's force about to press east into Tunisia.

The French Fleet did not come over to the Allies, but nor did the French Admiral at Toulon allow it to fall into German hands. Here the French Fleet scuttles itself

Rommel's own thoughts were bitter indeed. As he retreated, in the first place to Fuka along the southern side of the railway, he remembered the desperate attempt they had made to reach Alexandria after their victory at Tobruk. Crossing the very same stretch of country as now but in the other direction, as dog tired then as they were now, they had nevertheless been afire with enthusiasm, eager to grasp their one and only chance of really seizing the initiative in Africa. But their supplies had let them down and now they were reaping the reward. Now in the pitch dark night with vehicles incessantly driving off the track into sand drifts up to their axles and having to be hauled out each time by manhandling back on to the track, they could do nothing but hope that Fate would come to their rescue.

'The authorization for the retreat', Rommel wrote,
which had now arrived – far too late – from the Fuehrer and the Duce, charged us with the duty of extricating all German and Italian troops especially the non-motorized units. We could do nothing but shrug our shoulders, for extricating the infantry was precisely what the original order had prevented us from doing.[8]

Even in retreat, however, the magic of Rommel's reputation induced caution in the pursuers.

No victory was certain as long as Rommel himself remained at large, and now providential downpours of rain helped the later stages of the getaway. By rights they should all have been trapped in the first few days. They were not.

Meanwhile our columns were steadily streaming westwards and were now approaching Sollum. In the afternoon the Italian General Gandin appeared on behalf of Marshal Cavallero to inquire about our situation and plans. This suited me very well. I gave him a detailed account of the battle, laying particular stress on the effects of the supply crisis and the Fuehrer's and Duce's order. I told him point-blank that with the present balance of forces there was not a chance of our making a stand anywhere, and that the British could keep on going right through to Tripolitania, if they chose to. We could never accept battle but would have to confine ourselves to trying to delay the British long enough to allow our columns, in which the utmost confusion reigned, to get across the Libyan frontier . . . Gandin left my H.Q. visibly shaken. It was clear that to the Commando Supremo war was simple. When, for instance, during the July crisis at Alamein, I had told Marshal Cavallero that in the event of a British break-through threatening, only two possibilities would exist – either to stay in our line and be forced to surrender in two or three days by lack of water, or to beat a fighting retreat to the west – Cavallero had said he could give no guidance for such an event; one simply should not contemplate it. That was no doubt an easy way out.[9]

Nevertheless Rommel's skill – and luck – became as evident in retreat as in attack. Even as early as 7 November, it became clear to the British that Rommel was slipping out of reach and that the follow-up would be a long race, not a short one. Now it was the British who were suffering the hazards and delays of an ever-lengthening supply line.

That night – the night of the North African invasion – Rommel gave orders to retire to Sidi Barrani. During that same night the British, correctly, turned north to cut off the German retreat. But the trap proved to be empty but for a small number of burnt-out vehicles destroyed by the Germans for lack of petrol. As Rommel commented:

> There is never any point in attempting an outflanking movement round an enemy force unless it has first been tied down frontally, because the defending force can always use its motorized forces – assuming it has petrol and vehicles – to hold up the outflanking columns while it slips out of the trap.[10]

The problem for Rommel at that moment was twofold. One, of course, was whether the petrol would hold out. The other was whether they could get their columns through the Halfaya Pass.

There was a 25-mile queue of vehicles waiting to get through, and these were subject to incessant harassment from the R.A.F. Indomitably they still plugged on.

> At about 0800 (8 November) I met Bayerlein and informed him that a convoy of about 104 ships was approaching Africa, and it was possible that the British and Americans were about to strike at us from the west. At about 1100 this was confirmed. The Anglo-Americans had, in fact, landed in North-West Africa during the night – as I heard shortly afterwards from Westphal. This spelt the end of the Army in Africa.[11]

It was now proving impossible to bring east the petrol stored in Benghazi because of the heavy burden which the non-motorized troops, the sick and the wounded were placing on the German lorry columns and because the Italians had already blown up the railway track to Barce. Rommel therefore had to ask Kesselring for the Luftwaffe to fly in 250 tons of petrol a day. He actually received about sixty tons.

Since neither Cavallero nor Kesselring considered it necessary to come to Africa, Rommel sent his A.D.C. Lieutenant Berndt, to Hitler's Headquarters to report the position. He found the master far from amiable. Although Rommel received an assurance of 'his very special confidence', this did not extend to any understanding of the real position. Rommel was assured of Hitler's active support in the matter of supplies – nothing would be denied him, but the Mersa el Brega line was to be held at all costs. It would then form the springboard for a new offensive.

So far as Tunis was concerned, Rommel was told to leave it out of his calculations. He was to act on the simple assumption that the bridgehead would be held. Rommel commented acidly that 'this was typical of the attitude of the highest command. It was to be the characteristic of, and at the same time to determine, the coming series of reverses.'[12]

Benghazi's harbour and dock installations were destroyed on 18 November, and shortly afterwards the sorely tried town changed hands for the fifth time.

> When we arrived in Agedabia, we had virtually no petrol left. There were 500 tons lying in Tripoli and another 10 tons in Buerat, but even the latter was still 250 miles away. The principal cause of this crisis was the fact that the front was now out of reach of transport aircraft from Italy. That day an Italian tanker carrying 4,000 tons of petrol was sunk off Misurata, although a small tanker with 1,200 tons aboard succeeded in reaching Tripoli. Every supply lorry that would run was immediately sent off to Tripoli to bring it up. It was an ugly situation to have to stand immobilized for any length of time in the desert.[13]

However, just behind them now stood the Mersa el Brega line where work on fortification was going on at full pressure. This was a key position since, a few miles south of the coast, it abutted on a salt marsh some ten miles across, beyond which there was a long stretch of very heavy going for vehicles. Thus for the British to outflank this position entailed them hauling well down to the south and it soon became obvious to Rommel that the British needed to organize their supplies, and thus that both sides were in for another mutual build-up of strength.

Meanwhile the Axis take-over of Tunisia and the compressing of the sea supply line to Bizerta, Tunis and Tripoli from Sicily and the Italian mainland drew Malta into even sharper focus than before. The battered, brave population of 300,000 was still subsisting on a just-above-starvation diet, but now relief was in sight. Special supplies were rushed through in a couple of the Navy's fastest minelayers, the 40-knot *Welshman* and *Manxman*,

one of these cargoes being a consignment of seed potatoes (Malta normally has three crops of potatoes a year but they had been forced to eat their seed potatoes during the worst period of crisis).

Militarily Malta became of even greater importance. The main Axis supply line to Bizerta and Tunis involved a short open sea passage of little more than 100 miles. Ships could cover this in under ten hours and at the outset Italian ships were making these passages by day and by night. After 'Torch' however, the Royal Navy stationed a force of cruisers and destroyers, known as Force Q, at Bône, its most easterly port in Algeria. This was only 200 miles from the Axis convoy route and on the night of 1–2 December Force Q made a smashing attack on a night convoy which, thereafter, though temporarily, caused the Italians to prefer a daylight passage in spite of the risks of air attack.

Another immediate result of the invasion of North Africa was an intensification of the U-boat war inside the Mediterranean. Whilst Allied shipping naturally suffered, this was not a one-sided affair. The Royal Navy moved the depot

ship *Maidstone* and the 8th Submarine Flotilla to Algiers, and the 10th Flotilla continued to operate successfully from Malta. Three submarines from these two flotillas were lost during November and December working in the heavily mined Sicilian channel, but a total of 14 merchant vessels, 2 destroyers, 1 U-boat and 2 small craft were sunk and another 10 merchant ships, an Italian cruiser, destroyer and torpedo boat were damaged. In the first four months of 1943 a further mixed bag of seventy-seven warships and merchantmen were similarly disposed of. The tide had turned.

The main snag, however, still remained: the two long Axis minefields stretching from Cape Bon almost to the coast of Sicily. Through the canal, so to speak, between these two minefields convoys were able to pass to and fro by day and by night without much risk of attack from British light surface forces. As Admiral Cunningham wrote:

These minefields certainly added to our difficulties. They had to be avoided, which meant that our ships from Bône or Malta had to steam a circuitous and lengthier course before reaching the enemy's convoy area, which was within easy reach of the airfields in Sicily. We lacked adequate fighter protection, and the consequence in practice was

that we had to accept the risk of our cruisers or destroyers being at sea without air cover during daylight either at the beginning or end of their operations, probably both.

We eventually countered this move by using our fast minelayers *Abdiel* and *Welshman* and the submarine *Rorqual* to lay lines of mines across and between the two enemy fields, starting as close to the Tunisian coast as possible and gradually working northward, rather like fitting rungs into a ladder.

Aircraft from Malta co-operated by laying mines close inshore; but the bulk of the work was done by the *Abdiel*, Captain David Orr-Ewing, and as the minelayers were unescorted, the task was particularly risky. But the risk was worthwhile. These cross minefields in what the enemy thought was clear water lost him several ships and I remember that one of the first victims was a vessel called the *Ankara*, specially fitted for carrying tanks, which we had often tried to catch from the Eastern Mediterranean but had never succeeded.[14]

Further to the west Force H, under Vice-Admiral Sir Neville Syfret, consisting of the battleships *Nelson, Rodney,* one or more aircraft-carriers and attendant destroyers divided its time between Gibraltar and Mers-el-Kebir (Oran). They were to provide heavy cover should the Italian fleet put in an appearance. However, Italian battleships and cruisers decided to remain peacefully 'in being' in their harbours. No doubt,

the Royal Navy thought, this was wise.

But the Italians were specialists in a particularly brave and hazardous form of warfare – the midget submarine and the 'limpet' mine attacks on shipping in what were thought to be safe harbours. They had disposed of two battleships in Alexandria by this daring method, and now they turned their attention with success to shipping in Algiers. On 12 December one merchant ship was sunk and three were damaged.

Christmas in Algiers, however, saw another event which was to have far-reaching results. On Christmas Eve a young fanatic named Bonnier de la Chapelle gained access to Admiral Darlan's office in the Palais d'Été and when Darlan was returning after lunch he emptied a revolver into him. Darlan died almost at once.

The murder of Darlan took place on the very day that Eisenhower, having spent two days examining the front line at Souk-el-Khemis, was forced to a bitter decision. The attack on Tunis would have to be indefinitely postponed. At one stage, a month previously, advanced elements of the British First Army had reached to within twelve

miles of Tunis. They had then been pushed back in appalling weather conditions to a line running south-east from a few miles east of Tabarka and in front of Medjez-el-Bab.

The cause of this setback was mud. Just as the prime conditioning factor in the Western Desert was sand, so on the Algerian-Tunisian front it was mud, caused by continuing and torrential rain. Christmas for the Eighth Army found them 1,200 miles from Alamein 'needing a halt during which it could pull itself together' in readiness for the final jump to Tripoli. Christmas for the First Army found them 700 miles east of Oran but at the end of a rickety single-track railway bogged down in unfriendly mountain passes in very uncomfortable proximity to Axis forces being rapidly reinforced from Sicily and the Italian mainland. The condition of the two fronts could not have been more different. The gap between the two arms of the pincer was still 1,000 miles as the crow flies.

Montgomery wrote,

> The officers and men deserved a rest and I was determined they should have it. I ordered that we would halt where we stood, that no offensive operations would take place until

after Christmas, and we would all spend that day in the happiest way that conditions in the desert allowed. It was very cold. Turkeys, plum puddings, beer were all ordered up from Egypt and the staff concentrated on ensuring that it all arrived in time: and it did.[15]

Eisenhower's Christmas was to be concerned with the problems of straightening out the line, assembling units into proper formations, collecting local reserves and protecting his southern flank to permit operations throughout the winter whilst holding firmly to the gains already made, pending the arrival of better weather in the spring. The rain fell constantly.

'I observed an incident', Eisenhower wrote,

> which as much as anything else, I think, convinced me of the hopelessness of an attack. About thirty feet off the road, in a field that appeared to be covered with winter wheat, a motor cycle had become stuck in the mud. Four soldiers were struggling to extricate it but, in spite of their most strenuous efforts, succeeded only in getting themselves mired into the sticky clay. They finally had to give up the attempt and left the motor cycle more deeply bogged down than when they started.[16]

Eisenhower returned to Algiers after thirty hours of non-stop driving through rain, snow and sleet. He was a profoundly worried man. The assassination of Darlan would mean, inevitably, more tricky negotiations with the unreliable French who up to now had obstinately refused to serve under British command and whose control of a German-infiltrated Arab population was at that moment essential. How could they be persuaded or driven to co-operate? At that dark moment it seemed impossible. It was scarcely surprising that on Christmas Day Eisenhower contracted a severe case of flu and for four days became very ill indeed.

The British War Cabinet had sent Harold Macmillan to Algiers as their man on the spot, and Britain's future Prime Minister worked tirelessly and in easy harness with Robert Murphy, his American counterpart. But the problems they faced appeared to be all but unresolvable. No one really understood the French – or if he did could do very much about them.

'My entire acquaintanceship with Darlan', Eisenhower wrote,

> covered a period of six weeks. His reputation was that of a notorious collaborator with Hitler, but during the time that he served as the administrator of French North Africa he never once, to our knowledge, violated any commitment or promise. On the other hand his mannerisms and personality did not inspire confidence and in view of his reputation we were always uneasy in dealing with him. In any event his death presented me with new problems.[17]

The French General in Morocco, Noguès, was untrustworthy or worse, but he still remained the Foreign Minister to the Sultan. He enjoyed the full confidence of the fierce Moroccan tribesmen, who were a force to be reckoned with. Patton, still a political child, reckoned that if the Moroccans grew antagonistic he would need 60,000 fully equipped American troops to keep order and he therefore strongly advised Eisenhower to let Noguès alone.

Another complication was the ancient antagonism between Arab and Jew. The former outnumbered the latter by forty to one in North Africa, so local policy perforce had to placate the Arab at the expense of the Jew. Nazi propaganda had put it about that Eisenhower was Jewish and had been sent to North Africa by the Jew, Roosevelt, to grind down the Arabs and turn North Africa over to Jewish rule. This was generally believed, and Eisenhower's political staff had to work overtime to try to correct this propaganda.

Local hatred of de Gaulle in the French Army and in all echelons of civil government was also intense. Giraud, though honest, virtually refused to interest himself in politics, and the forcibly reinstated Generals Mast and Béthouart were ostracized and their wives insulted by the wives of other officers. Indeed, the internal situation in French North Africa became so serious in the first six weeks of 1943 that Eisenhower, with the greatest reluctance, imposed a censorship on any political news.

This infuriated the French and was misinterpreted in Great Britain and in the United States. However, it did secure a breathing space and the ban was lifted shortly after Churchill and Roosevelt had forced Giraud and de Gaulle, almost at gun point, to meet and to shake hands at the Casablanca Conference in January.

The ugly situation in French North Africa was aptly summed up by Darlan when Eisenhower had earlier asked for the replacement both of Noguès in Morocco and of the weak Yves Chatel in Algeria. 'I don't want them either,' Darlan had replied, 'but the governing of Arab tribes is a tricky business that requires much experience with them. As quickly as you can produce any men, of your own choice, who are experienced in this regard and are loyal Frenchmen, I will instantly dismiss the incumbents and appoint the men you desire.'[18]

But now Darlan had gone. Meanwhile, up at the front it had proved impossible to set up a unified command. The British First Army was on the left, French forces – still claiming their troops would rebel if they were put under overall British command – held the centre and weak 'unblooded' American forces stood to the right. All were part of a closely interrelated battle front and all depended upon a single, wildly inadequate line of communication. Such a state of affairs was manna from heaven for the Germans, who took full advantage of it. The situation became critical in mid-January, when the French broke and gave way before small but determined German attacks.

'Under these conditions', Eisenhower wrote,

I peremptorily ordered General Anderson to take charge of the entire battle line. I personally visited General Juin, in command of the French forces in the line, to assure myself that he would take orders from General Anderson. Later I informed General Giraud of what I had done. He interposed no objection – the need had become too obvious.[19]

Italian wheeled vehicles near the Kasserine Pass

12
AFRICA REDEEMED

The great world event of January 1943 was the Casablanca Conference attended by the American President, the British Prime Minister, the Combined Chiefs of Staff, Eisenhower, Alexander, Giraud and, with the utmost reluctance, de Gaulle. The latter at first haughtily refused, and eventually turned up after the heaviest pressure had been put upon him, 'even to the point of saying that if he would not come, we should insist on his being replaced by someone else at the head of the French Liberation Committee in London.'[1]

At the various historic meetings which took place during the ten days of the Casablanca Conference, the Allied strategy for the future conduct of the war in Europe was agreed. After the liberation of the whole of North Africa from Egypt to Morocco, Italy was now definitely to be the next on the list – the invasion of the northern coast of France being actively planned for 1944. 'Admiral King, of course, considers the Pacific should be a first charge on all resources . . . on the other hand I am satisfied that the President is strongly in favour of the Mediterranean being given prime place.'[2] And so it was to be.

General Mark Clark had been appointed away

from the North African theatre to the U.S. Fifth Army, and it was agreed that at the right time Alexander should replace him as Eisenhower's Deputy. Alexander had brought the excellent news that Montgomery would soon be in Tripoli.

'It was fortunate indeed that we all met here', Churchill wrote,

and that I brought General Alexander to the scene. General Eisenhower was about to begin an operation most daring and spirited but also most hazardous against Sfax, which he intended to try to hold, supplying himself partly from Malta. This operation ought evidently to be concerted with Alexander's advance, for otherwise the Americans might find themselves heavily attacked in Sfax just at the very period when the Desert Army would be motionless in Tripoli, regathering petrol and supplies and dependent upon conditions of the port.

I therefore brought together Alexander and Eisenhower who got on extremely well, both alone and also with the C.I.G.S. and Marshall. The result has been a perfect understanding between them and arrangements for visits when necessary. Eisenhower is greatly relieved to realize how soon and with what great forces Alexander can arrive, and instead of an isolated operation to keep things going, he is now in a position to make a really good combination.

The feeling of all four generally was that we have very good prospects in Tunisia provided we do not make a mistake. Personally I am very well satisfied with the way this has gone.[3]

Mistakes were, of course, still going to be made, but this overall accord at the top contrasts with the overall disaccord which Rommel had to put up with 1,500 miles to the east. Indeed, the odds against the Desert Fox were such that his achievements in retreat are almost as astonishing as his genius in advance. Time and again Rommel slipped through every trap so carefully prepared, managing somehow or other to rally his men and to stand again in the face of overwhelming Eighth Army pressure and the incessantly broken promises of the Commando Supremo and of the O.K.W.

The Eighth Army entered Tripoli on 23 January, three months to the day after Alamein. 'I've been over all the plans,' Alexander had remarked casually at Casablanca, 'and there's really nothing for me to do now but leave things to Monty.' Ten days later Churchill himself visited Tripoli on his return journey from a conference with the Turkish Government at Adana and a stop-over in Cairo. That day Alexander made the Prime Minister his short definitive signal:

The orders you gave me on August 10th 1942 have been fulfilled. His Majesty's enemies, together with their

impedimenta, have been completely eliminated from Egypt, Cyrenaica, Libya and Tripolitania. I now await your further instructions.[4]

Commander Tommy Thompson, Churchill's inseparable bodyguard, describes that historic day:

The P.M. drove into the city to watch the ceremonial entry of the Eighth Army. I was worried about this as the route was overlooked by houses which could not as yet have been thoroughly searched. Montgomery seemed quite satisfied that everything would be all right but I spent a very uncomfortable forenoon.

On the seafront the greater part of the 51st Highland Division were lined up. They looked magnificent. We had last seen them on our arrival in Egypt, pink as lobsters from their first painful days in the African sun. Now they were bronzed and fit. Men and vehicles were turned out as though there had been a month to prepare for the parade.

There was one superb touch of showmanship. Silhouetted against the clear blue sky, a lone kilted soldier stood motionless on top of Mussolini's triumphal arch as the troops marched past with pipes playing. It was a sight I shall never forget. Nor will the P.M. who was in tears.[5]

Later that day Churchill addressed Montgomery's Headquarter troops and it was then that he said:

Ever since your victory at Alamein, you have nightly pitched your tents a day's march nearer home. In days to come when people ask you what you did in the Second World War, it will be enough to say: I marched with the Eighth Army.[6]

Meanwhile, Rommel was skilfully retiring into Tunisia to the next defensible line – the Mareth – which could be held long enough for supplies coming in through Bizerta and Tunis to be built up for another offensive. He was still a sick man and it must have seemed at times that his only friends and supporters were the troops he led. His enemies at the Fuehrer's Headquarters, at C.-in-C. South and, of course, at the Italian Commando Supremo – all of them desk generals – now felt themselves strong enough to demand his recall. They pitched this on the fact that he had given up the Tarhuna-Homs position against the Fuehrer's and the Duce's orders.

At midday on January 26th 1943 I received a signal from the Commando Supremo informing me that on account of my bad state of health, I was to be released from my command when we reached the Mareth line, the actual date being left to me. An Italian Army Command was to be formed under General Messe, who had led the Italian Expeditionary Corps in Russia. After my experience during the retreat, I had little desire to go on any longer playing the scapegoat for a pack of incompetents and requested the Commando Supremo to send General Messe

to Africa as soon as possible, so that he could be initiated into his new command.[7]

Further north and on the Allied side of the line, command changes were also taking place. Just at the time when Montgomery was entering Tripoli, all the mixed nationality forces – British, American and French – on the Tunisian front had been put under the command of the British General Anderson. The line had virtually been static for ten vital weeks, during which time, despite the best efforts of the Navy and the Air Force, the German build-up appeared to be gaining ground.

At the Casablanca Conference it had been decided that the British Eighth Army and the Desert Air Force would both come under Eisenhower's command upon entering Tunisia, and to effect this General Alexander was to become the Deputy Commander of the Allied forces. Admiral Cunningham remained the Naval Commander-in-Chief and Air Chief-Marshal Tedder the Commander-in-Chief of the joint air forces. Thus practical command of all the forces on the two fronts became British under the American 'supremo'. 'This development was extraordinarily pleasing to me,' Eisenhower wrote, 'because it meant, first and foremost, complete unity of action in the central Mediterranean. . . . I informed the President and the Chief of Staff that I would be delighted to serve under Alexander if it should be decided to give him the supreme authority.'[8]

Not the least of the qualities which Ike brought to the top command was a personal modesty, a total lack of chauvinism and a flexibility – all of which were to be severely tested during the next three months. This 'personality success' was, of course, to lead him to a much greater task the following year, but in those rather murky first few months of 1943, Ike's 'cohesive' ability played an essential part in the coming victory. On 11 February he was promoted to the temporary grade of a Four Star General. His substantive rank in the regular U.S. Army was still Lieutenant-Colonel.

Eisenhower's battle line in Tunisia was far from satisfactory in early February when intelligence was received that 'the enemy was preparing for a more ambitious counter-attack against our lines than any he had yet attempted. To provide additional strength for this counter-attack, some of Rommel's forces were hurried back from Tripoli to join von Arnim and Messe in Tunisia.'

Because General Anderson had originally been engaged entirely in the north, his communications and his command post were so situated as to make very difficult an effective control of the central and southern portions of the line. The Allied front then ran from the coast about midway between Bizerta and the Algerian frontier to a point about thirty miles south-west of Tunis, thence southwards for 150 miles or so to Maknassy, and from Maknassy south-westwards to the more or less impassable Chott el Jerid. Gafsa was some twelve miles behind the front. The most dangerous area was that held by the American II Corps, stretching from Gafsa to Fondouk and it was through the pass at Fondouk that the coming attack was expected.

On 12 February Eisenhower left Algiers to inspect the front line. In the American II Corps area (U.S. 1st Armoured, 1st Infantry and 34th Divisions),

> I found a number of things that were disturbing. The first of these was a certain complacency, illustrated by an unconscionable delay in perfecting defensive positions in the passes. Lack of training and experience on the part of commanders was responsible. At one point where mine-fields were not yet planted the excuse was given that the defending infantry had been present in the area only two days.
>
> The commander explained, with an air of pride, that he had prepared a map for his mine defence and would start the next day to put out the mines. Our experience in north Tunisia had been that the enemy was able to prepare a strong defensive position ready to resist counter-attack within two hours after his arrival on the spot. . . . I gave orders for immediate correction.[9]

This was but a part of what was wrong. Although frequent and accurate reports were submitted by the American troops to General Anderson about the strength and direction of the German attack through Faid, these reports were discounted by the Army and A.F.H.Q. Intelligence Divisions as 'the exaggeration of green, untried troops'. They were no such thing and this mistake was expensive. 'After the battle I replaced the Head of my Intelligence organization at A.F.H.Q.'[10]

The Panzer attack through the Kasserine Pass which immediately followed was the tragic 'blooding' which it seems any army has to endure to come of age. It certainly had this effect on the U.S. II Corps. In a few short days they had lost 150 tanks and 1,600 men captured. Panzer losses had

been very small indeed. As Rommel commented: 'The Americans had as yet no practical battle experience, and it was now up to us to instil in them from the outset an inferiority complex of no mean order.'[11]

In the series of engagements which came to be known as the battle of the Kasserine Pass, British and French troops were also involved as well as the Americans. Rommel planned to encircle the First Army by seizing the Kasserine Pass, advancing to Tebessa and then wheeling in a northerly direction to reach the coast at Bône.

He began by using the 21st Panzer Division to overwhelm the French garrison of the Faid Pass. The Allies, regarding this as a diversion, expected the main attack to come some thirty miles north of Faid, at Fondouk. They were thus unprepared for the convergent thrusts by which Rommel took Sidi Bou Zid on 14 February and his advance to Gafsa on the following day. On 17 February Rommel's right reached Sbeitla (twenty-five miles north-west of Sidi Bou Zid) and his left pushed on to Feriana, where it turned in a north-easterly direction towards the Kasserine Pass.

But Rommel's control of von Arnim's forces was conditional, so far as this battle was concerned, on using them in accordance with the Commando Supremo's wishes. At this point, therefore, he had to await authority from Rome to continue his offensive. On 18 February he received orders to advance north towards Thala, but not north-west towards Tebessa as he wanted to do.

As a result of the above, the Americans withdrew their Gafsa garrison on the night of 14 February and elements of the Afrika Korps and the Centauro occupied Gafsa on the afternoon of the 15th without a fight. Rommel wrote:

> Driving along the road to Gafsa on the morning of the 16th, we passed long columns of Arabs driving pack animals laden with loot. They were carrying away everything movable that could be stripped from the abandoned houses and buildings. Anything of wood was particularly prized. The Arabs were delighted with this good business and presented my men with chickens and eggs. The Americans had blown up their ammunition in the citadel without warning to the people living in the neighbourhood and thirty houses had collapsed on their occupants. The bodies of thirty Arabs had been dug out of their ruins and eighty were still missing. The people were consequently feeling very bitter towards the Americans and were noisily celebrating their liberation.[12]

The Americans as yet did not appreciate how

essential was a good relationship with the Arabs, a mistake Rommel never made. Only a month previously he had surprised a British column of the Long-Range Desert Group in Tunisia and had captured the Commander of the 1st S.A.S. Regiment, Lieutenant-Colonel David Stirling.

> Insufficiently guarded, he managed to escape and made his way to some Arabs, to whom he offered a reward if they would get him back to the British lines. But his bid must have been too small, for the Arabs with their usual eye to business, offered him to us for eleven pounds of tea – a bargain which we soon clinched. Thus the British lost the very able and adaptable commander of the desert group which had caused us more damage than any other British unit of equal strength.[13]

Rommel's thrust through the Kasserine Pass penetrated as far as Thala, and was to be the last major action Rommel undertook in Africa. He felt that the advantage should have been exploited by a deep thrust to ensure the collapse of the whole Tunisian front, but he had been at loggerheads with General von Arnim, the Commander in the north, who did not support this idea. So on 22 February:

> I met Field-Marshal Kesselring, who arrived at my H.Q. with Westphal and Seidemann. We agreed that a continuation of the attack towards Le Kef held no prospect of success and decided to break off the offensive by stages . . . Kesselring asked me whether I would like to take over command of the Army Group. Apparently, as a result of the Kasserine offensive, I had ceased to be *persona non grata* and had become acceptable again, in spite of my defeatism. After what I had been through in the last few months, however, and knowing in any case that the Fuehrer had already earmarked Colonel-General von Arnim for command of the Army Group, I declined the offer. Anyhow I had no great wish to hold a command under the Luftwaffe and Commando Supremo and to have to go on suffering their interference in tactical questions.[14]

Nevertheless on the following evening an order arrived from the Commando Supremo stating that to satisfy the urgent need for a unified command in Tunisia, Army Group 'Afrika' was to be formed under Rommel's command. On the other side of the line General Alexander took command of the whole front in the last week of February.

On 27 February he sent a signal to Churchill after three days' inspection of the American and French front lines. 'I hate to disappoint you,' he said, 'but final victory in North Africa is not just around the corner. A very great deal is required to be done on both land and in the air. General Eisenhower could not be more helpful.'

In the reorganization he called for, Alexander declared:

> Broadly speaking, Americans require experience and French require arms. For Americans I am sending best officers available to give instructions in battle technique and to help them train for war. For French I have wired to home and Mid-East for essential arms and light equipment to be flown here, and am helping as far as possible from my own resources. The repulse of the enemy in the south and re-establishment of former positions have put heart into Americans. I have ordered vigorous but in the meantime minor offensive action in south to regain initiative.
>
> I am frankly shocked at whole situation as I found it. Although Anderson should have been quicker to realize true state of affairs and to have started what I am now doing, he was only put in command of the whole front on January 24th. I am regrouping whole force into three parts as follows: British and French under Anderson, all Americans under Fredendall, Eighth Army under Montgomery.[15]

A few days later Eisenhower took this reorganization further by replacing General Fredendall with General Patton in command of the U.S. II Corps. 'Morale in the II Corps was shaken and the troops had to be picked up quickly. For such a job Patton had no superior in the Army.'[16]

It was, perhaps, at this point that the Americans showed their true mettle. Their war effort in North Africa suddenly came into sharp focus. Now, as if a switch had been turned, they began to display the extraordinary resilience, the real guts and the steady determination which were to turn them into the major world power. In the early days they had not done well. Disparaged by the Germans who – except for Rommel – regarded them as children in the art of warfare, they had now, almost overnight, come of age.

The battle of Kasserine was in no way on the scale of Dunkirk. It also took place thousands of miles from home. However, it had a similar effect on the Americans as Dunkirk had on the British. They had been pushed around enough. Now they were fighting mad and there was no better General than Patton to capitalize on this surge of will. Now they had been blooded, they knew what it was all about, knew what they were up against and knew that whatever tactical losses they might sustain, they were backed up – intelligently – by the most powerful war effort the world has ever seen. From then on there was no holding them back.

This dangerous event (for the Germans) took place at a moment when, although the Allies had no means of knowing it, Rommel was about to bow out. On 26 February his A.D.C., Berndt, had written to Frau Rommel saying:

> At the beginning of February the physical and mental condition of your husband had reached such a state that Professor Horster considered an immediate course of at least eight weeks' treatment to be indispensable. The latest date for this was given to the Fuehrer's H.Q. through C.-in-C. South as 20th February.[17]

But Hitler's 'best offensive general' was never going to let his troops down. On 3 March he wrote to his wife:

> I can't get away for the moment. I'll just have to go on for a bit. I wouldn't mind having a different job. I'm dictated to by Rome in every single thing, yet the full responsibility is mine. That I find intolerable. I often think my nerves will snap. One is continually having to take paths very close beside the abyss. If it goes wrong the consequences will be incalculable.[18]

On 6 March Rommel made four major attacks using all three of the German Panzer Divisions. It was a week too late and the British were ready for him, each attack being beaten off with heavy loss. In fact fifty-two German tanks were destroyed with no loss of armour to the British and only 130 men killed or wounded. Churchill commented that no comparable example of the power of massed anti-tank artillery against armour had yet been seen. This was – for Rommel – the *coup de grâce*. 'A great gloom settled over us all,' he wrote. 'The Eighth Army's attack was now imminent and we had to face it. For the Army Group to remain longer in Africa was now plain suicide.'[19]

On 8 March 1943 Rommel handed over the Army Group to von Arnim and the next day took off for Rome. 'I told Mussolini briefly and plainly what I thought of the situation . . . but he seemed to lack any sense of reality in adversity and spent the whole time searching for arguments to justify his views.'[20]

On the afternoon of 10 March Rommel arrived at Hitler's Headquarters. 'I received an invitation to take tea with Hitler and was thus able to talk to him in private. He seemed very upset and depressed about the Stalingrad disaster . . . it was all hopeless. He instructed me to take some sick leave and get myself put right. . . . All my efforts to save my men and get them back to the Continent had been fruitless. I flew back to Wiener Neustadt and then went off to Semmering to start my treatment.'[21]

The end in Africa was now in sight, although there was still fierce fighting ahead. On 10 April, after a tough fight at Mareth and Wadi Akarit, the Eighth Army captured Sfax, and on the same day Montgomery wrote to Alexander saying that a decision was required as to which army should make the main effort for the final phase in Tunisia. The plain west of Tunis was suitable for manœuvring armour, whereas mountainous country at Enfidaville and Takrouna blocked the southern approach. Montgomery accordingly recommended that the First Army should take Tunis. To this Alexander agreed, ordering Montgomery to detach one armoured division and one armoured car regiment from the Eighth Army to help. In the meantime he was to continue to exert pressure from the south in such a way as to lead the Germans to think that the main attack would be made by the Eighth Army.

Accordingly Montgomery attacked the Enfidaville position on the night of 19–20 April. He advanced about three miles through very difficult country and planned to put in another attack in a week's time. The initial attempt of the First Army to break through to Tunis, however, on 23 April was not successful, although after five days' heavy fighting ground had been gained and the Germans forced back.

Alexander then decided to regroup the First and Eighth Armies so that the attack on Tunis could be made with the maximum strength in the most appropriate place. One more heavy punch was needed to break Army Group 'Afrika'. This was set out in a signal Alexander made to Churchill on 30 April:

> I had a long conference with Montgomery today, and have decided that owing to the extreme difficulties of the ground and the fact that the enemy has concentrated a strong force of guns against Eighth Army in the coastal sector his operations towards Bou Ficha would have been very costly in casualties and were not certain of success.
>
> I have therefore cancelled his large-scale operations and Eighth Army will undertake local action, with the chief object of preventing the enemy transferring troops from their front to First Army front.
>
> 4th Indian Division, 7th Armoured Division and 201st Guards Brigade are moving over to First Army, starting tonight. A very strong attack with all available air and artillery support will be launched by Vth Corps probably on May 4 on the axis Medjez-Tunis. IXth Corps with two or three armoured divisions, to pass through Vth Corps, directed on Tunis. I have every hope that this attack will lead to decisive results.

He went on to say that the 4th and 1st Divisions

and II U.S. Army Corps had been continuously counter-attacked over the past two days with particularly heavy fighting on V Corps' front. Localities had changed hands several times and enemy losses had been severe. Tanks had been used in these counter-attacks and seven of the new Mark VIs had been knocked out. General Crocker had been wounded and Horrocks was taking over IX Corps, Freyberg X. As an instance of the desperate nature of the enemy's resistance, Alexander finished by saying that, 'Fifty men of the Hermann Goering Division had just surrendered, when one of them persuaded them to take up arms again, and the whole party had to be shot to a man.'[22]

On 6 May the final attack was launched, the main assault being made by the veteran Eighth Army Desert Divisions which had been transferred to the First Army for this purpose. The Axis Air Force now in remnants could only make sixty sorties and, as a subsequent German report stated:

The Anglo-American Air Forces played a decisive part in the operational success which led to the destruction of the German-Italian bridgehead in Tunisia. They took part in the ground fighting to an extent never before attempted.[23]

IX Corps smashed straight through the enemy front to Massicault and the following day the 6th and 7th Armoured Divisions pressed on to Tunis, the old Desert 7th entering the city first.

They then turned north to Bizerta, which the 9th U.S. Infantry Division had reached the same day. Three German Divisions were thus trapped between the Anglo-American armies and surrendered on 9 May. 'It was a real thunderbolt,' Alexander said, and on 11 May he was signalling to Churchill that he expected all organized resistance to collapse within the next forty-eight hours.

I calculate that prisoners up to date exceed 100,000 but this is not yet confirmed and they are still coming in. Yesterday I saw a horse-drawn gig laden with Germans driving themselves to the prisoners' cage. As they passed we could not help laughing, and they laughed too. The whole affair was more like Derby Day. The equipment of all sorts will take some time to count up; some is destroyed but a lot intact.

No one has got away except a mere handful by air.

We have recovered 2,000 of our own prisoners, including wounded. It is all very satisfying and augurs well for the future.[24]

The next day von Arnim was captured and the tally of prisoners rose to 248,000, plus over 1,000

guns, 250 tanks and thousands of motor vehicles, many of which were serviceable. The pincers had snapped shut, the enemy had laid down his arms.

Perhaps the best end piece to the vast North African War is composed of the two congratulatory messages from Churchill to Alexander and to Eisenhower. To Alexander he said:

It has fallen to you to conduct series of battles which have ended in destruction of the German and Italian power in Africa. All the way from Alamein to Tunis in ceaseless fighting and marching of last six months you and your brilliant lieutenant Montgomery have added a glorious chapter to annals of British Commonwealth and Empire. Your combinations in the final great battle will be judged by history as a model of the military art.

But more than this, you have known how to inspire your soldiers with confidence and ardour which overcame all obstacles and outlasted all fatigue and hardship. They and their trusty United States and French Allied soldiers and airmen together can now be told of the admiration and gratitude with which entire British nation and Empire regard them and their famous deeds.

The generous rivalry in arms of the First and Eighth British Armies has achieved victory, full honour for each and all.[25]

To Eisenhower in Algiers, Churchill cabled:

Let me add my heartfelt congratulations to those which have been sent you by His Majesty and the War Cabinet on the brilliant result of the North African campaign by the army under your supreme direction.

The comradeship and conduct with which you have sustained the troops engaged in the fierce and prolonged battle in Tunisia and the perfect understanding and harmony preserved amidst the shock of war between British and United States forces and with our French allies have proved solid foundation of victory.

The simultaneous advance of British and United States Armies side by side into Tunis and Bizerta is an augury full of hope for the future of the world. Long may they march together, striking down the tyrants and oppressors of mankind.[26]

So the fighting ceased and the sound of guns died away from the North African battlefield. What had been achieved now that all Africa was once more in Allied hands? The next step would be a progression of the idea of attacking the Axis via its 'soft underbelly', that is by the invasion of Sicily and the mainland of Italy. This could not be undertaken without control of the sea but now the Mediterranean was once again to be opened up, Malta restored and the passage of ships from the United Kingdom to the Far East restarted through the Suez Canal.

The Italian Empire in Africa had ceased to exist

and the brief German presence of just over two
years had come and gone like a short act in a play
in which the star puts in only a brief appearance.
But it had been a very near thing. Rommel had
been stopped, more by a shortage of supplies than
by the British Army, a mere sixty miles from
Alexandria. Who knows what would have happened had the Panzers penetrated into the rich
Delta of Egypt? Rommel's exploits illuminate the
power of a single extraordinary man to persevere
and achieve against all odds and a lack of essential
practical support from his own Fuehrer – to which
must be added the lip-service war waged by the
Italians.

It is easy, with hindsight, to say that Hitler
made his great mistake in attacking Russia. He
very nearly succeeded. That he dodged certain
unpleasant facts in North Africa which, faced
earlier, might have been turned to his advantage
is the penalty a dictator pays for surrounding himself with yes-men. Rommel gave Hitler far more
and received far less than he deserved in Africa –
and perhaps the most appropriate comment is
that made by Rommel himself on being elevated
to the rank of Field-Marshal – 'I would rather the

Fuehrer had given me one more division.'

Both sides in the Desert War had their full share
of good and bad luck, well reasoned and unsound
judgement. To the Italians in December 1940 it
was inconceivable that the British, who had been
thrown out of Belgium, Norway and France and
who had even retreated before the Italians themselves in British Somaliland and the Western
Desert, would ever seriously attack. They did. To
Hitler when the crunch came, it was inconceivable
to permit even a tactical let alone a strategic
retreat. Both were forced upon him.

The North African War – more than any other
campaign – revealed the essential qualities and
defects of the German, Italian, French, British and
American forces involved. The German Army
was the most precise and efficient war machine the
world has seen. Their organization, even nega-
tively aided by the Italian Commando Supremo,
remained consistently superior to anything on the
Allied side. The German front-line soldier trusted
this machine implicitly. Almost never did it let him
down, even providing him with his mail from
home twice a week. The Wehrmacht paid for this
with an inability to adapt or to develop such

maverick talents as were to be found in the British Long-Range Desert Group.

Italian genius came out in the drive, the courage and the skill of individual officers and men operating most effectively in guerrilla activities. It is difficult to summarize French qualities and defects – as always one has to ask which French? The British, basically incapable of ever accepting the possibility of losing in the end, muddled along and were at their stubborn best when forced to use their initiative in relatively small fighting units, although this generalization does no justice to Wavell's offensive, which was a masterpiece of administrative and strategic planning and of tactical skill. Auchinleck's refusal to abandon the offensive when 'Crusader' seemed to be going badly was also decisive. To the Americans the North African adventure proved to be the essential first aggressive step towards the vast operations which they would later undertake and in which they would prove to be supreme in Europe and in the Pacific. It is true they made mistakes but these generated in them that unique American quality of quick adaptation, of recovery and of never looking back for long. Their innate frontier spirit

caused them always to pitch their ideas on a generous scale, ever bearing in mind the psychology of success.

One factor, however, was common to all. The proportion of those who risked being brewed up in their tanks and who suffered the front-line pestilence of sand and sun or the equivalent at sea or in the air, rarely exceeded twenty per cent of all those in uniform in the area. It took an enormous number of Groppi Grenadiers (the local name for army elements based in Cairo) to keep one armoured division in the desert. Perhaps the inevitable and resulting bond between front-line enemies now stands as the most remarkable single memory of that gruelling three-year campaign. The real comradeship of the desert together with the enduring and steely understanding it engendered remains, perhaps, the only plus to set against the huge minus of chaos, destruction, mutilation and death.

In the North African desert all were in it together, all were committed and the story must therefore end with a simple, reflective salute to those on either side who never returned and whose sacrifice should long be remembered.

NOTES

Chapter 1
1. Liddell Hart, *The Rommel Papers*, Collins 1953
2. F. W. von Mellenthin, *Panzer Battles 1939–45*, Cassell 1955
3. H. W. Schmidt, *With Rommel in the Desert*, Harrap 1951
4. Liddell Hart, op. cit.
5. Ibid.
6. Ibid.
7. Ibid.
8. Ibid.
9. Ibid.
10. Von Mellenthin, op. cit.
11. Sir Winston Churchill, *The Second World War*, Cassell 1948–54
12. Ibid.
13. Liddell Hart, op. cit.
14. Ibid.
15. Ibid.
16. Ibid.
17. Ibid.
18. Ibid.
19. Ibid.
20. Ibid.
21. Ibid.
22. Ibid.
23. Ibid.
24. Ibid.
25. Ibid.

Chapter 2
1. Churchill, *The Second World War*
2. Robert Murphy, *Diplomat Among Warriors*, Collins 1964
3. Ibid.
4. Ibid.
5. Churchill, op. cit.
6. Ibid. (Grand Admiral Raeder)
7. Ibid.
8. Ibid.
9. Liddell Hart, *The Rommel Papers*
10. Churchill, op. cit.
11. Churchill, op. cit.
12. Liddell Hart, op. cit.
13. Churchill, op. cit.
14. Ibid.
15. Ibid.
16. Liddell Hart, op. cit.
17. Ibid.
18. Ibid.
19. Ibid.
20. Churchill, op. cit.
21. Liddell Hart, op. cit.

Chapter 3
1. Churchill, *The Second World War*
2. Ibid.
3. Mountbatten, Foreword to *D Day*, Tute, Costello and Hughes, Sidgwick & Jackson 1974
4. Cunningham of Hyndhope, *A Sailor's Odyssey*, Arrow Books 1961
5. Amiral Auphon et Jacques Mordal, *La Marine Française pendant la Seconde Guerre Mondiale*, Hachette 1958
6. Murphy, *Diplomat Among Warriors*
7. Liddell Hart, *The Rommel Papers*
8. Ibid.
9. Schmidt, *With Rommel in the Desert*

Chapter 4
1. Churchill, *The Second World War*
2. Ibid.
3. Ibid.
4. Ibid.
5. Ibid.
6. Ibid.
7. Ibid.
8. Ibid.
9. Ibid.
10. Ibid.
11. Ibid.
12. Ibid.
13. Ibid.
14. Ibid.
15. Ibid.
16. Ibid.
17. Dwight D. Eisenhower, *Crusade in Europe*, Heinemann 1948
18. Churchill, op. cit.
19. Ibid.
20. Ibid.
21. Ibid.

Chapter 5
1. Eisenhower, *Crusade in Europe*
2. H. C. Butcher, *Three Years with Eisenhower*, Heinemann 1946
3. Eisenhower, op. cit.
4. Butcher, op. cit.
5. Ibid.
6. Ladislas Farago, *Patton*, Barker 1966
7. Eisenhower, op. cit.
8. W. S. Chalmers, *Full Cycle* (Biography of Admiral Ramsay), Hodder 1959
9. Cunningham, *A Sailor's Odyssey*
10. Butcher, op. cit.
11. Chalmers, op. cit.
12. Ibid.
13. Ibid.
14. Churchill, *The Second World War*

Chapter 6
1. Murphy, *Diplomat Among Warriors*
2. Ibid.
3. Hoare, *Ambassador on a Special Mission*
4. Eisenhower, *Crusade in Europe*
5. Murphy, op. cit.
6. Ibid.
7. Ibid.
8. Ibid.
9. Ibid.
10. Ladislas Farago, *The Game of Foxes*, Hodder 1971
11. Ibid.

Chapter 7
1. Montgomery, *The Memoirs of Field Marshal Montgomery*, Collins 1958
2. Ibid.
3. Ibid.
4. Ibid.
5. Ibid.
6. Ibid.
7. Ibid.
8. Ibid.
9. Liddell Hart, *The Rommel Papers*
10. *The Eighth Army*, H.M.S.O. (1944)
11. Ibid.
12. Von Mellenthin, *Panzer Battles 1939–45*
13. Churchill, *The Second World War*
14. Ibid.
15. Ibid.
16. Ibid.
17. Ibid.
18. Liddell Hart, op. cit.

19. Ibid.
20. Ibid.
21. Ibid.
22. Ibid.
23. Ibid.
24. Ibid.
25. Montgomery, op. cit.
26. Ibid.
27. Von Mellenthin, op. cit.
28. Liddell Hart, op. cit.
29. Montgomery, op. cit.
30. Von Mellenthin, op. cit.

Chapter 8
1. Battle Summary no. 38 – Operation Torch, BR. 1736(31), Admiralty 1948
2. Ibid.
3. Ibid.
4. Eisenhower, *Crusade in Europe*
5. Ibid.
6. Chalmers, *Full Cycle*
7. Ibid.
8. Ibid.
9. Ibid.
10. Murphy, *Diplomat Among Warriors*
11. Farago, *Patton*
12. Ibid.
13. Ibid.
14. Ibid.
15. Cunningham, *A Sailor's Odyssey*
16. Farago, op. cit.

Chapter 9
1. Montgomery, *Memoirs*
2. Ibid.
3. Liddell Hart, *The Rommel Papers*
4. Ibid.
5. Ibid.
6. Ibid.
7. Ibid.
8. Ibid.
9. A. W. Tedder, *With Prejudice*, Cassell 1966
10. Liddell Hart, op. cit.
11. *The Eighth Army*
12. Liddell Hart, op. cit.
13. Montgomery, op. cit.
14. Liddell Hart, op. cit.
15. Montgomery, op. cit.
16. Ibid.
17. Ibid.
18. *The Eighth Army*
19. Montgomery, op. cit.
20. Ibid.
21. *The Eighth Army*
22. Lieutenant-Colonel J. O. Ewart, quoted in Alan Moorehead, *The Desert War*, Hamish Hamilton 1965
23. Montgomery, op. cit.
24. Liddell Hart, op. cit.
25. Ibid.

Chapter 10
1. Churchill, *The Second World War*
2. Eisenhower, *Crusade in Europe*
3. Ibid.
4. Battle Summary – Operation Torch
5. Ibid.
6. Ibid.
7. Churchill, op. cit.

8. Ibid.
9. Battle Summary – Operation Torch
10. Ibid.
11. Farago, *The Game of Foxes*
12. Chalmers, *Full Cycle*
13. Eisenhower, op. cit.
14. Churchill, op. cit.
15. Ibid.
16. Ibid.
17. Battle Summary – Operation Torch
18. Ibid.
19. Churchill, op. cit.
20. Farago, *Patton*
21. Eisenhower, op. cit.

Chapter 11
1. Murphy, op. cit.
2. Eisenhower, *Crusade in Europe*
3. Ibid.
4. Ibid.
5. Ibid.
6. Ibid.
7. Ibid.
8. Liddell Hart, *The Rommel Papers*
9. Ibid.
10. Ibid.
11. Ibid.
12. Ibid.
13. Ibid.
14. Cunningham, *A Sailor's Odyssey*
15. Montgomery, *Memoirs*
16. Eisenhower, op. cit.
17. Ibid.
18. Murphy, op. cit.
19. Eisenhower, op. cit.

Chapter 12
1. Churchill, *The Second World War*
2. Ibid.
2. Ibid.
3. Ibid.
4. Ibid.
5. Gerald Pawle, *The War and Colonel Warden*, Harrap 1963
6. Churchill, op. cit.
7. Liddell Hart, *The Rommel Papers*
8. Eisenhower, *Crusade in Europe*
9. Ibid.
10. Ibid.
11. Liddell Hart, op. cit.
12. Ibid.
13. Ibid.
14. Ibid.
15. Churchill, op. cit.
16. Eisenhower, op. cit.
17. Liddell Hart, op. cit.
18. Ibid.
19. Ibid.
20. Ibid.
21. Ibid.
22. Churchill, op. cit.
23. Ibid.
24. Ibid.
25. Ibid.
26. Ibid.

Index

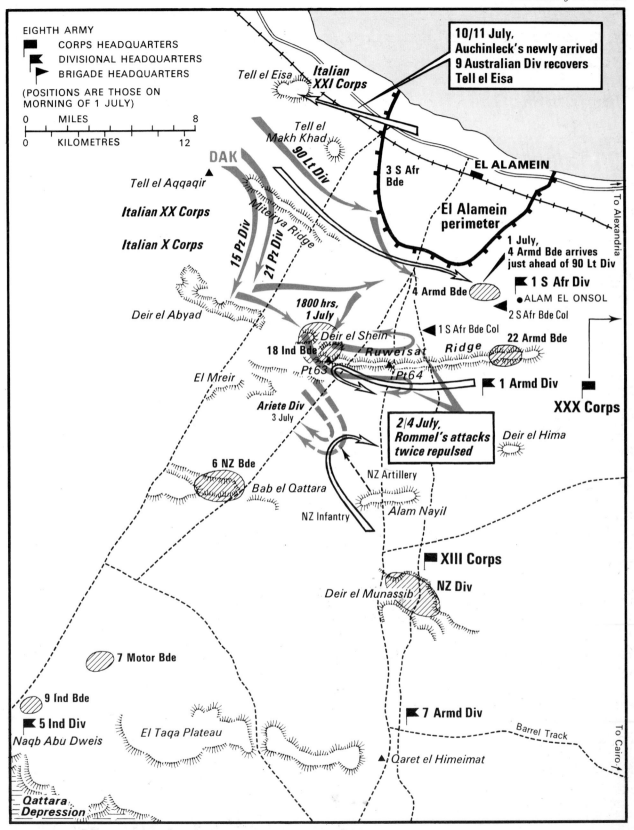

EIGHT ARMY
■ CORPS HEADQUARTERS
◣ DIVISIONAL HEADQUARTERS
◣ BRIGADE HEADQUARTERS
(POSITIONS ARE THOSE ON
MORNING OF 1 JULY)

MILES 0 — 8
KILOMETRES 0 — 12

Tell el Eisa
Italian XXI Corps

**10/11 July,
Auchinleck's newly arrived
9 Australian Div recovers
Tell el Eisa**

Tell el Makh Khad

DAK

90 Lt Div

3 S Afr Bde

EL ALAMEIN

To Alexandria

Tell el Aqqaqir

Italian XX Corps

Italian X Corps

Miteirya Ridge

El Alamein perimeter

**1 July,
4 Armd Bde arrives
just ahead of 90 Lt Div**

15 Pz Div *21 Pz Div*

4 Armd Bde

◣ **1 S Afr Div**
• ALAM EL ONSOL

◣ 2 S Afr Bde Col

Deir el Abyad

*1800 hrs,
1 July*

◣ 1 S Afr Bde Col

22 Armd Bde

Deir el Shein

18 Ind Bde

Ruweisat   Ridge

El Mreir

Pt 63   Pt 64

◣ **1 Armd Div**

XXX Corps

Ariete Div
3 July

**2/4 July,
Rommel's attacks
twice repulsed**

Deir el Hima

6 NZ Bde

Bab el Qattara

NZ Artillery

NZ Infantry   *Alam Nayil*

XIII Corps

Deir el Munassib   **NZ Div**

7 Motor Bde

9 Ind Bde

◣ **5 Ind Div**
Naqb Abu Dweis

El Taqa Plateau

◣ **7 Armd Div**

Barrel Track

To Cairo

▲ *Qaret el Himeimat*

**Qattara
Depression**

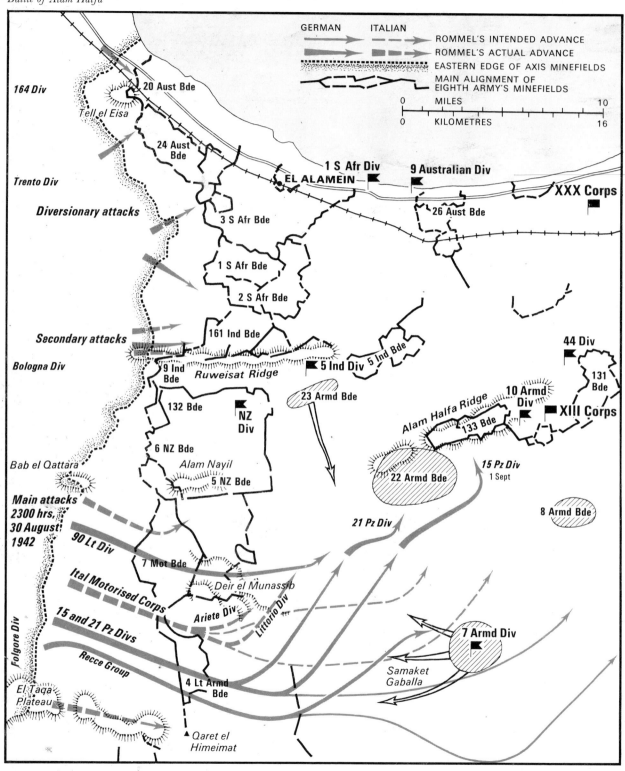

GERMAN **ITALIAN**

ROMMEL'S INTENDED ADVANCE

ROMMEL'S ACTUAL ADVANCE

EASTERN EDGE OF AXIS MINEFIELDS

MAIN ALIGNMENT OF
EIGHTH ARMY'S MINEFIELDS

MILES
0 ————————————————— 10

KILOMETRES
0 ————————————————— 16

164 Div

Tell el Eisa

20 Aust Bde

Trento Div

24 Aust Bde

Diversionary attacks

1 S Afr Div 9 Australian Div

EL ALAMEIN **XXX Corps**

26 Aust Bde

3 S Afr Bde

1 S Afr Bde

2 S Afr Bde

161 Ind Bde 44 Div

Secondary attacks

5 Ind Div 5 Ind Bde

131
Bde

Bologna Div

9 Ind Bde *Ruweisat Ridge*

10 Armd Div

23 Armd Bde *Alam Halfa Ridge* 133 Bde **XIII Corps**

132 Bde **NZ Div**

6 NZ Bde *Alam Nayil* 22 Armd Bde **15 Pz Div** 1 Sept

Bab el Qattara 5 NZ Bde 8 Armd Bde

*Main attacks
2300 hrs.
30 August
1942* **21 Pz Div**

90 Lt Div

7 Mot Bde

Ital Motorised Corps *Deir el Munassib* 7 Armd Div

Ariete Div *Littorio Div* *Samaket
Gaballa*

15 and 21 Pz Divs

Recce Group

Folgore Div

4 Lt Armd Bde

*El Taqa
Plateau*

▲ *Qaret el
Himeimat*